GOLF COURSES
OF THE
SOUTHWEST

ABOUT THE AUTHOR

Author of the acclaimed **Florida Golf Guide** and the forthcoming **New York/ New Jersey Golf Guide**, Jimmy Shacky is a golf writer, free-lance photographer, and full-time avid golfer. Jimmy and his wife Suzanne make their home in Ft. Lauderdale, Florida.

ACKNOWLEDGMENTS

I would like to thank the many people who have contributed their time and patience. These include the hundreds of owners, pro-shop staf, golfing pro's, advertising consultants, and management personnel who have generously cooperated in the writing of this book. I would also like to thank Jonathan Stein andAvery Cardoza, for their helpful criticism and direction; to my wife Suzanne, for spending countless hours helping me verify the information in this book; to Jonathan, my brother-in-law; Kenny Wolf; David Fishman (PC Man); and the staf at Traister One Computing, who have collectively contributed to my computer knowledge and have always been there to answer my questions; and finally my good friends, Julian and Lindy Silberstang.

GOLF COURSES OF THE SOUTHWEST

JIMMY SHACKY

OPEN ROAD PUBLISHING

OPEN ROAD PUBLISHING

Open Road publishes golf guides to your favorite destinations, as well as travel guides to American and foreign locales. Write for your *free* catalogue of all our titles.

Catalogue Department, Open Road Publishing
P.O. Box 11249, Cleveland Park Station, Washington, D.C. 20008

*To my father and mother, David and Norma,
and to my in-laws, Jon and Sandra*

1st Edition

Front Cover photo courtesy of the Sheraton Tucson El Conquistador Golf & Tennis Resort, Tucson, Arizona.
Back Cover photo courtesy of Edgewood Tahoe Golf Course, Stateline, Nevada.

TABLE OF CONTENTS

1. INTRODUCTION

You'll find a wealth of great golfing experiences in America's great southwest!

The land is a chasm full of scenic beauty that offers a multitude of platforms for golf course architecture to flourish. From traditional designs to the avant garde, you'll find them all here, and you'll be elated that you chose this part of America to explore.

Endless horizons sit magically on a cushion of suspended air laced with beautiful, lush foliage, distinct desert cacti, and snow-filled mountains with high-rising peaks. Once experienced, you'll never have to wonder why golf's most important architectural names have come to the Southwest to take on the challenge of designing courses that will complement the region without disturbing the balance of natural life. Some of these designs are among the most original anywhere, while others are a wonderful blend of traditional designs spread along diferent local terrain. You're bound to find a course that will offer you a-once-in-a-lifetime-experience that you'll want to pass along to your golfing partners and friends.

The perpetual golfing season in the Southwest allows players to enjoy the game all year round. Many of the clubs featured in this book have made the prestigious **Golf Digest** "Top 100 Courses" list.

In this book you'll find comprehensive descriptions for every public, semi-private, resort, municipal, private, and military course in the Southwest. It gives you a feel for how each course looks and plays, with all the important statistics you need to make an informed decision on where to play.

Every detail is covered: course type, year built, architect, local pro, amount of holes per locale, yardage, rating and slope, how many days in advance to place a tee-time, price differences between peak and slow times, amenities, credit cards accepted, whether there's a driving range, practice greens, locker rooms, rental clubs, walkers, snack bars, restaurants, lounges, meeting rooms, and more! This book will also help you play a course that you've never had the pleasure of golfing before. By discovering these new courses, it is my hope that some hidden element will lift your game to a new level. It is my further hope that you will tell your friends about it, too.

Whether you're traveling for business or pleasure, whether you live in the region or visiting for the first time, **GOLF COURSES OF THE SOUTHWEST** is a unique, entertaining, and valuable resource that I'm certain you'll use for a long time to come.

Happy golfing!

2. HOW TO USE THIS BOOK

Each chapter begins with a map of the state. You'll be introduced to the general location of each course within each county of that state in the following two pages. Here is an example of the Arizona map:

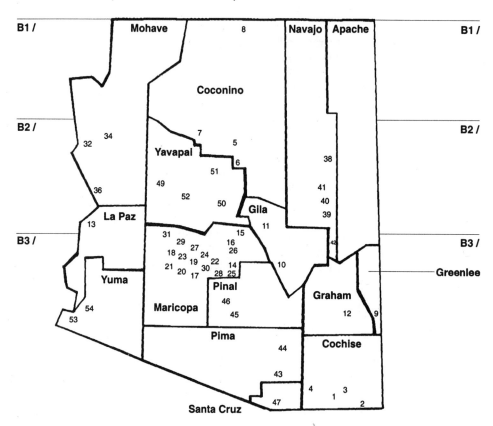

Below each map you'll find an alphabetical listing of all the counties and a numerical directive to the courses reviewed in each county. Before I breakdown the first county listing for the state of Arizona, notice the three sections labeled B1 (Block 1), B2, and B3, to the right and the left of the map above. All of the maps in this book are broken down into thirds to help you find the location of each county and city.

Below each map, the following will be found:

Cochise

B3 / Bisbee ... 1
B3 / Douglas ... 2

Cochise : This is the name of the first county listing.

B3 / : This indicates which third of the map the county can be located.

Bisbee ... 1 : Bisbee is the city. You can locate it by looking for its representative number (1) within the county

You can locate both Bisbee and the following city, Douglas (2), on the southeast section of the map provided in this example.

FINDING THE RIGHT COURSE

Each course listing can be found in one of three ways:

Region: Region names and their following page numbers are listed in the Table Of Contents.

County: County names and their following page numbers are listed in the Table Of Contents. The names are written in white type on the title bar located at the top of every page:

COCHISE COUNTY

County names are listed in alphabetical order. Each page covers two independent courses. If the second course listing is located in the following county, the following county will be written after the preceding county by a forward slash on the title bar as follows:

COCHISE/COCONINO COUNTY

The title bar above indicates the county location of the two courses featured on a page. The first is located in Cochise, and the second is located in Coconino.

Name: If you know the name of the course that you want to play, you can look it up in the Index.

COURSE LISTINGS

The following is a breakdown of the format used for each course listing:

Below the county title, you'll find the corresponding courses with their detailed information in alphabetical order. Look at the example on the following page (**ARIZONA SUNSITES COUNTRY CLUB**). It is the first section that you will see directly below the title bar.

ARIZONA SUNSITES COUNTRY CLUB
1105 Irene St., Pearce, AZ 85625 / (602) 826-3414

The **ARIZONA SUNSITES COUNTRY CLUB** is the name of the establishment and is followed by the course Address, City, State, Zip, Area Code and Phone Number.

The phone numbers listed are for the Pro Shop of each establishment (when made available). It is the quickest way to place your tee time or make an appointment with a golfing professional for a private lesson.

Below is the **BASIC INFORMATION** box that is included with every course description. Let's have a look at all of the individual sections.

BASIC INFORMATION	
Course Type: Semi-private	
Year Built: 1973 / 1982	
Architect: N/A	
Local Pro: Jim Hancock	
Course: N/A	
Holes: 18 / 71	
Back : 6,632 yds. Rating: 71.8 Slope: 127	
Middle: 6,324 yds. Rating: 68.9 Slope: 113	
Ladies: 5,980 yds. Rating: 72.0 Slope: 117	
Tee Time: 30 days in advance.	
Price: $20 - $25	

Credit Cards: ■	Restaurant:
Driving Range:	Lounge:
Practice Green: ■	Meeting Rooms:
Locker Room:	Tennis:
Rental Clubs: ■	Swimming: ■
Walkers: ■	Jogging Trails:
Snack Bar:	Boating:

Course Type: Most area golfers play on public courses, and this book's coverage of public courses is extensive. Many other types of courses allow non-members to play. Here is a listing and a definition for each title:

A **Municipal** course is one that is owned and operated by a local governing body. These courses are open to the general public without membership.

A **Public** course is one that is privately owned by a single owner or a corporation. Play is open to the general public. Many of these courses cater to local players by offering inviting memberships at discount rates. These memberships will usually allow advance tee-time privileges, too.

A **Semi-private** course is one that is owned privately or by a corporation. Like municipal and public courses, these courses are open to the general public. There is a slight difference between a semi-private course and a public or municipal course. The semi-private course members have priority in certain respects, especially in reservations.

A **Private** course is one that is reserved for membership play only. These courses are frequently called country clubs and are meticulously well-kept.

Private courses have a code of ethics that is strictly followed by golfers throughout the U.S.A. Please adhere to the following principles and practices:

If you happen to be a member of a private course, you may have the opportunity of playing other private courses too. The first thing you'll need to find out is whether the course you want to play will reciprocate with the course that you are a member of. Some courses will only reciprocate with courses in their immediate area and others will only reciprocate with courses out-of-state. There is no rule with whom they must reciprocate with. The proper method of communication is to have your golf professional set up an appointment with the pro at the course that you want to play.

One of the most popular ways of getting onto a private course is to make friends with one of its members. They have the power to set up an invitation for you to play the course when a time slot is open. It's a great way of getting to know people and hopefully being in the position to extend your gratitude by inviting them to play on your private course. If you're not a member of a private course, you can certainly invite them to a course you've enjoyed playing in the past.

A **Resort** course is one that is owned and operated by the resort-hotel. These courses offer excellent vacation packages for people both in and out of the state of the Southwestern states. Some of these courses are privately run for the guests of the resort only. The great majority of them do allow public play.

Course Type: Semi-private
Year Built: 1973 / 1982
Architect: N/A
Local Pro: Jim Hancock

This is the first section within the Basic Information box. Let's have a look at all of the individual subsections:

Course Type: Semi-private

Course Type tells you which type of play each course allows.

Year Built: 1973 / 1982

The **Year Built** corresponds to the year the course was opened. Over a certain period of time, courses lose their shape through the forces of nature. If any additional work has been done to the course by anyone after the original architect, a following date after a forward slash will indicate the year the change took place. There will be times when you'll see N/A following the colon marks, because no one is sure of the exact date or dates that the course was built or repaired.

Architect: N/A

The original **Architect's** name will be the one listed primarily. If any additional work had been done to the course by anyone after the original architect, the secondary architect's name will be listed after the forward slash. An **N/A** indicates that the architect's name is unknown.

Local Pro: Randy Webber

Local Pro: These are the people that you'll want to contact to book lessons. They often have the greatest knowledge of how the course should be played and the elements that you should watch out for.

Course: Champion
Holes: 18 / Par 72

This is the second section in the Basic Information box. The following will explain both sub-headings:

Course: Champion

Course: Some establishments have more than just one course for you to choose from. Each course is assigned a different name for easy identification. Many courses simply choose the location of each course from a certain starting point and end up calling their courses "East" or "West."

Whenever I was confronted with a two course situation, I chose the course that was most sought after. In this particular example, the N/A appears because this establishment only has one course, and thus does not need another name to differentiate it from another course. It's simply goes by the title name of the establishment: **ARIZONA SUNSITES COUNTRY CLUB.**

Holes: 18

Holes: The number of holes for this particular course. If more than one course is featured, the hole number and par move into parenthesis under the sub-heading **Course**. The new number in the sub-heading **Holes** indicates the amount of holes available to play.

Course: East (18/Par 72)
Holes: 36

Looking at the top example to the left, we know that the main body of the course description will be based on the **East** course. The numbers in the parenthesis tells us that it's an 18 hole/Par 72 layout. We also know that this establishment offers an additional course by the number 36 indicated in the sub-heading: **Holes**.

Note: Some courses offer 27 holes of golf. In most instances they'll tie two courses together to get a total of three layouts for the public to choose from. Others may have as many as 99 holes to play. Resort establishments are usually the ones that feature the greatest variety of courses under a single location.

Back: 6,632 yds.   Rating: 71.8   Slope: 127
Middle: 6,324 yds.   Rating: 68.9   Slope: 113
Ladies: 5,980 yds.   Rating: 72.0   Slope: 117

As you work your way down the **Basic Information** box, you'll see three sets of numbers (above and to the left in this example) will be the next section to appear. This is the most important and most informative section. These numbers indicate the length and severity of the course from a number of different starting positions called tee-markers. The order of difficulty for these tee-markers are as follows: Back-tees, Middle-tees, and the Ladies-tees. Knowing how to read and interpret the numbers in this section will help you make an educated choice as to the best course suited for your individual game.

Back: 6,632 yds.
Middle: 6,324 yds.
Ladies: 5,980 yds.

This sub-section indicates the total yardage from each of the individual tees. I chose to represent each course with these three sub-sections because it breaks down the entire playing field to its simplest form. Many of the newer courses offer additional tees for a wider spectrum of players. Most courses color code their tee-markers, from back to front, in the following way: Blue, White, and Red.

Rating: 71.8
Rating: 68.9
Rating: 72.0

Course ratings are an indication of how difficult a course is for a scratch golfer (a golfer who shoots par or better). This book includes the U.S.G.A. (United States Golf Association) ratings to the extent available. The best way to judge a course sight unseen is to evaluate both the course rating and the slope rating . Each tee marker will have a different course rating that will judge the difficulty by the distance the course is to be played from that marker.

Here is an example that will help you understand the system. If course #1 and #2 are rated at 71.4, would it be safe to assume that these courses are equally difficult? Can a person judge the severity of play without ever seeing the courses in the first place? Use this approach: When comparing two different courses, always look at the par rating for both courses. If course #1 is a par 72 at 6,624 yards, and course #2 is a par 70 at 6,515 yards, both of these courses are relatively the same. The biggest difference between the two is that course #1 is 109 yards longer than course #2; a possible one stroke difference. The shorter course is harder to play because it is a Par 70 course rather than a Par 72. With a two-stroke difference minus the one-stroke given to the first course, the shorter course is still one stroke harder than the first.

You can also picture it this way. If you could take that 109 yard difference and place it on any random hole on course #1, that hole will automatically change to a one-stroke par difference. Say we placed that 109 yard difference on a Par 4 hole that measures 408 yards. It can now be considered a Par 5 at 517 yards. Course #2 still has a one-stroke difference to make up despite its relative length. It is therefore the harder of the two.

Slope: 127
Slope: 113
Slope: 117

High handicap players (players that shoot well above par 72) can rely on this secondary system developed by the United States Golf Association (U.S.G.A.)

When comparing two or more courses, the one with the highest slope rating will be the most difficult to play. The U.S.G.A. considers a slope rating of 113 to be of average difficulty. The only way you'll get a full understanding of how this number relates to your personal game is if you write down your final score along with the course ratings for the next 10 courses you play in the future.

When you look back at these numbers, pick the courses that you posted similar numbers on. If their slope ratings are about even or closely related, the average number between them is the number best suited for your game. Always play from the tees that post the closest slope rating to the one you now consider your personal average. This will bring the course down to your playing style and will allow you to have the most amount of fun on a level that is challenging but not overbearing. If your game has been improving, start playing from the back tees. If you find playing from the back tees too lengthy, search for a course that offers a higher slope rating from the middle tees.

Tee Time: 30 days
Price: $20 - $25

This is the fourth section in the **Basic Information** box. The following will explain both sub-headings.

Tee Time: 30 days

The numbers in this sub-heading indicate how many days the course will allow you to book a tee time (a reservation to play) in advance.

Note: The numbers used in this book are based on a walk-in scenario. Keep in mind that most of the Resort courses listed in this book will allow you to book a tee-time well in advance if you plan to stay at their establishment. It isn't unusual to post a tee-time as far back as six months to a year.

Price: $20 - $25

Price: The numbers in this sub-heading indicate the price variance for the entire year based on the lowest to highest price. Prices are subject to change without notice. Please call to confirm.

Credit Cards:	■	Restaurant:	
Driving Range:		Lounge:	
Practice Green:	■	Meeting Rooms:	
Locker Room:		Tennis:	
Rental Clubs:	■	Swimming:	■
Walkers:	■	Jogging Trails:	
Snack Bar:		Boating:	

This is the fifth and last section in the **Basic Information** box. Any listing with a black box next to it indicates that the course offers that subject or amenity.

A black box by *Boating* indicates that the course is a half-hour away from a body of water by automobile.

Some courses only allow walking during certain hours of the day. If that happens to be an objective of yours, please call the course to confirm the proper time of the day.

Course Description

You'll find a concise course description for every listing with information that will help you choose the best course for you. Below is a sample piece:

"One of the most outstanding features on this course is the way it's set up for different types of players.

It gives you several options to drive your ball to different parts of the fairways from each of the tees. This will allow you to play within your game and not have to worry about hitting a shot you know you're not capable of.

Many of the holes are innovative and fun to play, and the overall design of the course should appeal to many different types of players."

Golf courses, or their particular holes, are often defined in one of three architectural terms: **Strategic**, **Penal**, and **Heroic**.

Strategic: Strategic holes allow a golfer two driving options off the tee. Think of a dog-leg left hole with water coming into play along the entire left side. Your first option would be to flirt with the water by playing your ball over the water, cutting off as much length from the hole as possible, and having the ball spin back and on to the fairway, leaving you with a simple short length shot to the green. If you're not successful and the ball ends up in the water, you'll be penalized two strokes. The next option would be to eliminate the water completely and play to the safest part of the fairway, known as the "bailout" area. From this point you'll have a long and difficult approach shot.

Penal: Penal holes are the most demanding. You can only play the hole one way or you'll end up in a lot of trouble. An island par-3 hole with water dividing the teeing area from the green is a great example. You're forced to hit the ball over water and land it on the green to be successful.

Heroic: Heroic holes are a matter of taste. The basic premise is based on the nature of the terrain that the course was built on. Mountain courses with high elevation changes, desert courses secluded among hundreds of cacti, and oceanside courses with par-3's playing over ocean water are classic heroic courses.

Some courses feature a healthy combination of all three types.

Directions

You'll find the directions to the course directly below each course description. They start from a major highway en route to the course. If you're visiting an area for the first time, please make sure you take along a concise map of the area with you.

It always helps to be prepared in case you venture off in the wrong direction and end up in an unfamiliar area. Nothing is more frustrating than waking up early in the morning and arriving at the course after your reserved tee-time!

ARIZONA

THE GRAND CANYON STATE

ARIZONA/COUNTIES AND CITIES

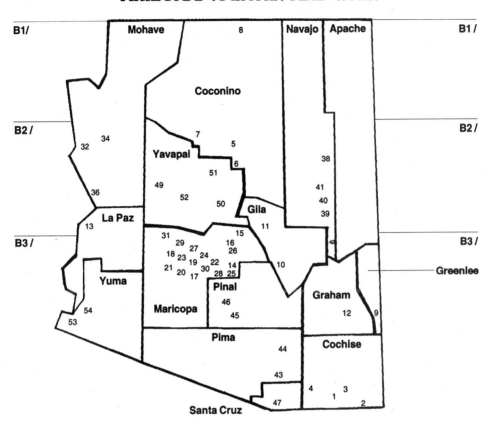

Cochise
B3 / Bisbee ... 1
B3 / Douglas ... 2
B3 / Pearce ... 3
B3 / Sierra Vista ... 4

Coconino
B2 / Flagstaff ... 5
B2 / Sedona ... 6
B2 / Williams ... 7
B1 / Page ... 8

Greenlee
B3 / York ... 9

Gila
B3 / Miami ... 10
B2 / Payson ... 11

Graham
B3 / Safford ... 12

Lapaz
B2 / Parker ...13

Maricopa
B3 / Apache ... 14
B3 / Carefree ... 15
B3 / Cave Creek ... 16

Mohave

Navajo

Pima

Pinal

Santa Cruz

Yavapai

Yuma

ARIZONA SUNSITES COUNTRY CLUB

1105 Irene St., Pearce, AZ 85625 / (602) 826-3414

BASIC INFORMATION

Course Type: Semi-private
Year Built: 1973 / 1982
Architect: N/A
Local Pro: Jim Hancock

Course: N/A
Holes: 18 / 71

Back : 6,632 yds. Rating: 71.8 Slope: 127
Middle: 6,324 yds. Rating: 68.9 Slope: 113
Ladies: 5,980 yds. Rating: 72.0 Slope: 117

Tee Time: 30 days in advance.
Price: $20 - $25

Credit Cards: ■	Restaurant:		
Driving Range:	Lounge:		
Practice Green: ■	Meeting Rooms:		
Locker Room:	Tennis:		
Rental Clubs: ■	Swimming: ■		
Walkers: ■	Jogging Trails:		
Snack Bar:	Boating:		

COURSE DESCRIPTION

One of the most outstanding features on this course is the way it's set up for different types of players.

It gives you several options to drive your ball to different parts of the fairways from each of the tees. This will allow you to play within your game and not have to worry about hitting a shot you know you're not capable of.

Many of the holes are innovative and fun to play, and the overall design of the course should appeal to many different types of players.

DIRECTIONS

Take I-10 east to Exit 318 (Dragoon Rd.) which will dead-end into Hwy.191. Go south for about 7 miles and follow the signs to the course.

PUEBLO DEL SOL GOLF COURSE

2770 S. St. Andrews Dr., Sierra Vista, AZ 85635 / (602) 378-6444

BASIC INFORMATION

Course Type: Public
Year Built: 1977
Architect: N/A
Local Pro: Pat Kelly

Course: N/A
Holes: 18 / Par 72

Back : 6,880 yds. Rating: 71.3 Slope: 121
Middle: 6,599 yds. Rating: 70.0 Slope: 118
Ladies: 5,818 yds. Rating: 72.2 Slope: 119

Tee Time: 1-3 days in advance.
Price: $11 - $25

Credit Cards: ■	Restaurant:
Driving Range: ■	Lounge:
Practice Green: ■	Meeting Rooms:
Locker Room: ■	Tennis:
Rental Clubs: ■	Swimming:
Walkers: ■	Jogging Trails:
Snack Bar: ■	Boating:

COURSE DESCRIPTION

If you've never had the pleasure of playing a links-styled course, you may want to consider this layout as an introduction. It's a wonderful test of golf that will challenge you from beginning to end.

The layout opens up immediately from the tees, allowing you plenty of room to work the ball as you choose, but you'll need to keep your eyes open for deeply hidden bunkers in the distance. If your ball rolls into one of them, it could easily cost you a stroke or two.

DIRECTIONS

From Tucson, go 40 miles east on I-10 to Benson, south on Hwy. 90 to Sierra Vista, and south through the main part of town to St. Andrews Dr.

ELDEN HILLS

2380 N. Oakmont Dr., Flagstaff, AZ 86004 / (602) 527-7997

BASIC INFORMATION

Course Type: Public
Year Built: 1960
Architect: N/A
Local Pro: Leon Schwebke

Course: N/A
Holes: 18 / Par 73

Back : 6,079 yds. Rating: 66.6 Slope: 115
Middle: N/A   Rating: N/A Slope: N/A
Ladies: 5,280 yds. Rating: 70.5 Slope: 120

Tee Time: 3 days in advance.
Price: $25 - $37

Credit Cards: ■   Restaurant: ■
Driving Range: ■   Lounge: ■
Practice Green: ■   Meeting Rooms: ■
Locker Room: Tennis: ■
Rental Clubs: ■   Swimming: ■
Walkers: Jogging Trails:
Snack Bar: ■   Boating:

COURSE DESCRIPTION

Elden Hills is not your typical golf course. It's a unique par-73 venue that features three par-5 holes.

The layout has beautiful mountain views you'll enjoy looking at. The terrain does get hilly at times, but not to the point in which you'll feel uncomfortable stepping up to your ball. Get to the range early and practice hitting balls above and below your feet.

You'll find wide open fairways along the front-nine as opposed to the tree-lined narrow ones in the back. Bring along your best fade shot!

DIRECTIONS

Take exit 201 off I-40 and go south on Country Club Dr. for approximately one mile. Make a right and proceed to the clubhouse.

OAKCREEK COUNTRY CLUB, THE

690 Bell Rock Blvd., Sedona, AZ 86336 / (602) 284-1660

BASIC INFORMATION

Course Type: Semi-private
Year Built: 1968
Architect: Robert Trent Jones
Local Pro: Gary Pearce

Course: N/A
Holes: 18 / Par 72

Back : 6,854 yds. Rating: 71.9 Slope: 129
Middle: 6,286 yds. Rating: 69.4 Slope: 121
Ladies: 5,555 yds. Rating: 71.6 Slope: 124

Tee Time: 7 days in advance.
Price: $45

Credit Cards: ■   Restaurant: ■
Driving Range: ■   Lounge:
Practice Green: ■   Meeting Rooms:
Locker Room: Tennis: ■
Rental Clubs: ■   Swimming:
Walkers: Jogging Trails:
Snack Bar: ■   Boating:

COURSE DESCRIPTION

Robert Trent Jones is considered by many to be one of the most innovative and prolific designers of all time.

He built this traditional course on moderately rolling terrain. Many of the holes allow you the option to bail out to a safe spot rather than having to play a shot that requires exact execution. This allows golfers of all levels a chance to be competitive without having to be intimidated by a better player in his/her group. The course is surrounded by beautiful trees and many gorgeous mountain views. Most of the holes tend to favor a draw over a fade.

DIRECTIONS

Take I-17 to Exit 179 to the Village of Oakcreek. Go west on Verde Valley School Rd. and north on Bell Rock Blvd. The course will be on your left.

SEDONA GOLF RESORT

7260 State Hwy. 179, Sedona, AZ 86336 / (602) 284-9355

BASIC INFORMATION

Course Type: Public
Year Built: 1988
Architect: Gary Panks
Local Pro: John Benzel (Director of Golf)

Course: N/A
Holes: 18 / Par 72

Back   : 6,642 yds. Rating: 70.3 Slope: 129
Middle: 6,126 yds. Rating: 67.8 Slope: 121
Ladies: 5,030 yds. Rating: 67.0 Slope: 109

Tee Time: 14 days in advance.
Price: $35-$50

Credit Cards:	■	Restaurant:	■
Driving Range:	■	Lounge:	
Practice Green:	■	Meeting Rooms:	
Locker Room:		Tennis:	■
Rental Clubs:	■	Swimming:	
Walkers:	■	Jogging Trails:	■
Snack Bar:	■	Boating:	

COURSE DESCRIPTION

The *Sedona Golf Resort*, offers great golf amidst the spectacular red rock cliffs along its mountain range.

Nestled in a picturesque region of America's Southwest, the new Sedona Golf Resort offers 18-holes of unequalled championship golf. Gary Panks, the architect, masterfully planned this course with a deep regard for the fragile environment of the Coconino National Forest. The unique setting of the course provides golfing enthusiast breathtaking views of landscapes that are often filled with beautiful wildlife.

This is one course you'll enjoy every time you play it!

DIRECTIONS

Take the Sedona exit west off I-17 on Hwy. 179 for seven miles to the Sedona Golf & Tennis Resort.

VILLAGE OF OAKCREEK CLUB

690 W. Bell Rock Blvd., Sedona, AZ 86336 / (602) 284-1660

BASIC INFORMATION

Course Type: Semi-private
Year Built: 1968
Architect: Robert Trent Jones, Sr.
Local Pro: Gary Pearce

Course: N/A
Holes: 18 / Par 72

Back   : 6,854 yds. Rating: 71.9 Slope: 129
Middle: 6,286 yds. Rating: 69.4 Slope: 121
Ladies: 5,355 yds. Rating: 71.6 Slope: 124

Tee Time: 14 days in advance.
Price: $20 - $45

Credit Cards:	■	Restaurant:	■
Driving Range:	■	Lounge:	■
Practice Green:	■	Meeting Rooms:	■
Locker Room:		Tennis:	■
Rental Clubs:		Swimming:	
Walkers:	■	Jogging Trails:	
Snack Bar:	■	Boating:	

COURSE DESCRIPTION

Robert Trent Jones, Sr., has once again designed one heck of a great golf course.

The most comforting part of playing the *Village Of Oakcreek Club* is that it's designed to appeal to a wide spectrum of golfers with respect to their various handicaps. The course features a nicely woven series of holes that play well together in their original design. Some will force you to hit long accurate drives for position, while others will require you to have a deft touch around the greens. Either way, the course is designed to challenge many different styles of play.

DIRECTIONS

Take I-10 north to Hwy. 179 and make a right at Birde Valley School Rd. Make a right at Bell Rock Blvd.

PAYSON GOLF COURSE

1504 W. Country Club Dr., Payson, AZ 85541 / (602) 474-2273

BASIC INFORMATION

Course Type: Public
Year Built: 1959 / 1975
Architect: F. Hughes / R. Zakarison
Local Pro: N/A

Course: N/A
Holes: 18 / Par 72

Back : 5,854 yds. Rating: 66.9 Slope: 114
Middle: N/A yds. Rating: N/A Slope: N/A
Ladies: 5,061 yds. Rating: 67.5 Slope: 110

Tee Time: 30 days in advance.
Price: $18 - $27

Credit Cards:		Restaurant:	
Driving Range:	■	Lounge:	■
Practice Green:	■	Meeting Rooms:	
Locker Room:		Tennis:	
Rental Clubs:	■	Swimming:	
Walkers:	■	Jogging Trails:	
Snack Bar:	■	Boating:	

COURSE DESCRIPTION

This is the type of course you'll like for the sheer enjoyment of playing the game rather than having to slug it out with an unbearably long and difficult desert layout.

You'll enjoy the pleasant cool weather that comes with being 5,200' above sea level and the many beautiful sights of nature that it features.

The course was built with Bluegrass on the fairways and Seaside Bent grass putting greens. The front-nine is open and features larger greens, while the back-nine features tighter fairways with smaller greens.

DIRECTIONS

Take Hwy. 87 from Phoenix and turn left to Main St. at the first stoplight. Follow the road for about 1 1/2 miles and look for the course on your right.

MT. GRAHAM GOLF COURSE

Golf Course Rd., Safford, AZ 85546 / (602) 428-1260

BASIC INFORMATION

Course Type: Municipal
Year Built: 1945
Architect: N/A
Local Pro: Burton Watkins

Course: N/A
Holes: 18 / Par 72

Back : 6,354 yds. Rating: 69.5 Slope: 116
Middle: N/A Rating: N/A Slope: N/A
Ladies: 5,691 yds. Rating: 71.3 Slope: 117

Tee Time: N/A
Price: $15

Credit Cards:		Restaurant:	
Driving Range:	■	Lounge:	■
Practice Green:	■	Meeting Rooms:	
Locker Room:		Tennis:	
Rental Clubs:	■	Swimming:	
Walkers:	■	Jogging Trails:	
Snack Bar:	■	Boating:	

COURSE DESCRIPTION

The *Mt. Graham Golf Course* offers inexpensive golf for the golfer who needs a break from the more expensive venues. Like most municipal courses, this one gets a lot of play during the year, making it a little more difficult to keep in prime shape — but it's a pleasant surprise. The terrain is mostly level along the fairways and features many mature trees throughout the playing field.

Because of its relative ease, this is not the type of course I would recommend for better players.

DIRECTIONS

Turn south off Hwy. 70 on 20th Ave. and that will take you to Golf Course Rd. Make a right and that will take you right into the course.

LAPAZ / MARICOPA COUNTIES

EMERALD CANYON GOLF COURSE

72 Emerald Canyon Dr., Parker, AZ 85344 / (602) 667-3366

BASIC INFORMATION

Course Type: Public
Year Built: 1989
Architect: Design Plus West
Local Pro: Steve Benton

Course: N/A
Holes: 72

Back : 6,657 yds. Rating: 71.5 Slope: 131
Middle: 5,989 yds. Rating: 68.1 Slope: 120
Ladies: 4,754 yds. Rating: 66.2 Slope: 119

Tee Time: 7 days in advance.
Price: $15 - $26

Credit Cards:	■	Restaurant:	
Driving Range:	■	Lounge:	■
Practice Green:	■	Meeting Rooms:	
Locker Room:		Tennis:	
Rental Clubs:	■	Swimming:	
Walkers:	■	Jogging Trails:	■
Snack Bar:	■	Boating:	■

COURSE DESCRIPTION

This scenic course is one you'll keep in mind for quite a long time. You'll find holes that run along canyon fields and mountainous terrains with spectacular views of landscapes that you'll want to capture with your camera.

It's a very hard challenge from the back tees and should only be played by low handicappers for maximum fun. This layout puts a premium on accuracy. Work on hitting the ball along a fairly straight path rather than using a fade or a draw.

This is a demanding course with many excellent rewards for the skillful shot-maker.

DIRECTIONS

Take Hwy. 95 north to I-10 or south from I-40, 8 miles north of Parker, AZ. Hwy. 95 runs right through the course.

APACHE WELLS COUNTRY CLUB

5601 E. Hermosa Vista Dr., Mesa, AZ 85205 / (602) 830-4725

BASIC INFORMATION

Course Type: Semi-private
Year Built: 1963
Architect: Hughes
Local Pro: Brian Grosswiler

Course: N/A
Holes: 18 / Par 71

Back : 6,047 yds. Rating: 66.7 Slope: 102
Middle: 5,756 yds. Rating: 65.4 Slope: 99
Ladies: 5,374 yds. Rating: 68.1 Slope: 100

Tee Time: 3 days in advance.
Price: $10 - $25

Credit Cards:		Restaurant:	■
Driving Range:	■	Lounge:	■
Practice Green:	■	Meeting Rooms:	■
Locker Room:		Tennis:	
Rental Clubs:	■	Swimming:	
Walkers:	■	Jogging Trails:	
Snack Bar:		Boating:	

COURSE DESCRIPTION

Apache Wells Country Club was built in the middle of a housing development. It was specifically designed for Senior golfers, yet also serves as a good layout for beginners who are looking for a course that is relatively easy and not at all intimidating. Many golfers are enticed to walk the course because of the flat terrain that it was built on.

With challenging par-3's and reachable par-5's, the course is easily open to low numbers. Plan your strategy and work on your short-irons and wedges.

The course is open to the public from May 1st through October 31st.

DIRECTIONS

Go east on 360 to Higley Rd. then north to McKellips. Make a right to 56th St. then a left to the course. Look for it on your right.

MARICOPA COUNTY

ARIZONA BILTMORE RESORT HOTEL
24TH St. & E. Missouri Ave., Phoenix, AZ 85016 / (602) 955-6600

BASIC INFORMATION

Course Type: Public
Year Built: 1979
Architect: Bill Johnson
Local Pro: Randy Beaupre

Course: Links (18 / Par 72)
Holes: 36

Back : 6,300 yds. Rating: 69.3 Slope: 122
Middle: 5,726 yds. Rating: 66.6 Slope: 115
Ladies: 4,747 yds. Rating: 68.0 Slope: 115

Tee Time: 5 days with credit-card.
Price: $35 - $87

Credit Cards: ■   Restaurant: ■
Driving Range: ■   Lounge: ■
Practice Green: ■   Meeting Rooms:
Locker Room: ■   Tennis:
Rental Clubs: ■   Swimming:
Walkers: Jogging Trails:
Snack Bar: ■   Boating:

COURSE DESCRIPTION
The Links, constructed in 1979 by Bill Johnson, offers a super layout with many solid hole designs. You'll find lush rolling fairways running between mature trees and dazzling lakes.

The Adobe course was constructed in 1932 by William Bell. Like most traditional courses, this one puts an emphasis on accuracy over distance. The 60-year-old-tree lined fairways are shaped around beautiful streams and lakes with many gorgeous views of Squaw Peak and Camelback Mountain.

The course's signature third-hole features a small lake with a 100-yard carry to the green.

DIRECTIONS
Take I-17 north to Missouri Ave. and go east to the course.

ARIZONA GOLF RESORT & CONFERENCE CENTER
425 S. Power Rd., Mesa, AZ 85206 / (602) 832-1661

BASIC INFORMATION

Course Type: Public (Resort Daily Fee)
Year Built: N/A
Architect: N/A
Local Pro: Donald L. Parker

Course: N/A
Holes: 18 / Par 72

Back : 6,574 yds. Rating: 71.1 Slope: 123
Middle: 6,195 yds. Rating: 69.4 Slope: 117
Ladies: 5,782 yds. Rating: 72.0 Slope: 115

Tee Time: Please call to confirm.
Price: $25 - $62

Credit Cards: ■   Restaurant: ■
Driving Range: ■   Lounge: ■
Practice Green: ■   Meeting Rooms: ■
Locker Room: ■   Tennis: ■
Rental Clubs: ■   Swimming: ■
Walkers: Jogging Trails:
Snack Bar: ■   Boating:

COURSE DESCRIPTION
This well-maintained golf course features rolling hills and elevated greens that flow between tall trees and a lot of real estate.

Long hitters will find the par-3's to their advantage with six of them playing over 200 yds. long. Ironically, the par-5's play rather short and are often reachable in two strokes. It makes for an interesting day of golf with many opportunities to score well.

The course caters to golfers of all abilities by offering four sets of tees to choose from.

DIRECTIONS
Go east on Hwy. 60 to Power Rd. (Exit 188). Turn left and go two miles to Broadway Rd. Make a right to the first entrance and that will be the course.

MARICOPA COUNTY

CAMELBACK GOLF CLUB
7847 N. Mocking Bird Lane, Scottsdale, AZ 85253 / (602) 948-6770

BASIC INFORMATION

Course Type: Resort / Semi-private
Year Built: 1980
Architect: Jack Snyder
Local Pro: Mark Bakeman

Course: Indian Bend (18 / Par 72)
Holes: 36

Back : 7,014 yds. Rating: 71.9 Slope: 116
Middle: 6,486 yds. Rating: 69.2 Slope: 114
Ladies: 5,917 yds. Rating: 72.0 Slope: 118

Tee Time: 7 days in advance.
Price: $30 - $85

Credit Cards:	■	Restaurant:	■
Driving Range:	■	Lounge:	■
Practice Green:	■	Meeting Rooms:	
Locker Room:	■	Tennis:	
Rental Clubs:	■	Swimming:	
Walkers:		Jogging Trails:	
Snack Bar:	■	Boating:	

COURSE DESCRIPTION

This is one of the finest golfing destinations in the city of Scottsdale and is part of the 5-Star Diamond Resort Camelback Inn. All 36-holes of golf are absolutely spectacular.

From the teeing area, you'll be looking across perfectly manicured fairways, mature trees, and lushly landscaped surroundings that lead to a wide assortment of putting greens. You'll find many creatively set greens that will challenge your putting stroke throughout the day.

DIRECTIONS

Take the McCorimick Ranch Pkwy. west to Scottsdale Rd. and head south to Cheney. Go east on Cheney and North on Mockingbird Lane to the course.

CAMELOT GOLF CLUB
6210 E. McKellips Rd., Mesa, AZ 85205 / (602) 832-0156

BASIC INFORMATION

Course Type: Municipal (Daily Fee)
Year Built: 1969
Architect: N/A
Local Pro: Mike Barnett

Course:N/A
Holes: 18 / Par 70

Back : 6,026 yds. Rating: 65.9 Slope: 95
Middle: 5,240 yds. Rating: 63.5 Slope: 90
Ladies: 4,660 yds. Rating: N/A Slope: N/A

Tee Time: 3 days in advance.
Price: $10 - $39

Credit Cards:	■	Restaurant:	■
Driving Range:	■	Lounge:	■
Practice Green:	■	Meeting Rooms:	■
Locker Room:		Tennis:	
Rental Clubs:	■	Swimming:	
Walkers:	■	Jogging Trails:	
Snack Bar:	■	Boating:	■

COURSE DESCRIPTION

Friendly is the operative word for this course. It's set up for the average golfer to have a fun experience without having to contend with overly difficult hazards.

The layout is consistently flat throughout and features nicely contoured fairways that are wide enough for the most sporadic of drives. Both the front-nine and the back-nine holes play consistently even, yet they do favor a high-flying fade over a low-flying draw.

If you'd like to take golf lessons, the course holds a division with the John Jacobs Golf School.

DIRECTIONS

Take the Superstition Freeway east to Power Rd. and go north to McKellips Rd. Make a left at McKellips Rd. and look for the course about a mile further on your right.

CAVE CREEK MUNICIPAL GOLF COURSE
15202 N. 19 Ave., Phoenix, AZ 85023 / (602) 866-8076

BASIC INFORMATION

Course Type: Municipal
Year Built: 1982-83
Architect: Jack Snyder
Local Pro: Jim Franko

Course: N/A
Holes: 18 / Par 72

Back : 6,876 yds. Rating: 71.1 Slope: 122
Middle: 6,290 yds. Rating: 68.3 Slope: 117
Ladies: 5,614 yds. Rating: 68.9 Slope: 109

Tee Time: 2 days in advance.
Price: $5 - $25.50

Credit Cards:	■	Restaurant:	■
Driving Range:	■	Lounge:	
Practice Green:	■	Meeting Rooms:	
Locker Room:		Tennis:	
Rental Clubs:	■	Swimming:	
Walkers:	■	Jogging Trails:	
Snack Bar:	■	Boating:	

COURSE DESCRIPTION

This understated course features innovative hole designs that appear much easier than they really are. The fairways are wide open and run between 10 year-old trees that are often small enough to hit over when needed.

Although the course favors long hitters, the true challenge begins on the large putting greens, which will cause you a lot of trouble if you don't get your ball close to the hole on your approach shots. They're undulating and at times hard to read.

This is a true shotmakers course!

DIRECTIONS

Take I-10 to Thunderbird and go east to 19th Ave. Make a left and the course will be only 3/4 miles on your left.

ENCANTO - 18 MUNICIPAL GOLF COURSE
2705 N. 15 Ave., Phoenix, AZ 85007 / (602) 253-3963

BASIC INFORMATION

Course Type: Public
Year Built: 1940
Architect: N/A
Local Pro: Jim Farkas

Course: N/A
Holes: 18 / Par 72

Back : 6,600 yds. Rating: 70.8 Slope: 111
Middle: 6,200 yds. Rating: 67.0 Slope: 105
Ladies: 5,900 yds. Rating: 71.0 Slope: 111

Tee Time: 2 days in advance.
Price: $6 - $25

Credit Cards:	■	Restaurant:	■
Driving Range:	■	Lounge:	■
Practice Green:	■	Meeting Rooms:	
Locker Room:		Tennis:	
Rental Clubs:	■	Swimming:	
Walkers:	■	Jogging Trails:	■
Snack Bar:	■	Boating:	■

COURSE DESCRIPTION

One of the most interesting features on this course is that it offers five par-3's and three par-5's. Yet it still has a total yardage of 6,600 yards from the back tees with a comforting 111 slope rating for amateur golfers.

It's not a tremendously hard course to play, but it's a surprisingly good layout to experience. If your natural shot is a draw, you'll find the majority of the course playing to the natural flight of your ball. Get your birdies early, for the back-nine plays much harder than the front.

You'll find some beautiful skyline views of downtown Phoenix from different vantage points along the course.

DIRECTIONS

Take I-10 north on 7th Ave. and go west on McDowell Rd. to 15th Ave. Make a right on 15th and that will take you to the course.

ESTRELLA MOUNTAIN GOLF COURSE
S. Bullard Ave., Goodyear, AZ 85338 / (602) 932-3714

BASIC INFORMATION

Course Type: Municipal
Year Built: 1962
Architect: N/A
Local Pro: Dick Mulvaine

Course: N/A
Holes: 18 / Par 72

Back : 6,415 yds. Rating: 69.5 Slope: 118
Middle: N/A Rating: N/A Slope: N/A
Ladies: 5,374 yds. Rating: 71.2 Slope: 116

Tee Time: 7 days in advance.
Price: $13 - $20

Credit Cards:	■	Restaurant:	
Driving Range:	■	Lounge:	
Practice Green:	■	Meeting Rooms:	
Locker Room:		Tennis:	
Rental Clubs:	■	Swimming:	
Walkers:	■	Jogging Trails:	
Snack Bar:	■	Boating:	

COURSE DESCRIPTION

If you're a 15 or higher handicapper, you're bound to have an excellent time at this course, for it offers many good opportunities to make par or better.

The course is set in the foothills of the Estrella Mountains featuring soft rolling fairways, lined with trees and desert rough. It makes for a fabulous setting to score low numbers.

Many of the locals feel that the course plays much harder than the numbers indicated on the scorecard for its rating and slope.

DIRECTIONS

Take I-10 west to exit Estrella Pkwy. Continue south for about five miles and make a left on Vineyaro. Make a right at the first gate, Golf Course Dr., and that will take you straight to the clubhouse.

500 CLUB GOLF COURSE
4707 W. Pinnicle Peak Rd., Glendale, AZ 85310 / (602) 492-9500

BASIC INFORMATION

Course Type: Public
Year Built: 1990
Architect: Brian Whitcomb
Local Pro: Craig Buckley

Course:N/A
Holes: 18 / Par 72

Back : 6,543 yds. Rating: 69.8 Slope: 116
Middle: 6,083 yds. Rating: 67.5 Slope: 113
Ladies: 5,557 yds. Rating: 69.8 Slope: 112

Tee Time: 3 days in advance.
Price: $20 - $39.50

Credit Cards:	■	Restaurant:	
Driving Range:	■	Lounge:	■
Practice Green:	■	Meeting Rooms:	
Locker Room:		Tennis:	
Rental Clubs:	■	Swimming:	
Walkers:	■	Jogging Trails:	
Snack Bar:	■	Boating:	

COURSE DESCRIPTION

This is another of Arizona's many friendly golf courses. Average golfers will most likely be the ones to get the most out of it for a number of reasons. The length of the course is neither long nor short, which makes the layout fun and interesting to play.

The fairways have been built wide and open, making them highly forgiving on misguided drives. The putting surfaces allow a two-club length variance for your approach shots, which on most occasions will make your target a little easier than normal to hit. Once on, two putting shouldn't be a problem.

DIRECTIONS

Take I-17 north to Pinnacle Peak, make a left, and follow the road to the course.

FOOTHILLS GOLF CLUB

22201 E. Clubhouse Dr. , Phoenix, AZ 85044 / (602) 460-8337

BASIC INFORMATION

Course Type: Public
Year Built: 1987
Architect: Tom Weiskopf / Jay Morrish
Local Pro: Jim Schade

Course: N/A
Holes: 18 / Par 72

Back : 6,967 yds. Rating: 72.7 Slope: 125
Middle: 6,406 yds. Rating: 69.9 Slope: 115
Ladies: 5,213 yds. Rating: 64.5 Slope: 102

Tee Time: 7 days in advance.
Price: $30 & $80

Credit Cards:	■	Restaurant:	■
Driving Range:	■	Lounge:	■
Practice Green:	■	Meeting Rooms:	■
Locker Room:	■	Tennis:	
Rental Clubs:	■	Swimming:	
Walkers:		Jogging Trails:	
Snack Bar:	■	Boating:	

COURSE DESCRIPTION

Designed by the award winning team of Tom Weiskopf and Jay Morrish, *The Foothills Golf Club* is a rewarding experience for golfers at every level.

Nestled in the Estrella Mountains, this desert links course offers some of the most spectacular golfing in the Southwest. The meticulously groomed championship course is complemented by strategic bunkering, grass mounding, naturally rolling Tif-Burmuda-grass fairways, and greens.

It's a wonderful place to experience the joy of playing golf in the Valley of the Sun.

DIRECTIONS

Exit I-10 at Chandler Blvd. and continue west until you get to 19th St. Turn left and follow the street to the clubhouse which will be on right side.

FOUNTAIN HILLS GOLF CLUB

10440 N. Indian Wells Dr., AZ 85268 / (602) 837-1173

BASIC INFORMATION

Course Type: Public
Year Built: 1970
Architect: John Allen
Local Pro: Hale Wittington

Course: N/A
Holes: 18 /Par 72

Back : 6,100 yds. Rating: 68.9 Slope: 119
Middle: N/A Rating: N/A Slope: N/A
Ladies: 5,898 yds. Rating: 71.5 Slope: 112

Tee Time: 3 days in advance.
Price: $29.50 - $69.50

Credit Cards:	■	Restaurant:	■
Driving Range:	■	Lounge:	
Practice Green:	■	Meeting Rooms:	
Locker Room:	■	Tennis:	
Rental Clubs:	■	Swimming:	
Walkers:		Jogging Trails:	
Snack Bar:	■	Boating:	

COURSE DESCRIPTION

High-handicap players and Senior citizens will get the most out of this course. They can comfortably hit their tee shots with a 3-wood throughout the entire day without having to worry about making up the distance on their approach shots with a difficult low-lofted-iron. Playing well here means having to place tee shots onto the proper landing areas of the fairways and following through with good short-iron approaches.

The rolling terrain of the course will often place your ball on an uneven lie. Practicing these types of shots on the range will help you gain the control that you'll want when you finally play the course.

DIRECTIONS

The course is east of Scottsdale on Shea Blvd., 11-miles to Saguaro Blvd. Make a left at Indian Wells to the course.

GOLF CLUB AT RANCHO MANAÑA

5734 E. Rancho Manaña Rd., Cave Creek, AZ 85331 / (602) 488-0398

BASIC INFORMATION

Course Type: Semi-private
Year Built: 1988
Architect: Bill Johnston
Local Pro: Ron Nicol

Course:N/A
Holes: 18 / par 72

Back : 6,378 yds. Rating: 69.7 Slope: 127
Middle: 5,910 yds. Rating: 69.1 Slope: 122
Ladies: 5,011 yds. Rating: 68.8 Slope: 114

Tee Time: 7 days in advance.
Price: $20 - $65

Credit Cards:	■	Restaurant:	■
Driving Range:	■	Lounge:	■
Practice Green:	■	Meeting Rooms:	
Locker Room:	■	Tennis:	
Rental Clubs:	■	Swimming:	
Walkers:		Jogging Trails:	
Snack Bar:	■	Boating:	■

COURSE DESCRIPTION

Nestled between the base of Black Mountain and Skull Mesa in the heart of Cave Creek's Sonoran Desert, *Rancho Manaña* is certainly one of the finest courses you'll find in the high desert plateau.

You'll be entranced by the pristine environment of this course, set as it is in a serene locale far away from the turbulence of the city. The fairways twist and turn between lush desert surroundings leading to small greens that are both undulating and demanding.

Accuracy takes high precedence over distance. Practice working the ball both left and right before you play this wonderful layout.

DIRECTIONS

1 1/2 miles north of Carefree Hwy. on Cave Creek Rd. Look for the course on your left.

HAPPY TRAILS GOLF RESORT

17200 W. Bell Rd., Surprise, AZ 85374 / (602) 584-6000

BASIC INFORMATION

Course Type: Semi-private
Year Built: 1985
Architect: Ken Kavanaugh / Greg Nash
Local Pro: Eric Grindereng

Course: N/A
Holes: 18 / Par 72

Back : 6,646 yds. Rating: 72.1 Slope: 124
Middle: 5,939 yds. Rating: 68.7 Slope: 119
Ladies: 5,146 yds. Rating: 69.7 Slope: 117

Tee Time: 3 days in advance.
Price: $15 - $45

Credit Cards:	■	Restaurant:	■
Driving Range:	■	Lounge:	■
Practice Green:	■	Meeting Rooms:	
Locker Room:	■	Tennis:	■
Rental Clubs:	■	Swimming:	■
Walkers:		Jogging Trails:	
Snack Bar:	■	Boating:	

COURSE DESCRIPTION

Happy Trails Golf Resort is located at the foot of the breathtaking White Tank Mountains in the heart of beautiful Arizona.

An inviting 18-hole, par-72 championship golf course offers you the best of both worlds. The original nine (which is now the back nine) was created by Ken Kavanaugh in 1985. The new nine, created by Greg Nash, is an equally challenging and complementary addition.

From the well-manicured tees and fairways to the lush bent grass greens, a challenging and enjoyable round of golf is awaiting your arrival.

DIRECTIONS

Take I-10 west to Cotton Lane and go North to Bell Rd. Make a left and look for the course on your right.

HILLSCREST GOLF COURSE

20002 N. Star Ridge Dr., Sun City West, AZ 85375 / (602) 584-1500

BASIC INFORMATION

Course Type: Public
Year Built: 1978
Architect: Greg Nash
Local Pro: Gary Balliet

Course:N/A
Holes: 18/ Par 72

Back : 6,960 yds. Rating: 72.5 Slope: 127
Middle: 6,421 yds. Rating: 69.8 Slope: 116
Ladies: 5,909 yds. Rating: 72.7 Slope: 121

Tee Time: 30 days in advance.
Price: $25 - $50

Credit Cards:	■	Restaurant:	
Driving Range:	■	Lounge:	
Practice Green:	■	Meeting Rooms:	
Locker Room:		Tennis:	
Rental Clubs:	■	Swimming:	
Walkers:		Jogging Trails:	
Snack Bar:	■	Boating:	

COURSE DESCRIPTION

The traditional layout of this course has inspired five Senior PGA competitions (1983-1988) and three LPGA competitions (1980-1982). The course features gently rolling hills with 72 sand-bunkers running along open fairways that lead to large undulating greens. The other obstacle you'll need to overcome is the twelve holes that play into water. If you've ever played golf in Florida, this course will make you feel right at home.

The following is a list of some of the champions on the Senior PGA Tour that have played here: Billy Casper, Al Geiberger, Don January, and Charles Owens.

DIRECTIONS

Take I-75 to Bell Rd., west to El Mirage Rd., north to Beardsley, west one mile to a dead-end, and look for the course on your left.

KARSTAN GOLF COURSE AT A.S.U.

Rio Salado Pkwy., Tempe, AZ 85281 / (602) 921-8070

BASIC INFORMATION

Course Type: Public
Year Built: 1989
Architect: Pete Dye
Local Pro: Scott Summers

Course:N/A
Holes: 18 / Par 72

Back : 7,057 yds. Rating: 74.3 Slope: 133
Middle: 6,272 yds. Rating: 70.3 Slope: 125
Ladies: 4,765 yds. Rating: 67.5 Slope: 115

Tee Time: 5 days in advance.
Price: $20 - $64

Credit Cards:	■	Restaurant:	
Driving Range:	■	Lounge:	
Practice Green:	■	Meeting Rooms:	
Locker Room:		Tennis:	
Rental Clubs:	■	Swimming:	
Walkers:	■	Jogging Trails:	
Snack Bar:	■	Boating:	

COURSE DESCRIPTION

This course takes a great amount of thought to play well on. The open architecture is reminiscent of the great Scottish links courses that have influenced architects since the beginning of golf. It's a fascinating challenge that you won't easily forget.

The 4th-hole (par-4/420 yds.) is the number one handicap design on the course. It requires a long straight tee shot to a fairway that features severe mounds on both sides. The green is protected by a pot bunker in the front-left along with water left and behind. The smart approach shot is always to the right-center.

DIRECTIONS

Exit I-10 to the east on University Dr. Turn left on Rural Rd. and right on Rio Salado Pkwy. The course will be about 300 yards on your right.

KEN MCDONALD GOLF COURSE

800 E. Divot Dr., Tempe, AZ 85283 / (602) 350-5250

BASIC INFORMATION

Course Type: Municipal
Year Built: 1974
Architect: Jack Snider
Local Pro: Dick Sanders

Course: N/A
Holes: 18 / Par 72

Back : 6,743 yds. Rating: 70.8 Slope: 115
Middle: 6,316 yds. Rating: 68.7 Slope: 111
Ladies: 5,872 yds. Rating: 70.4 Slope: 112

Tee Time: 2 days in advance.
Price: $11 - $17

Credit Cards: ■   Restaurant: ■
Driving Range: ■   Lounge: ■
Practice Green: ■   Meeting Rooms:
Locker Room: Tennis:
Rental Clubs: ■   Swimming:
Walkers: ■   Jogging Trails:
Snack Bar: ■   Boating:

COURSE DESCRIPTION

This course emphasizes fun above all else. Its relative ease makes it attractive for many different types of players.

You've got a flat layout that features a good variety of trees and a challeging series of golf holes. You'll find many of the fairways easy to hit because of thier relative width.

Most golfers tend to hit their balls with a left-to-right spin, and that's exactly what this course favors. Play your fades high-and-soft and you'll fare well.

DIRECTIONS

Take I-17 south and exit to Elliot Rd. Go east to Rural Rd. and turn left about a half-mile further. You'll see the course on your left behind the Y.M.C.A.

LEGEND GOLF CLUB, THE

21025 N. 67 Ave., Glendale, AZ 85308 / (800) GO TRY 18

BASIC INFORMATION

Course Type: Public
Year Built: 1987
Architect: Arnold Palmer
Local Pro: Todd Siel

Course: N/A
Holes: 18 / Par72

Back : 7,005 yds. Rating: 73.0 Slope: 129
Middle: 6,509 yds. Rating: 70.7 Slope: 124
Ladies: 5,233 yds. Rating: 71.2 Slope: 119

Tee Time: 7 days in advance.
Price: $28 - $69

Credit Cards: ■   Restaurant:
Driving Range: ■   Lounge:
Practice Green: ■   Meeting Rooms:
Locker Room: Tennis:
Rental Clubs: ■   Swimming:
Walkers: Jogging Trails:
Snack Bar: ■   Boating:

COURSE DESCRIPTION

The Legend is a traditionally designed golf course that features six sparkling blue lakes and hundreds of palm trees throughout its impressive layout.

Arnold Palmer once said the following about the course's signature hole: " Golf just doesn't come any better than hole number 5." It's a 426 yrd., par-4, that has an elevated tee overlooking a beautiful view of the Valley. It also feautures one of the most treacherous putting surfaces on the course: one of many that you'll need to master by the end of the day!

DIRECTIONS

Take I-17 north to the Union Hills Dr. exit. Go west to 67 Ave. Turn right and proceed two miles. The course will be on your right.

MARICOPA COUNTY

LOS CABALLEROS GOLF CLUB
1551 S. Vulture Mine Rd., Wickenburg, AZ 85390 / (602) 634-2704

BASIC INFORMATION

Course Type: Semi-private
Year Built: 1980
Architect: Hardin / Nash
Local Pro: Van Batchelder

Course: N/A
Holes: 18 / Par 72

Back : 6,962 yds. Rating: 73.4 Slope: 136
Middle: 6,554 yds. Rating: 71.3 Slope: 131
Ladies: 5,690 yds. Rating: 73.8 Slope: 128

Tee Time: 2 days in advance.
Price: $33 - $77

Credit Cards:		Restaurant:	■
Driving Range:	■	Lounge:	■
Practice Green:	■	Meeting Rooms:	■
Locker Room:	■	Tennis:	■
Rental Clubs:	■	Swimming:	■
Walkers:	■	Jogging Trails:	■
Snack Bar:	■	Boating:	

COURSE DESCRIPTION

If you're looking for a true PGA Tour caliber golf course that demands both distance and accuracy from tee-to-green, the *Los Caballeros Golf Club* won't let you down.

The 136 slope rating from the back-tees says it all. Making par requires long accurate drives to strategic landing areas. The greens are both large and undulating and can often cost you a stroke if you don't know where to place your ball on your approach shots.

This is a very competitive course that demands absolute concentration to play well on. Get to the course early to practice your putting game.

DIRECTIONS

Go west on I-10 to Cotton Ln. (Exit 124) to Loop-303. Go 20 miles north to Hwy. 60, west for another 20 miles to Wickenburg, and left on Vulture Mine Rd. to the course.

MARYVALE MUNICIPAL GOLF COURSE
5902 W. Indian School Rd., Phoenix, AZ 85033 / (602) 846-4022

BASIC INFORMATION

Course Type: Municipal
Year Built: 1961
Architect: William Bell
Local Pro: John Marin

Course: N/A
Holes: 18 / Par 72

Back : 6,539 yds. Rating: 70.0 Slope: 115
Middle: 6,191 yds. Rating: 68.1 Slope: 111
Ladies: 5,656 yds. Rating: 70.0 Slope: 111

Tee Time: 2 days in advance.
Price: $12 - $25.50

Credit Cards:	■	Restaurant:	
Driving Range:	■	Lounge:	
Practice Green:	■	Meeting Rooms:	
Locker Room:		Tennis:	
Rental Clubs:	■	Swimming:	
Walkers:	■	Jogging Trails:	
Snack Bar:	■	Boating:	

COURSE DESCRIPTION

You can't knock these unique little courses for their size. After all, they do have the same traits as the longer courses, yet they are less punishing for the average golfer.

That is exactly what you'll find at the *Maryvale Municipal Golf Course*. It's a clean layout that features interesting holes set up for aggressive play. All you need to do is keep the ball in good position and you should finish off the day with a good number.

The course features many tree lined fairways, four lakes, and a good variety of sand. The flat design will give your ball plenty of roll off the tees.

DIRECTIONS

Take I-10 west to 59 Ave. 4 miles north to Indian School Rd. The course will be on the northwest corner.

MCCORMICK RANCH GOLF CLUB

7505 E. McCormick Pkwy., Scottsdale, AZ 85258 / (602) 948-0260

BASIC INFORMATION

Course Type: Public
Year Built: 1972
Architect: Desmond Muirhead
Local Pro: Kirk Padgett

Course: Palm (18 / Par 72)
Holes: 36

Back : 7,032 yds. Rating: 73.7 Slope: 133
Middle: 6,279 yds. Rating: 69.9 Slope: 127
Ladies: 5,210 yds. Rating: 70.2 Slope: 120

Tee Time: 2 days public / 7 days for hotels.
Price: $32 - $79

Credit Cards:	■	Restaurant:	■
Driving Range:	■	Lounge:	■
Practice Green:	■	Meeting Rooms:	■
Locker Room:	■	Tennis:	
Rental Clubs:	■	Swimming:	
Walkers:		Jogging Trails:	
Snack Bar:	■	Boating:	■

COURSE DESCRIPTION

Each one of the two available courses offer spectacular golf for players of all levels, but beware — the courses are extremely long and difficult from the back tees and should not be attempted by anyone holding a 10-handicap and above.

If you're a mid-to-high handicapper, the middle tees will offer you the greatest amount of challenge and fun without penalizing you for minor mistakes.

With over 100,000 rounds of golf played here each year, the McCormick Ranch Golf Club is unquestionably one of the most popular attractions in Scottsdale.

DIRECTIONS

Take Scottsdale Rd. north of downtown Scottsdale and make a right at McCormick Pkwy. Go 1/4 mile further and you'll see the clubhouse on the right side of the street.

OCOTILLO GOLF COURSE

3751 S. Clubhouse Dr., Chandler, AZ 85248 / (602) 275-4355

BASIC INFORMATION

Course Type: Public
Year Built: 1986
Architect: Ted Robinson
Local Pro: Tim Heffuer

Course: White / Golf (18 / Par 72)
Holes: 27

Back : 6,605 yds. Rating: 71.7 Slope: 126
Middle: 6,200 yds. Rating: 70.2 Slope: 123
Ladies: 6,100 yds. Rating: 69.0 Slope: 120

Tee Time: 2 days in advance.
Price: $29 - $75

Credit Cards:	■	Restaurant:	■
Driving Range:	■	Lounge:	■
Practice Green:	■	Meeting Rooms:	
Locker Room:		Tennis:	
Rental Clubs:	■	Swimming:	
Walkers:		Jogging Trails:	
Snack Bar:	■	Boating:	

COURSE DESCRIPTION

The three nines at the *Ocotillo Golf Club* are absolutely spectacular. Each one is impeccably kept, with offerings of great strategically designed holes to conquer on your way to par.

Water is featured on many of the holes making proper club selection an important ingredient to a low scoring round. Strategy means everything here! Play the course to your individual ability and don't get tempted into playing a shot over water that requires a long carry. The beauty behind these 27 holes is that they offer you a variety of choices on your way to par. Choose the best route for your particular style and have fun!

DIRECTIONS

Take I-10 south towards Tucson and exit on Chandler Blvd. Proceed east to Price Rd. and south on Price Rd. to the course.

ORANGE TREE GOLF RESORT

10601 N. 56 St., Scottsdale, AZ 85254 / (602) 948-6100

BASIC INFORMATION

Course Type: Public
Year Built: 1957
Architect: Jonathan Bulla
Local Pro: Randy Wittig

Course: N/A
Holes: 18 / Par 72

Back : 6,762 yds. Rating: 71.3 Slope: 122
Middle: 6,398 yds. Rating: 69.5 Slope: 118
Ladies: 5,632 yds. Rating: 71.8 Slope: 116

Tee Time: 7 days in advance.
Price: $27 - $90

Credit Cards:	■	Restaurant:	■
Driving Range:	■	Lounge:	■
Practice Green:	■	Meeting Rooms:	■
Locker Room:	■	Tennis:	
Rental Clubs:	■	Swimming:	
Walkers:		Jogging Trails:	■
Snack Bar:	■	Boating:	

COURSE DESCRIPTION

The *Orange Tree Golf Resort* is a nice public design with a good mixture of holes that play comfortably in their selective positions. The course favors neither a fade nor a draw, which adds to its appeal by offering a great selection of playable options on every hole.

This is a well-conditioned course with many inviting tree lined fairways built on a fairly level playing field. You won't find any drastic elevation changes to complicate your playing stance. The course is fairly straightforward and simple to understand.

DIRECTIONS

Take Scottsdale Rd., 2 miles west to Shea Blvd. Go north on 56th St. for about two blocks and look for the course on your right.

PAPAGO MUNICIPAL GOLF COURSE

5595 E. Moreland St., Phoenix, AZ 85008 / (602) 495-0555

BASIC INFORMATION

Course Type: Municipal
Year Built: 1963
Architect: William Bell
Local Pro: Joe Huber

Course: N/A
Holes: 18 / Par 72

Back : 7,068 yds. Rating: 73.3 Slope: 132
Middle: 6,590 yds. Rating: 70.7 Slope: 123
Ladies: 5,936 yds. Rating: 72.4 Slope: 119

Tee Time: 2 days in advance.
Price: $15.50 - $25

Credit Cards:		Restaurant:	■
Driving Range:	■	Lounge:	
Practice Green:	■	Meeting Rooms:	■
Locker Room:		Tennis:	
Rental Clubs:	■	Swimming:	
Walkers:	■	Jogging Trails:	
Snack Bar:	■	Boating:	

COURSE DESCRIPTION

The *Papago Municipal Golf Course* may very well be the greatest "Muni" in the country. One authoritative publication has notably referred to it as the "75th Top Course In The Nation."

The course is professionally noted for hosting a qualifying tournament on behalf of the Phoenix Open and the PGA Tour. The back-tees are set up for professional competition, the middle-tees are set up to challenge the most accomplished 9-24 handicapper, and the ladies-tees offer a tremendous playing field from a distance of 5,936 yards.

DIRECTIONS

Take I-10 east to Hwy. 202 ("the loop") and take the off ramp to 52 St. Make a left and proceed for about 1/4 mile. The course will be on your right.

PHOENICIAN, THE

6000 E. Camel Back Rd., Scottsdale, AZ 85251 / (602) 423-2449

BASIC INFORMATION

Course Type: Semi-private
Year Built: 1988
Architect: Homer Flint
Local Pro: Doug Hoskins / Dir: John Jackson

Course:N/A
Holes: 18 / Par 71

Back : 6,487 yds. Rating: 71.2 Slope: 134
Middle: 6,033 yds. Rating: 68.7 Slope: 128
Ladies: 5,058 yds. Rating: 68.2 Slope: 122

Tee Time: One week to 60 days in advance.
Price: $70 - $115

Credit Cards:	■	Restaurant:	■
Driving Range:	■	Lounge:	■
Practice Green:	■	Meeting Rooms:	■
Locker Room:	■	Tennis:	■
Rental Clubs:	■	Swimming:	■
Walkers:		Jogging Trails:	■
Snack Bar:	■	Boating:	

COURSE DESCRIPTION

The Phoenician offers 6,500 yards of spectacular golf that is accentuated by a tranquil and beautiful environment. With lavishly landscaped fairways, meticulously manicured greens, arid desert bunkers, needle-sharp cacti, and deep-water hazards, every outing is guaranteed to be an adventure.

The course consists of six par-3's, five par-5's, and four par-4's that accentuate the resort in both an elegant and functional matter.

This is certainly a playing field you'll want to come back to, again and again.

DIRECTIONS

Take I-10 (Hwy.202) east to 44th St. Go north to Camelback rd. and east to the stoplight at Jokake Rd. Turn left and that will take you directly into the Phoenician.

PIMA COUNTRY CLUB

7331 N. Pima Rd., Scottsdale, AZ 85258 / (602) 948-3370

BASIC INFORMATION

Course Type: Public
Year Built: 1963 / 1992 1/2
Architect: Dale Rittenhouse (1992 1/2)
Local Pro: Tom O'Connell

Course: N/A
Holes: 18 / Par 70

Back : 6,324 yds. Rating: 69.6 Slope: 118
Middle: 6,094 yds. Rating: 68.5 Slope: 116
Ladies: 5,898 yds. Rating: 71.5 Slope: 112

Tee Time: 5 days in advance.
Price: $13 - $48

Credit Cards:	■	Restaurant:	
Driving Range:	■	Lounge:	
Practice Green:	■	Meeting Rooms:	
Locker Room:		Tennis:	
Rental Clubs:	■	Swimming:	
Walkers:	■	Jogging Trails:	
Snack Bar:	■	Boating:	

COURSE DESCRIPTION

At a distance of only 6,324 yards from the back-tees with a slope rating of 118, you wouldn't normally associate this course with the type that the PGA Tour would be searching for its qualifying tournaments ... yet this course is one of a selective group that the PGA did pick for the Phoenix Open. Another notable tournament worth mentioning is the Arizona Open, which is played by PGA Club Professionals from across the country.

This is a great course with a rich history of golfing excitement. You won't want to miss this one.

DIRECTIONS

Take I-10 to Bell Rd. and go east to Pima Rd. Make a right and drive about 5-miles to the traffic lights on Indian Bend. The course is located behind the huge Scottsdale Pavilion Mall.

38

POINTE GOLF CLUB, THE
7777 S. Pointe Pkwy., Phoenix, AZ 85044 / (602) 438-9000

BASIC INFORMATION

Course Type: Public
Year Built: 1988
Architect: Forest Richardson
Local Pro: Bret Greenwald

Course:N/A
Holes: 18 / Par 70

Back : 6,003 yds. Rating: 68.1 Slope: 117
Middle: 5,814 yds. Rating: 65.7 Slope: 112
Ladies: 5,201 yds. Rating: 66.2 Slope: 107

Tee Time: 30 days in advance.
Price: $29 - $80

Credit Cards: ■   Restaurant: ■
Driving Range: Lounge: ■
Practice Green: ■   Meeting Rooms:■
Locker Room: ■   Tennis: ■
Rental Clubs: ■   Swimming: ■
Walkers: Jogging Trails: ■
Snack Bar: ■   Boating:

COURSE DESCRIPTION

Carved out of the Sonoran Desert with breathtaking views into the Valley of the Sun, this well-respected golf course is a fun challenge to play.

With a slope rating of only 117 from the back tees, this course was obviously designed for the double-digit handicapper who enjoys the game immensely, but doesn't want to deal with U.S. Open conditions. If you're a single digit handicapper, you shouldn't settle for anything less than a par round.

Play the course aggressively!

DIRECTIONS

Take I-10 east and exit at Baseline Rd. Proceed west to Pointe Pkwy. The course will be 15 minutes away from the airport.

POINTE GOLF CLUB ON LOOKOUT MOUNTAIN, THE
11111 N. 7 St., Phoenix, AZ 85020 / (602) 866-6356

BASIC INFORMATION

Course Type: Semi-private
Year Built: 1989
Architect: Bill Johnston
Local Pro: Dale Williams

Course: N/A
Holes: 18 / Par 72

Back : 6,700 yds. Rating: 71.7 Slope: 131
Middle: 5,900 yds. Rating: 69.1 Slope: 126
Ladies: 4,600 yds. Rating: 65.3 Slope: 113

Tee Time: 2-30 days in advance.
Price: $50 - $120

Credit Cards: ■   Restaurant: ■
Driving Range: ■   Lounge: ■
Practice Green: ■   Meeting Rooms:■
Locker Room: ■   Tennis: ■
Rental Clubs: ■   Swimming: ■
Walkers: Jogging Trails: ■
Snack Bar: ■   Boating:

COURSE DESCRIPTION

The Pointe Golf Club on Lookout Mountain is home to the Senior PGA Tour Arizona Classic. It features lots of hills with undulations and flowing elevation changes throughout — none more dramatic than the 175' elevated tee on their famous 10th hole.

You'll be playing golf on the best possible platform available to modern course designs, such as Hybrid 828 Bermuda grass on the fairways and Bent grass on the putting-greens.

Practice hitting the ball below and above your feet. It will help you overcome the many uneven lies your ball will inevitably roll onto.

DIRECTIONS

Take I-75 north and make a right on Thunderbird Rd. Make another right on 7th St. and the Resort will appear on your left.

PUEBLO EL MIRAGE COUNTRY CLUB

11201 N. El Mirage Rd., El Mirage, AZ 85335 / (602) 583-0425

BASIC INFORMATION

Course Type: Public
Year Built: 1985
Architect: Fuzzy Zoellor
Local Pro: George Castle

Course: N/A
Holes: 18 / Par 72

Back   : 6,521 yds. Rating: 70.0 Slope: 119
Middle: 6,125 yds. Rating: 68.1 Slope: 114
Ladies: 5,563 yds. Rating: 71.0 Slope: 117

Tee Time: 3 days in advance.
Price: $15 - $36

Credit Cards:	■	Restaurant:	■
Driving Range:	■	Lounge:	
Practice Green:	■	Meeting Rooms:	
Locker Room:		Tennis:	
Rental Clubs:	■	Swimming:	
Walkers:	■	Jogging Trails:	
Snack Bar:	■	Boating:	

COURSE DESCRIPTION

This course was never meant to be a daring challenge that would defy anything built before it. What it does do exceptionally well is offer a playing field that will delight the average to high-handicapper, which as you probably know, makes up the majority of the people who play this game in the first place.

The course does have subtle undulations and contours that run along the fairways, although most are comprised of flat fields of well-manicured grass. The trees are young and mostly too low to cause a great deal of difficulty.

DIRECTIONS

Go north on El Mirage Rd. 1 1/2-miles from Olive. The course will appear on your right.

RED MOUNTAIN RANCH COUNTRY CLUB

6425 E. Teton, Mesa, AZ 85205 / (602) 981-6501

BASIC INFORMATION

Course Type: Semi-private
Year Built: 1987
Architect: Pete Dye
Local Pro: Bill Pearce

Course: N/A
Holes: 18 / Par 72

Back   : 6,797 yds. Rating: 73.8 Slope: 134
Middle: 6,112 yds. Rating: 69.5 Slope: 123
Ladies: 4,982 yds. Rating: 69.4 Slope: 120

Tee Time: 3 days in advance.
Price: $25 - $125

Credit Cards:	■	Restaurant:	■
Driving Range:	■	Lounge:	■
Practice Green:	■	Meeting Rooms:	■
Locker Room:	■	Tennis:	■
Rental Clubs:	■	Swimming:	■
Walkers:		Jogging Trails:	■
Snack Bar:	■	Boating:	■

COURSE DESCRIPTION

Pete Dye has gained a notable following for his personal brand of golf architecture. His designs are incredibly innovative and unique, but often difficult and demanding. This shotmakers' course will challenge the greatest professional from the back-tees and the most focused amateur from the middle-tees. It's truly a competitive course with a great assortment of hole designs.

The locals love this layout, for it seems to change with each passing day. Don't forget to bring your best putter ... the undulating greens are absolutely spectacular!

DIRECTIONS

Take I-10 east on U.S. 60 to Power Rd. The course will be about 7 1/2 miles on the left side of Red Mountain.

SAN MARCOS COUNTRY CLUB

100 N. Okata St., Chandler, AZ 85224 / (602) 963-3358

BASIC INFORMATION

Course Type: Semi-private
Year Built: 1914 / 1928
Architect: William Watson / Harry Collis
Local Pro: Jim Lawrence

Course: N/A
Holes: 18 / Par 72

Back   : 6,500 yds. Rating: 70.0 Slope: 117
Middle: 6,172 yds. Rating: 68.5 Slope: 114
Ladies: 5,386 yds. Rating: 69.4 Slope: 112

Tee Time: 7 days in advance.
Price: $29 - $69

Credit Cards:	■	Restaurant:	■
Driving Range:	■	Lounge:	■
Practice Green:	■	Meeting Rooms:	■
Locker Room:	■	Tennis:	■
Rental Clubs:	■	Swimming:	■
Walkers:	■	Jogging Trails:	■
Snack Bar:	■	Boating:	

COURSE DESCRIPTION

Wouldn't it be nice to get a feel for what it must have been like to play golf in the early part of its American history?

The *San Marcos Country Club*, Arizona's oldest course, is the perfect answer to that question! It was first built in 1914 by William Watson, and later reconstructed in 1928 by Harry Collins. It's a special treat for the golfing aficionado searching for a physical experience of history.

The playability of this flat layout is easily taught, and thus allows for many opportunities to score below par. The course plays consistently from start to finish, and neither favors a fade nor a draw.

DIRECTIONS

Take I-10, south to Chandler Blvd., east for about 7 miles, and look for the course on your right side.

SCOTTSDALE COUNTRY CLUB

7702 E. Shea Blvd., Scottsdale, AZ 85260 / (602) 948-6000

BASIC INFORMATION

Course Type: Semi-private
Year Built: 1950
Architect: Arnold Palmer
Local Pro: Larry Meister

Course: South / East (18 / Par 71)
Holes: 27

Back   : 6,335 yds. Rating: 69.6 Slope: 118
Middle: 5,866 yds. Rating: 69.7 Slope: 119
Ladies: 5,246 yds. Rating: 69.6 Slope: 118

Tee Time: 2 days in advance.
Price: $23 - $80

Credit Cards:	■	Restaurant:	■
Driving Range:		Lounge:	■
Practice Green:	■	Meeting Rooms:	■
Locker Room:	■	Tennis:	■
Rental Clubs:	■	Swimming:	■
Walkers:		Jogging Trails:	
Snack Bar:	■	Boating:	

COURSE DESCRIPTION

All three courses represented at the *Scottsdale Country Club* are challenging and fun to play.

It's a well rounded golf course featuring facinating holes that will challenge you to work the ball both left and right. The playing field will undoubtedly accommodate the mid-to-high handicapper, but better players should get a kick out of it, too.

If you were to match up two equally favored players, on this course the one with the ability to hit balls from an assortment of uneven lies will rule the day!

DIRECTIONS

Take Exit I-17 east to Scottsdale Rd., south to Shea Blvd., and east 1/2 mile on the north side of Shea Blvd.

STONECREEK, THE GOLF CLUB

4435 E. Paradise Village Pkwy. N., Phoenix, AZ 85032 / (602) 953-9110

BASIC INFORMATION

Course Type: Semi-private
Year Built: N/A
Architect: Aurthor Hills
Local Pro: Leo Simonetta

Course: N/A
Holes: 18 / Par 71

Back : 6,839 yds. Rating: 73.5 Slope: 133
Middle: 6,280 yds. Rating: 70.2 Slope: 126
Ladies: 5,909 yds. Rating: 69.8 Slope: 118

Tee Time: 3 days in advance.
Price: $20 - $85

Credit Cards:	■	Restaurant:	■
Driving Range:	■	Lounge:	■
Practice Green:	■	Meeting Rooms:	■
Locker Room:	■	Tennis:	
Rental Clubs:	■	Swimming:	
Walkers:		Jogging Trails:	■
Snack Bar:	■	Boating:	

COURSE DESCRIPTION

Stonecreek is a links style golf course that offers lush green fairways, water, rolling hills, and smooth undulating Bent grass greens.

The average golfer should consider playing the course from the middle-tees because of the significant difficulties that the course brings forth from the back-tees.

You'll be playing through a serene piece of property that magically spreads a mood of relaxation and comfort.

DIRECTIONS

Go north on 44th St. until it winds around the Camelback Mountain. Turn left on Tatum Blvd. and continue north until you see the clubhouse on the left side of the road.

SUPERSTITION SPRINGS GOLF CLUB

6542 E. Baseline Rd., Mesa, AZ 85206 / (602) 985-5622

BASIC INFORMATION

Course Type: Public
Year Built: 1986
Architect: Greg H. Nash
Local Pro: Jeff Lessig

Course: N/A
Holes: 18 / Par 72

Back : 7,005 yds. Rating: 74.1 Slope: 135
Middle: 6,405 yds. Rating: 71.0 Slope: 132
Ladies: 5,328 yds. Rating: 70.9 Slope: 120

Tee Time: 7-60 days in advance.
Price: $31 - $85

Credit Cards:	■	Restaurant:	■
Driving Range:	■	Lounge:	■
Practice Green:	■	Meeting Rooms:	■
Locker Room:	■	Tennis:	
Rental Clubs:	■	Swimming:	
Walkers:		Jogging Trails:	
Snack Bar:	■	Boating:	

COURSE DESCRIPTION

Listed as one of "America's Best Courses" by **Golfweek** magazine in 1992 and 1993, the *Superstition Springs Golf Club* has hosted regional qualifying events for the PGA Tour on more than one occasion.

You'll find numerous water holes, hurricane palms, large bunkers, unique contoured mounds, and much more! Multiple tees are set to accommodate all types of players. You'll need to reach for every club in your bag to make the many different shots that the course requires.

It's a great challenge of golf.

DIRECTIONS

Exit U.S. Rt. 60 at Power Rd. and turn right on Baseline Rd. Make another right on Baseline Rd. and look for the course on your right.

TATUM RANCH GOLF CLUB

29888 N. Tatum Ranch Dr., Cave Creek, AZ 85331 / (602) 585-2399

BASIC INFORMATION

Course Type: Public
Year Built: 1985
Architect: Robert Cupp
Local Pro: Gary Klein

Course: N/A
Holes: 18 / Par 72

Back : 6,870 yds. Rating: 73.4 Slope: 128
Middle: 6,357 yds. Rating: 71.0 Slope: 123
Ladies: 5,609 yds. Rating: 71.5 Slope: 116

Tee Time: 7 days in advance.
Price: $32 - $85

Credit Cards:	■	Restaurant:	■
Driving Range:	■	Lounge:	■
Practice Green:	■	Meeting Rooms:	
Locker Room:	■	Tennis:	
Rental Clubs:	■	Swimming:	
Walkers:		Jogging Trails:	
Snack Bar:	■	Boating:	

COURSE DESCRIPTION

This challenging desert course was designed in 1993 Golf Course Architect of the year: Robert Cupp.

It's a flat layout that features many wonderful holes to play through. The front-nine plays a little tighter than the longer and wider back-nine, which allows you to be a little more aggressive over the ball.

Many of the holes are shaped differently than their counterparts, which is one of the reasons you'll get a chance to play a wide assortment of shots.

Directions

Go north on Hwy. 17 towards Flagstaff, take Yorkshire to Beardsley, make a right to Cove Creek, left to Tatum Blvd., right to Tatum Ranch Dr., and left to the course.

THUNDERBIRD COUNTRY CLUB

701 E. Thunderbird Trail, Phoenix, AZ 85040 / (602) 243-1262

BASIC INFORMATION

Course Type: Public
Year Built: 1955
Architect: N/A
Local Pro: John Reckard

Course: N/A
Holes: 18 / 72

Back : 6,469 yds. Rating: 70.2 Slope: 110
Middle: 6,209 yds. Rating: 68.9 Slope: 107
Ladies: 5,852 yds. Rating: 72.8 Slope: 115

Tee Time: 7 days in advance.
Price: $10 - $40

Credit Cards:	■	Restaurant:	■
Driving Range:	■	Lounge:	■
Practice Green:	■	Meeting Rooms:	■
Locker Room:	■	Tennis:	
Rental Clubs:	■	Swimming:	
Walkers:	■	Jogging Trails:	
Snack Bar:	■	Boating:	

COURSE DESCRIPTION

If you're looking for a course that will allow you to take chances without penalizing you too much for a misdirected shot, this may be the one you've been searching for. It serves its purpose perfectly by offering a nice platform for high-handicappers and Senior golfers alike. If your handicap is close to 15, you shouldn't have much trouble setting yourself up for birdies on the majority of the holes. Both the front-nine and the back-nine play relatively the same.

This flat desert course features beautiful city and mountain views from many of its holes.

DIRECTIONS

Take Hwy. I-10 and get off on 7th St. The course will be about 1 1/2 miles south of Baseline Rd. Look for it on your left.

TOM WEISKOPF'S FOOTHILLS GOLF

2201 E. Clubhouse Dr., AZ 85044 / (602) 460-8337

BASIC INFORMATION

Course Type: Semi-private
Year Built: 1987
Architect: Tom Weiskopf
Local Pro: Tammy Anderson

Course: N/A
Holes: 18 / 72

Back : 6,976 yds. Rating: 72.7 Slope: 122
Middle: 6,406 yds. Rating: 73.4 Slope: 110
Ladies: 6,027 yds. Rating: 68.9 Slope: 110

Tee Time: 7 days in advance.
Price: $35 - $75

Credit Cards:	■	Restaurant:	■
Driving Range:	■	Lounge:	■
Practice Green:	■	Meeting Rooms:	■
Locker Room:	■	Tennis:	
Rental Clubs:	■	Swimming:	
Walkers:		Jogging Trails:	
Snack Bar:	■	Boating:	

COURSE DESCRIPTION

You can't underestimate the unique qualities that come with having a golfing professional such as Tom Weiskopf designing golf courses. It didn't take the public too long to figure out the amount of thought that had gone into this fabulous course. Today, it's become one of the leading locales for golfers to test their skills to the limit!

The fairways on this course are wide, undulating, and generous, allowing aggressive play off the tees, which makes for a wonderful platform to play golf.

If you're in the area, make it a point to play this remarkable layout – you won't be disappointed.

DIRECTIONS

Take I-10 east to Tucson and exit onto Chandler Blvd. Go west to 24th St. and look for the course on your left.

TOURNAMENT PLAYERS CLUB

17020 N. Hayden Rd., Scottsdale, AZ 85255 / (602) 585-3600

BASIC INFORMATION

Course Type: Public
Year Built: 1986
Architect: Tom Weiskopf & Jay Morrish
Local Pro: Tim Eleeson

Course: Stadium (18 / Par 72)
Holes: 36

Back : 6,508 yds. Rating: 71.0 Slope: 124
Middle: 6,049 yds. Rating: 68.9 Slope: 120
Ladies: 5,567 yds. Rating: 71.6 Slope: 122

Tee Time: 7 days in advance.
Price: $60 - $113.11

Credit Cards:	■	Restaurant:	■
Driving Range:	■	Lounge:	■
Practice Green:	■	Meeting Rooms:	
Locker Room:	■	Tennis:	
Rental Clubs:	■	Swimming:	
Walkers:		Jogging Trails:	
Snack Bar:	■	Boating:	

COURSE DESCRIPTION

The TPC is well known for constructing quality layouts that appeal to both professionals and amateurs alike. Tom Weiskopf and Jay Morrish put their collective wisdom into this design and it immediately caught the attention of the PGA Tour. Today, the course hosts an exciting "Tour" event called the Phoenix Open.

If you want to experience the feeling of playing a professional caliber golf course, this is one of the few that you can actually play. It's a tremendous tribute to the game and one you'll inevitably talk about with your golfing friends back home.

DIRECTIONS

Take Pima Rd. north until you pass Frank Lloyd Wright Blvd., make your first left and proceed down Bell Rd. You'll be heading straight for the course.

TROON NORTH GOLF CLUB

10320 E. Dynamite Blvd., Scottsdale, AZ 85255 / (602) 585-5300

BASIC INFORMATION

Course Type: Semi-private
Year Built: 1990
Architect: Tom Weiskopf & Jay Morrish
Local Pro: Dana Garmany

Course: N/A
Holes: 18 /Par 72

Back : 7,008 yds. Rating: 73.1 Slope: 146
Middle: 6,474 yds. Rating: 70.1 Slope: 131
Ladies: 5,050 yds. Rating: 69.0 Slope: 116

Tee Time: 5 days in advance.
Price: $90 - $125

Credit Cards: ■	Restaurant: ■
Driving Range: ■	Lounge: ■
Practice Green: ■	Meeting Rooms: ■
Locker Room:	Tennis:
Rental Clubs: ■	Swimming:
Walkers: ■	Jogging Trails:
Snack Bar: ■	Boating:

COURSE DESCRIPTION

Note: the course is presently building a new 3,300 sq. ft. clubhouse due to open some time in July 1994.

How good is this course? It was rated #1 for the last three years by **GolfWeek** magazine, 65th in the country by **Golf Digest** magazine, and 70th in the country by **Golf** magazine.

The course is very difficult from the back-tees and should only be played by single-digit-handicappers for maximum fun. It's a "target" type course that will eat you up alive if you're not prepared for the challenge.

DIRECTIONS

From Scottsdale Rd. go north to Dynamite Blvd. Make a right and stay on Dynamite Blvd. for about 4-miles east. The course will be on your left.

VILLA DE PAZ GOLF COURSE

4220 N. 103 Ave., Phoenix, AZ 85039 / (602) 877-1172

BASIC INFORMATION

Course Type: Public
Year Built: 1971 / 1977
Architect: N/A
Local Pro: Doug Wilkerson

Course: N/A
Holes: 18 / Par 72

Back : 6,140 yds. Rating: 68.6 Slope: 114
Middle: 5,868 yds. Rating: 67.2 Slope: 111
Ladies: 5,288 yds. Rating: 69.1 Slope: 117

Tee Time: 60 days at 1-602-962-GOLF
Price: $15 - $36

Credit Cards: ■	Restaurant:
Driving Range: ■	Lounge:
Practice Green: ■	Meeting Rooms: ■
Locker Room:	Tennis:
Rental Clubs: ■	Swimming:
Walkers: ■	Jogging Trails:
Snack Bar: ■	Boating:

COURSE DESCRIPTION

The *Villa De Paz Golf Course* offers a great playing field for high handicappers and golfers short on distance.

The course features narrow fairways that will force you to hit accurate tee shots with your 3-wood. Remember, accuracy above distance is the golden rule.

This course is the perfect retreat for a weekend golfer in search of a fun playing field. The terrain is moderately undulating throughout and features a tougher platform on the back-nine, so if you're searching for some birdies, get them on the front.

Bring your best fade to the course!

DIRECTIONS

Take I-10 west to 99 Ave. and go north to Indian School Rd. Make a left, heading west, to 103 Rd. Go right on 103 Rd. and look for the course on your left.

WESTBROOK VILLAGE COUNTRY CLUB
19260 N. Westbrook Pkwy., Peoria, AZ 85345 / (602) 933-0174

BASIC INFORMATION

Course Type: Semi-private
Year Built: 1982
Architect: Ted Robinson
Local Pro: Bob Bower

Course:N/A
Holes: 18 / Par 72

Back : 6,412 yds. Rating: 69.2 Slope: 112
Middle: 6,033 yds. Rating: 67.0 Slope: 107
Ladies: 5,388 yds. Rating: 69.5 Slope: 112

Tee Time: 2 days in advance.
Price: $14 - $45

Credit Cards:	■	Restaurant:	■
Driving Range:	■	Lounge:	■
Practice Green:	■	Meeting Rooms:	■
Locker Room:	■	Tennis:	
Rental Clubs:	■	Swimming:	
Walkers:	■	Jogging Trails:	
Snack Bar:	■	Boating:	

COURSE DESCRIPTION

When playing this course for the first time, you may find it a little harder than the numbers indicated on the score-card – so much so that one golfing professional I spoke with felt that the course could easily add up to a 124 slope rating from the back-tees. It's due to be reevaluated in the near future.

You'll find a strong combination of holes that hold up well together despite their relative short distance. This faders' course features water coming into play on four holes.

DIRECTIONS

Take I-17 to Union Hills and go west to 96th Ave., which is slightly north. Look for the course on your left.

WIGWAM, THE
4344 N. Litchfield Rd., Litchfield, AZ 85340 / (602) 935-3811

BASIC INFORMATION

Course Type: Public / Semi-private
Year Built: 1932 / 1974
Architect: Robert Trent Jones, Sr.
Local Pro: Keith Kalny / Craig Allen

Course: Gold (18 / Par 72)
Holes: 54

Back : 7,074 yds. Rating: 74.5 Slope: 133
Middle: 6,504 yds. Rating: 71.7 Slope: 129
Ladies: 5,657 yds. Rating: 71.9 Slope: 128

Tee Time: 3-5 days in advance.
Price: $30 - $90

Credit Cards:	■	Restaurant:	■
Driving Range:	■	Lounge:	■
Practice Green:	■	Meeting Rooms:	■
Locker Room:	■	Tennis:	■
Rental Clubs:	■	Swimming:	■
Walkers:	■	Jogging Trails:	■
Snack Bar:	■	Boating:	

COURSE DESCRIPTION

The Gold course is the most difficult and most renowned of *The Wigwam's* three championship layouts. Rated as one of the nation's top 75 resort courses by **Golf** magazine, this classic Robert Trent Jones, Sr. design features elevated greens with many undulations, devilish bunkering, tall palms, grand old eucalyptus', and a variety of pine trees that work beautifully in accentuating the natural beauty of the course. The playing field was originally designed for Good Year executives and VIP's.

DIRECTIONS

Take I-10 west to Litchfield Rd. (Exit 128) and make a right. Head north two stoplights to a four way stop-sign. The resort will be left and the courses will be on your right.

DESERT LAKES GOLF COURSE

5835 Desert Laks Dr., Ft. Mohave, AZ 86427 / (602) 768-1000

BASIC INFORMATION

Course Type: Municipal
Year Built: 1989
Architect: Bob Balldock
Local Pro: Steve Buller

Course: N/A
Holes: 18 / Par 72

Back : 6,569 yds. Rating: 69.5 Slope: 114
Middle: 6,267 yds. Rating: 68.5 Slope: 110
Ladies: 5,440 yds. Rating: 79.6 Slope: 112

Tee Time: 14 days in advance.
Price: $30

Credit Cards:	■	Restaurant:	■
Driving Range:	■	Lounge:	
Practice Green:	■	Meeting Rooms:	
Locker Room:		Tennis:	
Rental Clubs:	■	Swimming:	
Walkers:	■	Jogging Trails:	
Snack Bar:	■	Boating:	

COURSE DESCRIPTION

This course doesn't over-penalize you, yet it does require a variety of shots with a number of different clubs.

The back-nine will force you to play some finesse shots that you won't normally find on the front-nine, making it the harder of the two sides. The course also favors a draw over a fade!

The layout tends to take on a new character in accordance to the varying wind conditions of each particular day.

DIRECTIONS

From Laughlin: Cross the Laughlin Bridge by the Riverside Casino. Turn right on Hwy. 95 and proceed 13-miles to Joy Lane, turn left to the fairway estates and make a right. Follow the signs to the course.

VALLE VISTA COUNTRY CLUB

9686 Concho Dr., Kingman, AZ 86401 / (602) 757-8744

BASIC INFORMATION

Course Type: Semi-private
Year Built: 1972
Architect: N/A
Local Pro: Dean Lott

Course: N/A
Holes: 18 / Par 72

Back : 6,266 yds. Rating: 68.3 Slope: 112
Middle: 5,877 yds. Rating: 66.6 Slope: 108
Ladies: 5,585 yds. Rating: 67.9 Slope: 111

Tee Time: 3 days in advance.
Price: $10 - $12

Credit Cards:	■	Restaurant:	■
Driving Range:	■	Lounge:	■
Practice Green:	■	Meeting Rooms:	
Locker Room:		Tennis:	
Rental Clubs:	■	Swimming:	
Walkers:	■	Jogging Trails:	
Snack Bar:	■	Boating:	

COURSE DESCRIPTION

This course will appeal to high-handicappers and golfers who can't get much distance on their iron play.

The fairways are mostly flat and feature man-made mounds to make them a little more challenging off the tees. You don't need an incredible amount of distance to play well here, accuracy is rewarded quite generously by supplying advantageous circumstances for par or better. If you're a natural long hitter, play the course to your game. The open architecture of the layout often makes it easy to play your following approach shot even from the rough.

DIRECTIONS

Take I-40 to Andy Divine (Rt. 66) eastbound for about 15-miles to Mile-Post 71. The course will be on your left side.

NAVAJO COUNTY

SHOW LOW COUNTRY CLUB
860 N. 36 Dr., Show Low, AZ 85901 / (602) 537-4564

BASIC INFORMATION

Course Type: Public
Year Built: N/A
Architect: N/A
Local Pro: Mary Samcha

Course: N/A
Holes: 18 / Par 70

Back : 5,916 yds. Rating: 67.3 Slope: 108
Middle: 5,572 yds. Rating: 65.2 Slope: 104
Ladies: 5,195 yds. Rating: 67.9 Slope: 116

Tee Time: 7 days in advance.
Price: $15 - $25

Credit Cards: ■	Restaurant:	
Driving Range: ■	Lounge:	■
Practice Green: ■	Meeting Rooms:	
Locker Room:	Tennis:	
Rental Clubs: ■	Swimming:	
Walkers: ■	Jogging Trails:	
Snack Bar: ■	Boating:	■

COURSE DESCRIPTION

The **Show Low Country Club** is geared mostly to high-handicappers and Senior Citizens alike. It's a short course with a strong layout conducive to short-iron play.

It features only three par-5's, the longest reaching 533 yds., ten par-4's and five par-3's. Seven of the holes favor a draw, three favor a fade, and the remaining holes play relatively straight.

Maturely grown Ponderosa pine trees make it a pleasure to play the course in its peaceful and isolated environment.

DIRECTIONS

Located on Old Linden Rd., a quarter mile east of Hwy. 260 north, on the north side of the road.

SILVER CREEK GOLF CLUB
P.O. Box 965, White Mountain Lake, AZ 85912 / (602) 537-2744

BASIC INFORMATION

Course Type: Semi-private
Year Built: 1984-85
Architect: Gary Panks
Local Pro: Mark Sillaman

Course: N/A
Holes: 18 / Par 71

Back : 6,813 yds. Rating: 71.5 Slope: 131
Middle: 6,075 yds. Rating: 68.2 Slope: 119
Ladies: 5,616 yds. Rating: 68.0 Slope: 112

Tee Time: 3 days in advance.
Price: $15.50 - $31

Credit Cards: ■	Restaurant:	■
Driving Range: ■	Lounge:	■
Practice Green: ■	Meeting Rooms:	
Locker Room: ■	Tennis:	
Rental Clubs: ■	Swimming:	
Walkers: ■	Jogging Trails:	
Snack Bar: ■	Boating:	■

COURSE DESCRIPTION

Silver Creek Golf Club is a links type design that rambles through high country filled with juniper trees and picture-perfect views of Arizona's White Mountains.

Having hosted many state championships, including the annual Navapache Amateur in July, the course has gained a reputation for being an excellent tournament site, and, at the same time, allows golfers of different abilities to play well from its multiple tees.

To compliment everyone's golfing experience, a new clubhouse facility opened in October 1993.

DIRECTIONS

Follow Hwy. 60 east from Show Low and turn north at Mile Post 347 at Bourdon Ranch Rd. Look for the course 7 miles further on your left.

48

SNOW FLAKE MUNICIPAL GOLF

90 North Country Club Dr., Snowflake, AZ 85937 / (602) 536-7233

BASIC INFORMATION

Course Type: Municipal
Year Built: 1980 / 1993
Architect: Ed Hunt / Lynn Elsworth
Local Pro: Steve Schnieder

Course: N/A
Holes: 18 / Par 72

Back : 6,352 yds. Rating: 68.1 Slope: 110
Middle: 6,122 yds. Rating: 67.2 Slope: 110
Ladies: 5,206 yds. Rating: 70.0 Slope: 108

Tee Time: 7 days in advance.
Price: $6 - $12

Credit Cards:		Restaurant:	
Driving Range:	■	Lounge:	
Practice Green:	■	Meeting Rooms:	
Locker Room:		Tennis:	
Rental Clubs:	■	Swimming:	
Walkers:	■	Jogging Trails:	
Snack Bar:	■	Boating:	

COURSE DESCRIPTION

This gentle little course will be appreciated by high-handicap players. From beginning to end, the design is both straightforward and simple.

This is an excellent venue to build up your confidence. With a slope rating of only 110, many of you should find the layout an easy challenge both off the tees and on the putting surfaces.

Many of the greens vary in size and are consistently smooth with slight undulations that can trick you if you're not checking your line before you putt.

DIRECTIONS

Take Hwy. 77 north to Hwy. 277 and go west to the course. Look for it on your left.

ARTHUR PACK DESERT GOLF

9101 N. Thornydale Rd., Tucson, AZ 85741 / (602) 744-3322

BASIC INFORMATION

Course Type: Public
Year Built: 1975
Architect: Lee Trevino
Local Pro: Steve Porter

Course: N/A
Holes: 18 / Par 72

Back : 6,900 yds. Rating: 71.6 Slope: 118
Middle: 6,400 yds. Rating: 69.2 Slope: 113
Ladies: 5,068 yds. Rating: 67.6 Slope: 108

Tee Time: 7 days in advance.
Price: $10 - $20

Credit Cards:	■	Restaurant:	■
Driving Range:	■	Lounge:	■
Practice Green:	■	Meeting Rooms:	
Locker Room:		Tennis:	
Rental Clubs:	■	Swimming:	
Walkers:	■	Jogging Trails:	
Snack Bar:	■	Boating:	

COURSE DESCRIPTION

This terrific course combines many exciting holes of golf that are intertwined with beautiful mountain sites and stunning views of Tucson.

No secrets are held; everything will open up in front of you as you take your stance over the ball. The fairways are wide and flat, underscored by dense desert flora, leading to highly demanding greens. These meticulously-kept greens attract a lot of golfers who choose to play the course on a weekly basis.

Neither a fade nor a draw is favored, opening up the course to many different styles of play.

DIRECTIONS

Take I-10 and Ina Rd. east for about a mile to Thornydale and go north to the course. The entrance will be on your left.

CANOA HILLS GOLF COURSE

1401 Calle Urbano, Green Valley, AZ 85614 / (602) 648-1880

BASIC INFORMATION

Course Type: Semi-private
Year Built: 1984
Architect: Bob Bennett
Local Pro: TomTatum

Course: N/A
Holes: 18 / Par 72

Back : 6,600 yds. Rating: 69.7 Slope: 126
Middle: 6,077 yds. Rating: 68.5 Slope: 122
Ladies: 5,158 yds. Rating: 68.5 Slope: 112

Tee Time: 2 days in advance.
Price: $21 - $55

Credit Cards: ■	Restaurant: ■
Driving Range: ■	Lounge: ■
Practice Green: ■	Meeting Rooms:
Locker Room:	Tennis:
Rental Clubs: ■	Swimming:
Walkers: ■	Jogging Trails:
Snack Bar: ■	Boating:

COURSE DESCRIPTION

The *Canoa Hills Golf Course* offers a fun challenge for many different types of players by offering multiple tees that make it easy to choose the game that is best suited for your particular style of play.

The layout of the course runs along a canyon vista that features beautiful views of the Santa Rita mountain range.

The 15th hole is the one to conquer. This par-5 measures 537 yards in length and requires a well-placed tee-shot onto a demanding fairway. The pro's play it with a 2-iron off the tee, followed with an 8-iron on the two approach shots it usually takes to hit the green.

DIRECTIONS

Take I-95 to Continental Rd. and go west to Camino del Sol. Turn left and go about three miles down the road. The course will be on your left.

EL CONQUISTADOR COUNTRY CLUB

10555 N. La Canada, Tucson, AZ 85737 / (602) 544-1800

BASIC INFORMATION

Course Type: Semi-private / Private
Year Built: 1984
Architect: Jeff Haroin / Greg Nash
Local Pro: Steve Phelps / Joan Fails

Course: Sunrise (18 / Par 72)
Holes: 45

Back : 6,819 yds. Rating: 71.7 Slope: 123
Middle: 6,288 yds. Rating: 69.0 Slope: 113
Ladies: 5,255 yds. Rating: 69.4 Slope: 116

Tee Time: 2 days in advance.
Price: $40 - $95

Credit Cards: ■	Restaurant: ■
Driving Range: ■	Lounge: ■
Practice Green: ■	Meeting Rooms: ■
Locker Room: ■	Tennis: ■
Rental Clubs: ■	Swimming: ■
Walkers:	Jogging Trails:
Snack Bar: ■	Boating:

COURSE DESCRIPTION

With 45 holes of golf to choose from, you can be assured that one of these layouts is right for you.

The Sunrise course is the most sought after for better players. It features two distinct 9-hole designs that work beautifully together. The first runs through a hilly terrain that cuts through the Sonoran mountains. The sights are wonderful and the layout of the course is clearly visible from the tees. The back-nine is completely different with its flat-open field and slightly wider fairways.

The Sunrise course is preferred among better players in the area. It's like playing two different courses within the span of a single round.

DIRECTIONS

Take I-10 east to La Canada Dr., and go left for about 4 miles to the course.

PIMA COUNTY

EL RIO GOLF COURSE

1400 W. Speedway Blvd., Tucson, AZ 85745 / (602) 791-4229

BASIC INFORMATION

Course Type: Public
Year Built: 1940's
Architect: N/A
Local Pro: Angel Ballesteros

Course: N/A
Holes: 18 / Par 70

Back : 6,418 yds. Rating: 69.6 Slope: 110
Middle: 6,013 yds. Rating: 68.6 Slope: 108
Ladies: 5,824 yds. Rating: 72.2 Slope: 115

Tee Time: 7 days in advance.
Price: $11.50 - $13.50

Credit Cards:		Restaurant:	■
Driving Range:	■	Lounge:	■
Practice Green:	■	Meeting Rooms:	
Locker Room:	■	Tennis:	
Rental Clubs:	■	Swimming:	
Walkers:	■	Jogging Trails:	
Snack Bar:	■	Boating:	

COURSE DESCRIPTION

This is a simple and straightforward golf course that holds no surprises. All you have to do is keep your drives grooved to the right part of each fairway for a clear approach shot to the many small tapered greens.

If you're a better player, you may want to use this course to practice your short game, otherwise the course will probably be too easy to satisfy your golfing enthusiasm. If you're a golfer short on distance or new to the game, you'll feel less intimidated on this platform, which can add to your confidence and elevate your game to new heights.

DIRECTIONS

Take I-10, north and go west on Speedway Blvd. Look for the course on your left as you head in a westbound direction.

FRED ENKE GOLF COURSE

8251 E. Irvington Rd., Tucson, AZ 85730 / (602) 296-8607

BASIC INFORMATION

Course Type: Public
Year Built: 1984
Architect: Brad Benz
Local Pro: Terry Wilks

Course: N/A
Holes: 18 / Par 72

Back : 6,807 yds. Rating: 73.3 Slope: 137
Middle: 6,363 yds. Rating: 70.4 Slope: 129
Ladies: 4,700 yds. Rating: 68.8 Slope: 111

Tee Time: 7 days in advance.
Price: $14 - $19

Credit Cards:		Restaurant:	■
Driving Range:	■	Lounge:	■
Practice Green:	■	Meeting Rooms:	
Locker Room:		Tennis:	
Rental Clubs:	■	Swimming:	
Walkers:	■	Jogging Trails:	
Snack Bar:	■	Boating:	

COURSE DESCRIPTION

You'll be telling your friends back home about this course for a long time into the future. It's a formidable challenge with an outstanding array of golfing holes that are set up for both the professional and amateur alike.

Playing golf on this desert course has its moments of excitement ... especially when you have to hit your tee-shot over both the desert and a neighboring mountain range!

The majority of the course winds through a hilly mountainous foundation that will often have you hitting your approach shots from unusual lies.

DIRECTIONS

Take I-10 to Kold Rd. and go north to Irvington Rd. and make a right towards the course. Look for it on your left.

PIMA COUNTY

HAVEN GOLF COURSE
110 N. Abrego Dr., Green Valley, AZ 85614 / (602) 625-8869

BASIC INFORMATION

Course Type: Public
Year Built: 1967
Architect: N/A
Local Pro: Bob Floyd

Course: N/A
Holes: 18 / Par 72

Back : 6,829 yds. Rating: 71.6 Slope: 117
Middle: 6,336 yds. Rating: 69.2 Slope: 111
Ladies: 5,811 yds. Rating: 71.5 Slope: 113

Tee Time: 7 days in advance.
Price: $15.75 - $25

Credit Cards:	■	Restaurant:	
Driving Range:	■	Lounge:	■
Practice Green:	■	Meeting Rooms:	
Locker Room:		Tennis:	
Rental Clubs:	■	Swimming:	
Walkers:	■	Jogging Trails:	
Snack Bar:	■	Boating:	

COURSE DESCRIPTION
Many locals consider this course to be one of the best in Green Valley.

Big trees and ponds are featured in their natural settings giving the course a look and feel all its own. The Santa Rita mountains are yet another spectacular attraction here. Although the course was designed to be played long, accurate shotmakers will find many avenues to cut the playing field down on each hole.

You'll be playing through beautiful wide fairways that lead to wonderful Bermuda greens.

DIRECTIONS
Take I-19 to Esperanza and make a left at the following stoplight. At Abrego, turn left and the course will be on your right side.

RANDOLPH GOLF COURSE
600 S. Alvernon Way, Tucson, AZ 85716 / (602) 791-4161

BASIC INFORMATION

Course Type: Public
Year Built: 1962
Architect: N/A (Redesigned by Pete Dye)
Local Pro: Homero Blancas

Course:North (18 / Par72)
Holes: 36

Back : 6,902 yds. Rating: 72.5 Slope: 128
Middle: 6,436 yds. Rating: 70.0 Slope: 121
Ladies: 5,972 yds. Rating: 73.7 Slope: 124

Tee Time: 7 days in advance.
Price: $8 - $21

Credit Cards:		Restaurant:	■
Driving Range:	■	Lounge:	
Practice Green:	■	Meeting Rooms:	■
Locker Room:	■	Tennis:	■
Rental Clubs:	■	Swimming:	■
Walkers:	■	Jogging Trails:	■
Snack Bar:	■	Boating:	

COURSE DESCRIPTION
The North course has a rich history of hosting professional tournaments, such as the PGA Tucson Open, featured on the regular tour, the Seiko Match Play Championship (Senior PGA Tour), and the LPGA Tucson Open.

The South course plays shorter and a little bit easier. Although it was originally designed by W.F. Bell in 1925, Pete Dye added some inviting modifications to make the course a little more demanding and contemporary. The North is the longer of the two and features wider fairways that you're going to love hitting onto.

DIRECTIONS
Exit I-10 at Alvernon Way. The course is about 4 miles north, half-mile further than 22nd St. on your left.

PIMA COUNTY

SAN IGNACIO GOLF CLUB
4201 S. Camino Del Sol St., Tucson, AZ 85614 / (602) 648-3468

BASIC INFORMATION

Course Type: Public
Year Built: 1989
Architect: Arthur Hills
Local Pro: Kevin Lewis

Course: N/A
Holes: 18

Back : 6,704 yds. Rating: 71.4 Slope: 129
Middle: 6,288 yds. Rating: 69.8 Slope: 126
Ladies: 5,200 yds. Rating: 68.7 Slope: 112

Tee Time: 4 days in advance.
Price: $30 - $60

Credit Cards:	■	Restaurant:	■
Driving Range:	■	Lounge:	■
Practice Green:	■	Meeting Rooms:	
Locker Room:		Tennis:	
Rental Clubs:	■	Swimming:	
Walkers:		Jogging Trails:	
Snack Bar:	■	Boating:	

COURSE DESCRIPTION

This club offers a delightful desert layout that offers golfers of all abilities many options from different sets of tees.

Spectacular views of both the Santa Rita Mountains and the Arroyas of the Santa Cruz River Valley are unforgettable.

You'll find a variety of exciting holes that are uniquely demanding and fun to play. Arthur Hills put a lot of thought into the making of this particular course. It's a player's course from tee to green!

DIRECTIONS

Take I-19 south from Tucson to Green Valley. Exit on Continental Rd. and take West Side Frontage Rd. Go south to Camino Encanto, west to Camino Del Sol, and south to the golf club. It will be on your left.

SILVERBELL GOLF COURSE
3600 N. Silverbell Rd. Tucson, AZ 85745 / (602) 791-4336

BASIC INFORMATION

Course Type: Public
Year Built: 1978
Architect: Jack Synder
Local Pro: Fred Marti

Course: N/A
Holes: 18 / Par 72

Back : 6,824 yds. Rating: 71.2 Slope: 114
Middle: 6,361 yds. Rating: 68.8 Slope: 110
Ladies: 5,751 yds. Rating: 70.3 Slope: N/A

Tee Time: 7 days in advance.
Price: $12.50 - $18.50

Credit Cards:	■	Restaurant:	
Driving Range:	■	Lounge:	■
Practice Green:	■	Meeting Rooms:	
Locker Room:	■	Tennis:	
Rental Clubs:	■	Swimming:	
Walkers:	■	Jogging Trails:	
Snack Bar:	■	Boating:	

COURSE DESCRIPTION

This conventional type course features 153 acres of grassland. The terrain is filled with rolling hills that flow between two distinctive mountain ranges.

The three finishing holes work tremendously well together in elevating the level of play that is needed to score well on them.

The back-tees offer a very competitive platform for most golfers, but if you have a problem with the length of the course, you should consider playing from the middle-tees.

DIRECTIONS

Take I-10 to Grant Rd. and go west to Silverbell Rd. Turn left here, and look for the course to appear 2-miles further on your right.

PIMA COUNTY

STARR PASS GOLF CLUB
3645 W. 22 St., Tucson, AZ 85745 / (602) 622-4300

BASIC INFORMATION

Course Type: Semi-private
Year Built: 1986
Architect: Robert Cupp
Local Pro: Owen Compton

Course:N/A
Holes: 18 / Par 72

Back : 7.010 yds. Rating: 74.6 Slope: 139
Middle: 6,383 yds. Rating: 71.3 Slope: 127
Ladies: 5,210 yds. Rating: 70.7 Slope: 121

Tee Time: 7 days in advance.
Price: $48 - $89

Credit Cards: ■		Restaurant: ■
Driving Range: ■		Lounge: ■
Practice Green: ■		Meeting Rooms: ■
Locker Room:		Tennis: ■
Rental Clubs: ■		Swimming: ■
Walkers:		Jogging Trails:
Snack Bar: ■		Boating:

COURSE DESCRIPTION

Robert Cupp is one of America's most gifted golf architects who has carved out one of the most beautiful and exciting courses in Tucson. It's a jolting "target-oriented layout," both long and demanding on accuracy.

The challenge extends along vast desert stretches that feature cacti fields, rolling hills, and mountain ranges. The elements of the desert's natural beauty is heightened by the sheer brilliance of the layout.

With four sets of tees on every hole, the course easily accommodates all types of players. You may have spotted the course on television while watching the Northern Telecom Open on the PGA Tour.

DIRECTIONS

The course is 3-miles west of I-10 on 22nd St. and is located 5-miles west of downtown Tucson.

SUN CITY VISTOSO
1495 E. Rancho Vistoso Blvd., Tucson, AZ 85737 / (602) 825-3110

BASIC INFORMATION

Course Type: Semi-private
Year Built: 1986
Architect: Grag Nash
Local Pro: Mike Williams

Course:N/A
Holes: 18 / Par 72

Back : 6,723 yds. Rating: 71.8 Slope: 137
Middle: 6,163 yds. Rating: 69.5 Slope: 131
Ladies: 5,484 yds. Rating: 70.6 Slope: 120

Tee Time: 3 days in advance.
Price: $30 - $61

Credit Cards: ■		Restaurant:
Driving Range: ■		Lounge: ■
Practice Green: ■		Meeting Rooms:
Locker Room:		Tennis: ■
Rental Clubs: ■		Swimming: ■
Walkers:		Jogging Trails: ■
Snack Bar: ■		Boating: ■

COURSE DESCRIPTION

Arizona has certainly built a reputation for "target" style golf that is unique to its desert environment. This beautiful course is no exception, for it will test your ability to hit a golf ball long and accurate throughout its entire field.

The back-tees, with a slope rating of 137, will certainty annoy anyone playing with a double-digit handicap. If you choose to play the course from the middle tees, you'll find a greater variety of options from their vantage points, making the course much more manageable and fun to play.

DIRECTIONS

From Ina Rd. and Hwy 89 (Oracle Rd.) go north for 8 miles until you get to Rancho Vistoso Blvd. Make a left and look for the course 2 miles further on your right.

TUCSON NATIONAL GOLF & CONFERENCE RESORT

2727 W. Club Dr., Tucson, AZ 85741 / (602) 297-2271

BASIC INFORMATION

Course Type: Semi-private
Year Built: 1963
Architect: Bruce Devlin
Local Pro: Mike Boss

Course: Orange/Gold (18 / Par 73)
Holes: 27

Back   : 7,108 yds. Rating: 74.9 Slope: 136
Middle: 6,549 yds. Rating: 71.0 Slope: 122
Ladies: 5,647 yds. Rating: 72.4 Slope: 123

Tee Time: 2 days in advance.
Price: $46 - $99

Credit Cards:	■	Restaurant:	■
Driving Range:	■	Lounge:	■
Practice Green:	■	Meeting Rooms:	■
Locker Room:	■	Tennis:	■
Rental Clubs:	■	Swimming:	■
Walkers:		Jogging Trails:	■
Snack Bar:	■	Boating:	

COURSE DESCRIPTION

This traditional course offers a nice break from all the "target-type" courses that make up the majority of golf courses in Arizona.

It's the type of course that will inevitably have you reaching for every club in your bag by the time you step off the 18th green. It's also one of the sites for the PGA's Northern Telecom Tucson Open.

All three 9-hole designs offer championship golf with many fascinating holes that work beautifully together in all of their configurations.

DIRECTIONS

Take I-10 north to exit Cortaro Farms Rd and stay right (east) for about 5 miles and you'll drive through a set of street lights at Thornydale Rd. The course will be approximately 3/4 miles further east. The course will be on your left.

ARIZONA CITY GOLF COURSE

13270 S. Sunland Gin Rd., Arizona City, AZ 85223 / (602) 466-5248

BASIC INFORMATION

Course Type: Semi-private
Year Built: Jack Snyder
Architect: 1960
Local Pro: Bob L. Hickson

Course: N/A
Holes: 18/Par 72

Back   : 6,775 yds. Rating: 71.6 Slope: 117
Middle: 6,440 yds. Rating: 70.3 Slope: 114
Ladies: 5,959 yds. Rating: 72.7 Slope: 117

Tee Time: 5 days in advance.
Price: $14 - $28

Credit Cards:		Restaurant:	■
Driving Range:	■	Lounge:	■
Practice Green:	■	Meeting Rooms:	
Locker Room:		Tennis:	
Rental Clubs:	■	Swimming:	
Walkers:	■	Jogging Trails:	
Snack Bar:	■	Boating:	

COURSE DESCRIPTION

Most city courses have to endure an enormous amount of play, which makes them extremely hard to maintain — especially around the greens. Surprisingly enough, this course has stood the test of time in perfect shape.

The terrain is mostly flat and features five lakes scattered along its platform. It's not a tough course, but some of you will find it sneaky-long. You'll find plenty of room to shape your tee-shots to your most desired landing area. You'll find the course a little more demanding from around 150 yards to the greens.

DIRECTIONS

The course is halfway between Phoenix and Tucson. Exit 200, south 3 miles to Arizona City.

CASA GRANDE MUNICIPAL GOLF COURSE

2121 N. Thorton Rd., Casa Grande, AZ 85222 / (602) 836-9216

BASIC INFORMATION

Course Type: Municipal
Year Built: 1979
Architect: N/A
Local Pro: John Gunby

Course: N/A
Holes: 18 / Par 72

Back : 6,316 yds. Rating: 68.8 Slope: 115
Middle: 5,218 yds. Rating: 65.4 Slope: 108
Ladies: 5,038 yds. Rating: 66.5 Slope: 100

Tee Time: 3 days in advance.
Price: $4 - $15.25

Credit Cards: ■	Restaurant:
Driving Range: ■	Lounge:
Practice Green: ■	Meeting Rooms:
Locker Room:	Tennis: ■
Rental Clubs: ■	Swimming:
Walkers: ■	Jogging Trails: ■
Snack Bar: ■	Boating:

COURSE DESCRIPTION

The *Casa Grande Golf Course* represents a no-nonsense, straightforward, play-it-as-you-see-it layout. It can work wonders on your confidence if you're a high-handicapper or a player short on distance.

The wide open fairways of the front nine make it the easier half to play, and thus should be approached more aggressively for low numbers.

Having the ability to work the ball both left and right will get you into good scoring position off your drives.

DIRECTIONS

Going east-bound on I-10, take Florence Blvd. to Pinal Ave., north to Kortsen Rd, west about a mile to Thornton Rd. and make a right to the course.

FRANCISCO GRANDE RESORT

26000 W. Gila Bend Hwy., Casa Grande, AZ 85222 / (602) 836-6444

BASIC INFORMATION

Course Type: Public
Year Built: 1963
Architect: N/A
Local Pro: Kent Chase

Course: N/A
Holes: 18 / Par 72

Back : 7,594 yds. Rating: 74.9 Slope: 126
Middle: 6,975 yds. Rating: 72.2 Slope: 120
Ladies: 5,554 yds. Rating: 69.5 Slope: 114

Tee Time: 5 days in advance.
Price: $15 - $50

Credit Cards: ■	Restaurant: ■
Driving Range: ■	Lounge: ■
Practice Green: ■	Meeting Rooms: ■
Locker Room:	Tennis: ■
Rental Clubs: ■	Swimming: ■
Walkers: ■	Jogging Trails:
Snack Bar: ■	Boating:

COURSE DESCRIPTION

This may be one of the few courses built in the early 1960's to have had the foresight, the vision, and the belief that one day golfers would have the ability to hit a ball the way John Daly does today — at an average of 288 yards!

If you're a long hitter, this is definitely a course you'll want to play. It was originally built for the San Francisco Giants as an extension of their training camp. Perhaps that explains why the architect built this course in the grand scale that he did — it's the longest course in the state of Arizona.

DIRECTIONS

Take I-10 to Casa Grande and get onto Exit 185 (Route 387) heading south. When you get to the Hwy. 84 intersection, turn right (onto Hwy. 84), and proceed 5 miles further to the course. It will be on your right.

KINO SPRINGS GOLF COURSE

187 Kino Springs Dr., Nogales, AZ 85621 / (602) 287-8701

BASIC INFORMATION

Course Type: Semi-private
Year Built: 1969
Architect: Red Lawrence
Local Pro: Neal Stafford

Course: N/A
Holes: 18 / Par72

Back : 6,445 yds. Rating: 69.8 Slope: 117
Middle: 5,974yds. Rating: 67.6 Slope: 112
Ladies: 5,368yds. Rating: 64.9 Slope: 107

Tee Time: 7 days in advance.
Price: $20 - $25

Credit Cards: ■	Restaurant: ■
Driving Range: ■	Lounge: ■
Practice Green: ■	Meeting Rooms: ■
Locker Room: ■	Tennis:
Rental Clubs: ■	Swimming:
Walkers:	Jogging Trails:
Snack Bar:	Boating:

COURSE DESCRIPTION

The *Kino Springs Golf Course* offers a beautiful balance between two very distinctive 9-hole layouts. You'll feel as though you're playing two different courses — one side is flat, and the other runs along a rolling mountain terrain that features dramatic scenery.

Many people tend to underestimate the challenge of this course when judging it numerically on its total yardage, rating, and slope. But if you don't hit the ball consistently straight throughout the length of the course, it may turn out to be the longest 6,445 yards of play you'll ever have to contend with.

DIRECTIONS

From Tucson: First exit from 1-19 straight to 6th set of stoplights. Go right onto Hwy. 82 for about 5-miles and look for the course on your right.

RIO RICO GOLF COURSE

1410 Rio Rico Dr., Nogales, AZ 85621 / (602) 281-8567

BASIC INFORMATION

Course Type: Semi-private
Year Built: 1972
Architect: Robert Trent Jones, Sr.
Local Pro: Jack Cute

Course: N/A
Holes: 18 / Par 72

Back : 7,119 yds. Rating: 74.4 Slope: 130
Middle: 6,426 yds. Rating: 70.9 Slope: 122
Ladies: N/A yds. Rating: 70.2 Slope: 114

Tee Time: Call for availability.
Price: Call to confirm.

Credit Cards: ■	Restaurant: ■
Driving Range: ■	Lounge: ■
Practice Green: ■	Meeting Rooms: ■
Locker Room: ■	Tennis: ■
Rental Clubs: ■	Swimming: ■
Walkers: ■	Jogging Trails: ■
Snack Bar: ■	Boating: ■

COURSE DESCRIPTION

Robert Trent Jones, Sr. is undoubtedly one of the most influential golf architects of our century. The *Rio Rico Golf Course* is a splendid example of his work.

At 4,000 ft. above sea level, nestled in the foothills of these mountains just north of the Mexican border, the views here are absolutely spectacular. It's not a desert course at all, but rather a traditional design with lush fairways and greens.

The 9th hole (par-5/602 yds./dogleg left) is the number one handicap hole on the course. You'll need to drive the ball well to open up the fairway on your first approach shot. Because of the high elevation and the large size of the green, long hitters may want to go for the green in two.

DIRECTIONS

Exit I-19 at the Rio Rico exit and go east for a mile. Make a right Pendelton Rd. and proceed straight for another mile.

TUBAC GOLF RESORT

#1 Otera Rd. P.O. Box 1297, Tubac, AZ 85646 / (602) 398-2211

BASIC INFORMATION

Course Type: Semi-private
Year Built: 1960
Architect: Red Lawrence
Local Pro: Joan Lusk

Course: N/A
Holes: 18 / Par 71

Back : 6,839 yds. Rating: 72.6 Slope: 124
Middle: 6,345 yds. Rating: 70.2 Slope: 120
Ladies: 5,481 yds. Rating: 69.0 Slope: 112

Tee Time: 3-7 days .
Price: $21 - $36

Credit Cards:	■	Restaurant:	■
Driving Range:	■	Lounge:	■
Practice Green:	■	Meeting Rooms:	■
Locker Room:	■	Tennis:	■
Rental Clubs:	■	Swimming:	■
Walkers:	■	Jogging Trails:	■
Snack Bar:	■	Boating:	■

COURSE DESCRIPTION

The ambiance and natural beauty of this course is the first thing that most golfers notice upon their arrival. It's a mature course with many fabulous cottonwoods scrambled along rows of lush vegetation that run along hilly and flat terrain.

When comparing the front-nine to the back, most golfers agree that the back-nine is the more scenic of the two and that each is equally hard to play.

The layout is set inside a valley and is bisected by the Santa Cruz River.

DIRECTIONS

Take 1-19 south to Exit-40 (Chavez Siding Rd.) and turn left to east Frontage Rd. The course will be on your right.

ANTELOPE HILLS GOLF COURSE

19 Clubhouse Dr., Prescott, AZ 86301 / (602) 776-7888

BASIC INFORMATION

Course Type: Municipal
Year Built: 1956 / 1992
Architect: Lawrence Hughes / Gary Panks
Local Pro: Jim Noe

Course: North (18 / Par 72)
Holes: 36

Back : 6,778 yds. Rating: 71.4 Slope: 131
Middle: 6,380 yds. Rating: 67.9 Slope: 115
Ladies: 6,087 yds. Rating: 74.3 Slope: 126

Tee Time: 3 days in advance.
Price: $16 - $30

Credit Cards:	■	Restaurant:	■
Driving Range:	■	Lounge:	■
Practice Green:	■	Meeting Rooms:	
Locker Room:		Tennis:	
Rental Clubs:	■	Swimming:	
Walkers:	■	Jogging Trails:	
Snack Bar:	■	Boating:	

COURSE DESCRIPTION

If you've ever fancied playing golf through a picturesque English forest, then try the north course at *Antelope Hills Golf Course*.

You'll find a rich cultivated expanse of trees hugging the fairways through magnificent doglegs that demand accuracy above distance — not that distance should worry you, because the course is set at a 5,000 ft. elevation. The thin air will automatically add distance to your drives and approach shots.

It's a tightly built course with a well-planned series of holes.

DIRECTIONS

Take US Hwy 89 north; when you get to the city limits (by the Sheraton Hotel), then proceed for about 7 miles. Make a right by Love airport.

BEAVER CREEK GOLF RESORT

P.O. Box 248, Lake Montezuma, AZ 86342 / (602) 567-4487

BASIC INFORMATION

Course Type: Public
Year Built: 1962
Architect: Arthur Jack Snyder
Local Pro: David Gray

Course: N/A
Holes: 18 /Par 72

Back : 6,386 yds. Rating: 69.1 Slope: 120
Middle: 6,054 yds. Rating: 68.0 Slope: 116
Ladies: 5,485 yds. Rating: 69.8 Slope: 111

Tee Time: 2 days in advance.
Price: $12 - $18

Credit Cards:	■	Restaurant:	■
Driving Range:		Lounge:	■
Practice Green:	■	Meeting Rooms:	■
Locker Room:		Tennis:	
Rental Clubs:	■	Swimming:	■
Walkers:	■	Jogging Trails:	
Snack Bar:	■	Boating:	

COURSE DESCRIPTION

If you're an average golfer, this course is bound to offer you many memorable holes, but if you're good — say a single handicap player, the relative shortness of the course may not be competitive enough for you.

If you can place your ball onto the proper landing areas on the fairways, you shouldn't have much trouble playing your approach shots. More often than not, this course will have you reaching for a high-lofted club.

The layout rewards accuracy above distance. You won't have to hit your drives 260 yards here to play well.

DIRECTIONS

Take I-17 east to Exit 293 and follow the road for about 4-miles. That will take you straight to the front of the course.

PRESCOTT COUNTRY CLUB

1030 Prescott Country Club Blvd., Dewey, AZ 86327 / (602) 772-8984

BASIC INFORMATION

Course Type: Semi-private
Year Built: 1971
Architect: Milt Coggins
Local Pro: Mark Oswald

Course: N/A
Holes: 18 / Par 72

Back : 6,800 yds. Rating: 71.4 Slope: 123
Middle: 6,500 yds. Rating: 69.6 Slope: 118
Ladies: 2,900 yds. Rating: 71.1 Slope: 104

Tee Time: 3 days in advance.
Price: $22.50 - $40.00

Credit Cards:	■	Restaurant:	■
Driving Range:	■	Lounge:	■
Practice Green:	■	Meeting Rooms:	■
Locker Room:	■	Tennis:	■
Rental Clubs:	■	Swimming:	■
Walkers:	■	Jogging Trails:	
Snack Bar:	■	Boating:	

COURSE DESCRIPTION

This is a well-crafted course that features many fascinating holes.

You'll find the most amount of pressure on your approach shots and your putting game. Most of the fairways are wide open and will allow you to play aggressively off the tee, but be forewarned: accuracy off the tees is much more important than long drives.

The Bent grass greens are undulating and at times difficult to read. Be patient and work on your putting skills before you start your round.

DIRECTIONS

Take I-17 to Hwy. 69 and go west for about 20-miles. The course is in the town of Dewey off Hwy. 69 on the south side of the road 13-miles east of Prescott.

MESA DEL SOL GOLF & TENNIS CLUB

10583 South Camino Del Sol, Yuma, AZ 85365 / (602) 342-1283

BASIC INFORMATION

Course Type: Public
Year Built: 1980
Architect: Arnold Palmer (Back 9-holes)
Local Pro: Dick Walters

Course: N/A
Holes: 18 / Par 72

Back : 6,767 yds. Rating: 72.6 Slope: 124
Middle: 6,299 yds. Rating: 69.7 Slope: 116
Ladies: 5,388 yds. Rating: 69.5 Slope: 112

Tee Time: 2 days in advance.
Price: $5 - $25

Credit Cards:	■	Restaurant:	■
Driving Range:	■	Lounge:	■
Practice Green:	■	Meeting Rooms:	
Locker Room:		Tennis:	■
Rental Clubs:	■	Swimming:	
Walkers:	■	Jogging Trails:	
Snack Bar:	■	Boating:	

COURSE DESCRIPTION

If you've never played on a links-type course, the *Mesa del Sol Golf & Tennis Club* should not be missed. This beautiful course was built on a contoured platform that features demanding fairways and fast greens. The open architecture of the design makes it susceptible to different wind conditions, which often can change the structure of how you should play the course. If such is the case, try to keep the ball beneath the wind by playing low, boring knockdown shots throughout the day.

The course offers many dramatic mountain views from a variety of holes that add to the visual appeal of the game.

DIRECTIONS

The course can be found north of I-8, between the Foothills and Fortuna exits.

ARIZONA

ALTERNATIVE COURSES

Cochise
9-Hole

Douglas Golf Club
P.O. Box 1220
Douglas, AZ 85608
(602) 364-3722

**Turquoise Valley
Golf & RV Park**
Newell Rd.
Bisbee, AZ 85603
(602) 432-3091

Coconino
Private

Fairfeild Flagstaff Resort
1900 N. Country Club Dr.
Flagstaff, AZ 86004
(602) 526-3232

Forest Highland
657 Forest Highlands
Flagstaff, AZ 86001
(602) 525-9014

Coconino
9-Hole

Canyon Mesa Country Club
500 Jacks Canyon Rd.
Sedona, AZ 86336
(602) 284-2176

Elephant Rocks Golf Course
2200 Country Club Dr.
Williams, AZ 86046
(602) 635-4935

Glen Canyon Golf Club
Hwy. 89 P.O. Box 1333
Page, AZ 86040
(602) 645-2715

Paco Diablo Resort
1752 State Hwy. 179
Sedona, AZ 86336
(602) 282-7333

Gila
9-Hole

Cobre Valley Country Club
Apache Trail
Miami, AZ 85539
(602) 473-2542

Greenlee
9-Hole

Greenlee Country Club
P.O. Box 306 (off Hwy. 75)
York, AZ 85534
(602) 687-1099

Maricopa
Private

Alta Mesa Country Club
1460 N. Alta Mesa Dr.
Mesa, AZ 85205
(602) 832-3257

Ancala Country Club
11700 E. Via Linda St.
Scottsdale, AZ 85259
(602) 391-1000

Arizona Country Club
5668 E. Orange Blossom Lane
Phoenix, AZ 85018
(602) 947-7666

Arrowhead Country Club
19888 N. 73 Ave.
Glendale, AZ 85308
(602) 561-9600

Briarwood Country Club
20800 N. 135 Ave.
Sun City West, AZ 85375
(602) 584-5600

Cottonwood Country Club
25612 E. J. Robinson Blvd.
Sun Lakes, AZ 85248
(602) 895-9660

Desert Forest Golf Course
P.O. Box 1399
Carefree, AZ 85377
(602) 488-4589

Desert Highland Golf
10040 E. Happy Valley Rd.
Scottsdale, AZ 85255
(602) 585-5171

Desert Mountain Develop Co.
10333 Rock Away Hills
Cave Creek, AZ 85331
(602) 4881363

Echo Mesa Golf Course
20349 N. Echo Mesa Dr.
Sun City West, AZ 85375
(602) 584-0666

Fountain Of The Sun Country Club
500 S. 80 St.
Mesa, AZ 85208
(602) 986-3128

Gainey Ranch Golf Club
7600 E. Gainey Club Dr.
Scottsdale, AZ 85258
(602) 951-0022

Grandview Golf Course
14260 Meeker Blvd.
Sun City West, AZ 85375
(602) 584-8036

Leisure World Country Club
908 S. Power Rd.
Mesa, AZ 85206
(602) 832-0003

Mesa Country Club
660 W. Fairway Dr.
Mesa, AZ 85201
(602) 964-1797

Moon Valley Country Club
151 W. Moon Valley Dr.
Phoenix, AZ 85023
(602) 942-0000

Palm Brook Country Club
9350 W. Greenway Rd.
Sun City, AZ 85351
(602) 977-8383

Paradise Valley Country Club
7101 N. Tatum Blvd.
Paradise Valley, AZ 85254
(602) 840-8100

Pebble Brook Golf Course
18836 N. 128 Ave.
Sun City West, AZ 85375
(602) 584-2401

Phoenix Country Club
2901 N. 7 St.
Phoenix, AZ 85014
(602) 263-5208

Pinnacle Peak Country Club
8701 E. Pinnacle Rd.
Scottsdale, AZ 85255
(602) 585-0385

Rio Verde Country Club
E. Four Peaks Blvd.
Scottsdale, AZ 85255
(602) 991-3451

Stardust Golf Course
12702 Stardust Blvd.
Sun City West, AZ 85375
(602) 584-2918

Sun City Country Club
9433 N. 107 Ave.
Sun City, AZ 85351
(602) 933-1353

Union Hills Country Club
9860 W. Lindgren Ave.
Sun City, AZ 85373
(602) 974-5888

Troon Golf & Country Club
25000 N. Windy Walk Dr.
Scottsdale, AZ 85255
(602) 563-5200

Wickenburg Country Club
Country Club Dr.
Wickenburg, AZ 85
(602) 684-2011

Willowbrook Golf Course
10600 Boswell Blvd.
Sun City, AZ 85351

(602) 876-3020

Maricopa
9-Hole

Apache Sun Golf Course
919 E. Pima Rd.
Queen Creek, AZ 85242
(602) 987-9065

Coronado Golf Course
2829 N. Miller Rd.
Scottsdale, AZ. 85257
(602) 947-8364

Cypress Golf Course
10801 E. McDowell Rd.
Scottsdale, AZ 85256
(602) 946-5155

Dreamland Villa Golf Course
5641 E. Albany St.
Mesa, AZ 85205
(602) 985-6591

Encanto-9 Municipal Golf Course
2300 N. 17 Ave.
Phoenix, AZ 85007
(602) 253-3963

Fiesta Lakes Golf Club
1415 S. Westwood St.
Mesa, AZ 85210

Glen Lakes Municipal Golf
5450 W. Northern Ave.
Glendale, AZ 85301
(602) 939-7541

Palo Verde Golf Course
6215 N. 15 Ave.
Phoenix, AZ 85015
(602) 249-9930

Pepperwood Public Golf Course
647 W. Baseline Rd.
Tempe, AZ 85283
(602) 831-9457

Rio Salado Golf Course
1490 E. Weber Dr.
Tempe, AZ 85281
(602) 990-1233

Riverview Municipal Golf Course
2202 W. 8 St.
Mesa, AZ 85201
(602) 644-3515

Roadhaven Golf Course
1000 S. Idaho Rd.
Apache Junction, AZ 85219
(602) 982-4653

Royal Palms Golf Course
1415 E. McKellips Rd.
Mesa, AZ 85203
(602) 964-1709

Shalimar Public Country Club
2032 E. Golf Ave.
Tempe, AZ 85282
(602) 838-0488

View Point Golf Resort
8700 E. University Dr.
Mesa, AZ 85207
(602) 373-8715

Villa Monterey Golf Club
8100 E. Camelback Rd.
Scottsdale, AZ 85251
(602) 990-7100

Valley Club
5200 E. Camelback Rd.
Phoenix, AZ 85018
(602) 952-9313

Mohave
Private

Beaver Dam Resort & RV Park
P.O. Box 260
Little Field, AZ 86432
(602) 347-5111

Chaparral Golf Course
1260 E. Mohave Dr.
Bullhead City, AZ 86430
(602) 758-3939

Queens Bay Country Club
1477 Queens Bay Rd.
Lake Havasu City, AZ 86403
(602) 855-4777

Riverview Golf Club
2000 E. Ramar Rd.
Riviera, AZ 86442
(602) 763-1818

Navajo
Private

Pinetop Country Club
Hwy. 20
Pinetop, AZ 85935
(602) 369-4375

White Mountain Country Club
P.O. Box 1489
Pinetop, AZ 85935
(602) 367-4357

Navajo
9-Hole

Hidden Cove Golf Course
P.O. Box 70
Holbrook, AZ 86025
(602) 524-3097

Pinetop Country Club
Hwy. 20
Pinetop, AZ 85935
(602) 369-4375

Pima
Private

Country Club of Green Valley
77 Paseo De Golf
Green Valley, AZ 85614
(602) 625-8831

Desert Hills Golf Club
2500 S. Cirulo De Las Lomas
Green Valley, AZ 85614
(602) 625-5090

La Paloma Country Club
3660 East Sunrise Dr.
Tucson, AZ 85718
(602) 299-1500

Oro Valley Country Club
200 W. Valle Del Oro
Tucson, AZ 85737
(602) 297-3322

Quail Creek Country Club
2010 E. Quail Crossing Blvd.
Green Valley, AZ 85614
(602) 625-0133

Rolling Hills Country Club
8900 E. 29 St.
Tucson, AZ 85710
(602) 298-2401

Saddlebrook Country Club
64500 E. Saddlebrook Blvd.
Tucson, AZ 85737
(602) 825-2505

Skyline Country Club
5200 E. St. Andrew Dr.
Tucson, AZ 85718
(602) 299-0464

Tucson Country Club
2950 N. Camino Principal
Tucson, AZ 85715
(602) 298-2381

Tucson Estates Vagabond
2500 W. Way
Tucson, AZ 85713
(602) 883-5566

Ventana Canyon Golf Club
6200 N. Clubhouse Lane
Tucson, AZ 85715
(602) 577-1400

Willowbrook Golf Course
10600 Boswell Blvd.
Sun City, AZ 85351
(602) 876-3020

Pima
9-Hole

Ajo Country Club
77 W. Mead Rd.
Ajo, AZ 85321
(602) 387-5011

Sheraton 9-Hole Golf Course
10000 N. Oracle Road
Tucson, AZ 85737
(602) 742-7000

Pima
Executive

Cliff Valley Golf Course
5910 N. Oracle Rd.
Tucson, AZ 85704
(602) 887-6161

Dorado Golf Course
6601 E. Speedway Blvd.
Tuczon, AZ 85710
(602) 885-6751

Yavapai
Private

Mesa View Golf Course
4 Ash St.
Bagdad, AZ 86321
(602) 633-2818

Yuma
Private

Yuma Golf & Country Club
3150 S. Fortuna Ave.
Yuma, AZ 85365
(602) 726-4210

WHERE TO STAY IN ARIZONA

AJO
POPULATION: 3,308

GUEST HOUSE INN B&B
3 Guest House Rd.
Ajo, AZ 85321
(602) 387-6133

MARINE MOTEL
1966 N. 2nd Ave
Ajo, AZ 85321
(602) 387-7626

ALPINE
POPULATION: 600

TAL-WI-WI LODGE & REST.
40 County Rd. 2200
Alpine, AZ 85920
(602) 339-4319

APACHE JUNCTION
POPULATION: 18,130

GOLD CANYON RESORT
6100 S. Kings Ranch Rd.
Apche Junction, AZ 85219
(602) 982-9090

APACHE LAKE
POPULATION: N/A

APACHE LAKE MARINA & RESORT
AZ Hwy. 88
Apche Lake, AZ 85290
(602) 467-2511

ASHFORK
POPULATION: 525

STAGECOACH MOTEL
823 Park Ave
Ashfork, AZ 86320
(602) 637-2551

BISBEE
POPULATION: 8,080

BISBEE GRANDE HOTEL B&B
57 Main St.
Bisbee, AZ 85603
(602) 432-5900

COPPER QUEEN HOTEL
11 Howell Ave. P.O Drawer CQ
Bisbee, AZ 85603
(602) 432-2216

GREENWAY HOUSE, THE
401 Cole Ave.
Bisbee, AZ 85603
(800) 253-3325

MILE HIGH COURT B&B
901 Tombstone Canyon
Bisbee, AZ 85603
(602) 432-4636

OLIVER HOUSE B&B, THE
26 Sowles (Box 1897)
Bisbee, AZ 85603
(602) 432-4286

PARK PLACE B&B
200 East Vista
Bisbee, AZ 85603
(602) 432-3054

BISBEE

Continued

SAN JOSE LODGE
1002 Naco Hwy.
Bisbee, AZ 85603
(602) 432-5761

SCHOOL HOUSE B&B
818 Tombstone Canyon PO Box 32
Bisbee, AZ 85603
(800) 537-4333

BULLHEAD CITY

POPULATION: 23,710

**ARIZONA CLEARWATER RESORT
HOTEL**
1081 Main St. (PO Box 207)
Bullhead City, AZ 86430
(800) 443-2201

**BEST WESTERN GRAND VISTA
HOTEL**
1817 Arcadia Plaza
Bullhead City, AZ 86430
(602) 763-3300

COLORADO RIVER RESORT
434 Riverglen Dr.
Bullhead City, AZ 86440
(602) 754-4101

DESERT RANCHO MOTEL
1041 Hwy. 95
Bullhead City, AZ 86430
(602) 754-2578

ECONO LODGE
1717 Hwy. 95
Bullhead City, AZ 86442
(602) 758-8080

FIRST CHOICE INNS
2200 Karis Dr.
Bullhead City, AZ 85442
(800) 225-6903

LAKE MOHAVE RESORT & MARINA
Kathrine Landing
Bullhead City, AZ 86430
(800) 752-9669

LA PLAZA INN
1978 Hwy. 95
Bullhead City, AZ 86442
(602) 763-8080

OASIS PARK MOTEL
7th and Lee St.
Bullhead City, AZ 86430
(800) 624-2737

SILVER CREEK INN
1670 Hwy. 95
Bullhead City, AZ 86442
(800) 548-7739

CAREFREE / CAVE CREEK

POPULATION: 5,000

BOULDERS, THE
34631 N. Tom Darlington
(PO Box 2090)
Carefree, AZ 85377
(800) 553-1717

**CAVE CREEK TUMBLEWEED
HOTEL**
6333 E. Cave Creek Rd. (PO Box 312)
Carefree, AZ 85331
(602) 488-3668

CASA GRANDE
POPULATION: 20,000

BEST WESTERN CASA GRANDE SUITES
665 Via Del Cielo
Casa Grande, AZ 85222
(800) 528-1234

FRANCISCO GRANDE RESORT & GOLF CLUB
26000 Gila Bend Hwy.
Casa Grande, AZ 85222
(800) 237-4238

GOLDEN 9 MOTEL & REST.
Route 2, Box 660
Casa Grande, AZ 85222
(602) 836-3323

HOLIDAY INN CASA GRANDE
777 Pinal Ave.
Casa Grande, AZ 85222
(602) 426-3500

CHANDLER
POPULATION: 105,000

ALOHA MOTEL
445 N. Arizona Ave.
Chandler, AZ 85224
(602) 963-3403

SHERATON SAN MARCOS GOLF RESORT & CONFERENCE CENTER
Number One San Marcos Place
Chandler, AZ 85224
(800) 325-3535

CHINLE
POPULATION: N/A

THUNDERBIRD LODGE
Box 548
Chinle, AZ 86503
(602) 674-5842

CLIFTON
POPULATION: 3,605

RODE INN MOTEL
186 S. Coronado Blvd.
Chinle, AZ 86503
(602) 865-4536

COTTONWOOD
POPULATION: 13,305

BEST WESTERN COTTONWOOD INN
993 S. Main St.
Cottonwood, AZ 86326
(602) 634-5575

LITTLE DAISEY MOTEL
34 S. Main St. (PO Box 1341)
Cottonwood, AZ 86326
(602) 634-7865

VIEW MOTEL
818 S. Main St.
Cottonwood, AZ 86326
(602) 634-7581

EAGER
POPULATION: 4,197

BEST WESTERN SUNRISE INN
128 N. Main St.
Eager, AZ 85925
(602) 333-2540

FLAGSTAFF
POPULATION: 44,200

BEST WESTERN KING'S HOUSE MOTEL
1560 Santa Fe
Flagstaff, AZ 86001
(800) 528-1234

BEST WESTERN PONY SOLDIER MOTEL
3030 E. Route 66
Flagstaff, AZ 86001
(800) 356-4143

BEST WESTERN WOODLANDS PLAZA HOTEL
1175 W. Route 66
Flagstaff, AZ 86001
(800) 528-1234

BIRCH TREE INN B&B
824 W. Birch Ave.
Flagstaff, AZ 86001
(602) 774-1042

COMFORT INN
914 S. Milton Rd.
Flagstaff, AZ 86001
(602) 774-7326

DAYS INN HWY. 66
1000 W. Hwy. 66
Flagstaff, AZ 86001
(602) 774-5221

ECONOLODGE WEST
2355 S. Beulah Blvd.
Flagstaff, AZ 86001
(602) 774-2225

FAIRFEILD INN BY MARRIOTT
2005 S. Milton Rd.
Flagstaff, AZ 86001
(602) 773-1300

FIVE FLAGS INN
2610 E. Route 66
Flagstaff, AZ 86004
(800) 535-2466

FLAGSTAFF TRAVELODGE SUITES
2755 Woodlands Village Blvd.
Flagstaff, AZ 86001
(800) 255-3050

FLAGSTAFF UNIVERSITY / GRAND CANYON TRAVELODGE
801 W. Hwy. 66
Flagstaff, AZ 86001
(800) 255-3050

LITTLE AMERICA HOTEL
2515 E. Butler Ave.
Flagstaff, AZ 86001
Fax: (602) 779-7983

QUALITY INN
2000 S. Milton Rd.
Flagstaff, AZ 86001
(800) 228-5151

QUALITY SUITES HOTEL
706 S. Milton Rd.
Flagstaff, AZ 86001
(800) 228-5151

RODEWAY INN WEST
913 S. Milton Rd.
Flagstaff, AZ 86001
(602) 774-5038

SAGA MOTEL
820 W. Hwy. 66
Flagstaff, AZ 86001
(602) 779-3631

SKI LIFT LODGE
6355 Hwy. 180
Flagstaff, AZ 86001
(800) 472-3599

STARLITE MOTEL
500 S. Milton Rd.
Flagstaff, AZ 86001
(602) 774-7301

TRAVELODGE 1-40
2520 E. Lucky Lane
Flagstaff, AZ 86001
(800) 545-5525

TWILITE MOTEL
2010 E. Route 66
Flagstaff, AZ 86004
(800) 554-1883

WESTERN HILLS MOTEL
1580 E. Route 66
Flagstaff, AZ 86001
(602) 774-6633

WEST WIND MOTEL
1416 E. Santa Fe
Flagstaff, AZ 86001
(602) 774-5123

GILA BEND
POPULATION: 2,005

**BEST WESTERN SPACE AGE
LODGE & RESTAURANT**
401 East Pima (Drawer C)
Gila Bend, AZ 85337
(800) 528-1234

YUCCA MOTEL
836 E. Pima St.
Gila Bend, AZ 85337
(602) 683-2211

GLOBE
POPULATION: 6,685

EL REY MOTEL
1201 Ash St.
Globe, AZ 85501
(602) 425-4427

GOODYEAR
POPULATION: 4,835

**BEST WESTERN PHOENIX-
GOODYEAR INN**
1100 N. Litchfield Rd.
Goodyear, AZ 85338
(602) 932-3210

GRAND CANYON-NORTH RIM
POPULATION: N/A

KAIBAB LODGE
C/O Canyoneers Inc., Box 2997
Flagstaff, AZ 86003
(800) 525-0924

GRAND CANYON-NORTH RIM

Continued

RED FEATHER LODGE
PO BOX 1460 Hwy 64/ US 180
Grand Canyon, AZ 86023
(800) 538-2345

GRAND CANYON SOUTH RIM
POPULATION: 1,348

GRAND CANYON NATIONAL PARK LODGES:

1) BRIGHT ANGEL LODGES
2) EL TOVAR HOTEL
3) KACHINA LODGE
4) MASWIK LODGE
5) MOQUI LODGE
6) QUALITY INN GRAND CANYON
7) THUNDERBIRD LODGE
8) YAVAPAI LODGE

TEL: (602) 638-2401
FAX: (602) 638-9247
TELEX: (602) 297394

GRAND CANYON QUALITY INN-BEST WESTERN
P.O. Box 130
Grand Canyon, AZ 86023
(602) 638-2681

GREEN VALLEY
POPULATION: 17,264

QUALITY INN GREEN VALLEY
111 La Canada
Green Valley, AZ 85614
(800) 344-1441

GREER
POPULATION: 100

FOUR SEASONS CABINS
P.O. Box 219
Greer, AZ 85927
(602) 735-7333

HOLBROOK
POPULATION: 5,000

ADOBE INN B/W
615 W. Hopi Dr.
Holbrook, AZ 86025
(602) 524-3948

BEST WESTERN ARIZONIAN INN
2508 E. Navajo Blvd.
Holbrook, AZ 86025
(602) 524-2611

COMFORT INN
2602 Navajo Blvd.
Holbrook, AZ 86025
(800) 228-5150

ECONO LODGE
2596 Navajo Blvd.
Holbrook, AZ 86025
(800) 424-4777

HOLBROOK DAYS INN
2601 Navajo Blvd.
Holbrook, AZ 86025
(800) 325-2525

RAINBOW INN
2211 E. Navajo Blvd.
Holbrook, AZ 86025
(602) 524-2654

WESTERN HOLIDAY MOTEL
720 Navajo Blvd.
Holbrook, AZ 86025
(602) 524-6216

KAYENTA
POPULATION: N/A

WETHERILL INN
P.O. Box 175
Kayenta, AZ 86003
(602) 697-3231

KINGMAN
POPULATION: 12,345

BEST WESTERN KINGS INN
2930 E. Andy Devine
Kingman, AZ 86401
(602) 753-6101

BEST WESTERN A WAY FARER'S INN
2815 E. Andy Devine
Kingman, AZ 86401
(800) 753-6271

HOLIDAY INN
3100 E. Andy Devine
Kingman, AZ 86401
(800 HOLIDAY)

HUALAPAI MOUNTAIN LODGE RESORT
4565 Hualapai Mountain Rd.
Kingman, AZ 86401
(602) 757-3545

IMPERIAL MOTEL
1911 Andy Devine Ave.
Kingman, AZ 86401
(602) 753-2176

QUALITY INN
1400 E. Andy Devine Ave.
Kingman, AZ 86401
(800) 221-2222

SUNNY INN
3275 E. Andy Devine Ave.
Kingman, AZ 86401
(602) 757-1188

LAKE HAVASU CITY
POPULATION: 21,060

AZTEC MOTEL
2078 Swanson Ave.
Lake Havasu City, AZ 86403
(602) 453-7172

BLUE DANUBE INN
2176 Birch Square (McCulloch)
Lake Havasu City, AZ 86403
(602) 855-5566

LAKE PLACE INN, B/W
31 Wings Loop
Lake Havasu City, AZ 86403
(602) 855-2146

HIDDEN PALMS-ALL SUITE INN
2100 Swanson Ave.
Lake Havasu City, AZ 86403
(602) 855-7144

LAKE HAVASU CITY

Continued

INN AT TAMARISK
3101 Londen Bridge Rd.
Lake Havasu City, AZ 86403
(602) 764-3033

ISLAND INN HOTEL
1300 W. McCulloch Blvd.
Lake Havasu City, AZ 86403
(800) 243-9955

**NAUTICAL INN RESORT AND
CONFERENCE CENTER**
1000 McCulloch Blvd.
Lake Havasu City, AZ 86403
(602) 855-2141

**RAMADA LONDEN BRIDGE
RESORT**
1477 Queen's Bay Rd.
Lake Havasu City, AZ 86403
(800) 624-7939

SANDMAN INN
1700 McCulloch Blvd.
Lake Havasu City, AZ 86403
(800) 835-2410

SANDS VACATION RESORT
2040 Mesquite
Lake Havasu City, AZ 86403
(800) 521-0360

WINDSOR INN MOTEL
451 London Bridge Rd.
Lake Havasu City, AZ 86403
(800) 245-4145

LAKE MONTEZUMA

POPULATION: 1,480

BEAVER CREEK INN, THE
Montezuma Ave. (P.O. Box 506)
Lake Montezuma, AZ 86342
(602) 567-4475

LAKESIDE

POPULATION: N/A

HIDDEN REST RESORT
Rt. 3, Box 2590
Lakeside, AZ 85929
(602) 368-6336

LAKE OF THE WOODS
P.O. Box 777
Lakeside, AZ 85929
(602) 368-5353

MOONRIDGE LODGE & CABIN
P.O. Box 1058
Lakeside, AZ 85935
(602) 367-1906

PLACE RESORT, THE
Rt. 3, Box 2675
Lakeside, AZ 85929
(602) 368-6777

RAINBOW LAKES LODGE RESORT
P.O. Box 1140
Lakeside, AZ 85929
(602) 368-6364

MARBLE CANYON
POPULATION: N/A

CLIFF DWELLERS LODGE
Rt. 89A, (Nine miles west of Navajo)
Marble Canyon, AZ 86036
(602) 355-2228

LEE'S FERRY LODGE
Hw. 89A HC67 Box 1
Vermillion Cliff, AZ 86036
(602) 355-2231

MARBLE CANYON LODGE
Hwy. 89A (Box 1)
Marble Canyon, AZ 86036
(602) 355-2225

MAYER
POPULATION: 3,000

DUNCAN'S OAK HILLS
P.O. Box 97
Mayer, AZ 86333
(602) 632-9696

McNARY
POPULATION: N/A

SUNRISE PARK HOTEL
P.O. Box 217
McNary, AZ 85930
(800) 55-HOTEL

MEADVIEW
POPULATION: N/A

MEADVIEW LAKE MOTEL
30205 Escalante Blvd. (P.O. Box 517)
Meadview, AZ 86444
(602) 564-2343

MESA
POPULATION: 311,000

ARIZONA GOLF RESORT & GOLF CENTER
425 S. Power Rd.
Mesa, AZ 85201
(800) 528-8282

BEST WESTERN MESA INN
1625 E. Main
Mesa, AZ 85201
(800) 528-1234

BEST WESTERN MESONA
250 W. Main
Mesa, AZ 85201
(800) 528-8299

CLOVERDALE MOTEL
1301 W. Main St.
Mesa, AZ 85201
(602) 964-3570

DOBSON RANCH INN & RESORT
1666 S. Dobson Rd.
Mesa, AZ 85201
(800) 528-1356

MESA

Continued

FRONTIER MOTEL
1307 E. Main St.
Mesa, AZ 85201
(602) 964-8398

LEXINGTON HOTEL SUITES
1410 S. Country Club Dr.
Mesa, AZ 85210
(602) 964-2897

MARICOPA INN MOTOR HOTEL
3 E. Main
Mesa, AZ 85201
(800) 627-2144

NENDELS INN
4244 E. Main St.
Mesa, AZ 85201
(602) 832-5961

QUALITY INN MESA
951 W. Main St.
Mesa, AZ 85201
(800) 228-5151

REGIS INN
5531 E. Main St.
Mesa, AZ 85205
(800) 527-3447

SAGUARO LAKE RANCH
13020 Bush Hwy.
Mesa, AZ 85205
(800) 984-2194

SHERATON MESA HOTEL
200 N. Continental Way
Mesa, AZ 85201
(800) 465-6372

SUPER 8 MOTEL
6733 E. Main St.
Mesa, AZ 85201
(800) 800-8000

SURREY INN
1750 E. Main
Mesa, AZ 85201
(602) 969-1942

TRAVELODGE MESA
22 S. Country Club Dr.
Mesa, AZ 85210
(800) 255-3050

MIAMI
POPULATION: 2,690

BW COPPER HILLS INN
Rt. 1, Box 506
Miami, AZ 85539
(602) 425-7151

NOGALES
POPULATION: 23,000

ELDORADO MOTEL
884 N. Grand Ave.
Nogales, AZ 85621
(602) 287-4611

BEST WESTERN TIME MOTEL
921 N. Grand Ave.
Nogales, AZ 85621
(602) 287-4627

ORACLE
POPULATION: N/A

INN AT THE BIOSPHERE
P.O. Box 689
Oracle, AZ 85623
(602) 825-6222

PAGE
POPULATION: 7,196

BEST WESTERN WESTIN INN
207 N. Lake Powell Blvd.
Page, AZ 86040
(602) 645-2451

CACTUS LODGE
75 S. 8th Ave.
Page, AZ 86040
(602) 645-2858

ECONO LODGE
121 S. Lake Powell Blvd.
Page, AZ 86040
(602) 645-2488

iNN AT LAKE POWELL
P.O. Box C
Page, AZ 86040
(800) 826-2718

LAKE POWELL SUITES
P.O. Box 5054
Page, AZ 86040
(800) 525-3189

PAGE HOLIDAY INN
284 N. Lake Powell Blvd.
Page, AZ 86040
(800) Holiday

WAHWEAP LODGE
P.O. Box 1597
Page, AZ 86040
(800) 528-6154

PARKER
POPULATION: 3,305

ARIZONA SHORES RESORT
579 Riverside Dr.
Parker, AZ 85344
(602) 667-2685

BRANSON'S RESORT
Rural Route 2, Box 710
Parker, AZ 85344
(602) 667-3346

HAVASU SPRINGS RESORT
Rte. 2, Box 624
Parker, AZ 85344
(602) 667-3361

KOFA INN
P.O. Box 1069
Parker, AZ 85344
(602) 669-2101

STARDUST MOTEL
700 California Ave.
Parker, AZ 85344
(602) 669-2278

PAYSON

POPULATION: 7,940

CHARLETON MOTOR INN
302 S. Beeline Hwy.
Payson, AZ 85541
(602) 474-2201

CHRISTOPHER CREEK LODGE-MOTEL
Star Route Box 119
Payson, AZ 85541
(602) 478-4300

GREY HACKLE LODGE
Star Route Box 145
Payson, AZ 85541
(602) 478-4392

KOHLS RANCH RESORT
E. Hwy. 260
Payson, AZ 85541
(800) 331-KOHL

MOUNTAIN MEADOWS CABINS
HCR Box 162E
Payson, AZ 85541

PAYSON PUEBLO INN
Suite 809, E. Hwy. 260
Payson, AZ 85541
(800) 888-9828

PAYSON TRAVELODGE
101 W. Phoenix
Payson, AZ 85541
(800) 255-3050

STAR VALLEY MOTEL
HC Box 45A
Payson, AZ 85541
(602) 474-5182

SWISS VILLAGE LODGE
801 N. Beeline Hwy.
Payson, AZ 85541
(602) 474-3241

PHOENIX

POPULATION: 955,695

ARIZONA BILTMORE
24th St. & Missouri
Phoenix, AZ 85016
(800) 528-3696

BEST WESTERN AIRPORT INN
2425 S. 24 St.
Phoenix, AZ 85016
(800) 528-8199

BEST WESTERN BELL MOTEL
1721 N. Black Cayon Hwy.
Phoenix, AZ 85023
(800) 528-1234

BEST WESTERN EXECUTIVE PARK HOTEL
24th St. & Missouri
Phoenix, AZ 85004
(800) 528-1234

BEST WESTERN GRACE INN AT AHWATUKEE
I-10 at Elliot Rd.
Phoenix, AZ 85044
(800) 843-6010

BEST WESTERN INN SUITES PHOENIX
I-10 at Elliot Rd.
Phoenix, AZ 85020
(800) 752-2204

BUDGET INN MOTEL
424 W. Van Buran St.
Phoenix, AZ 85003
(602) 257-8331

BUDGET LODGE
402 W. Van Buran St.
Phoenix, AZ 85003
(602) 254-7247

**CAMELBACK COUTRTYARD BY
MARRIOT HOTEL**
2101 Camelback Rd.
Phoenix, AZ 85016
(800) 321-2211

COMFORT INN AIRPORT
4120 E. Van Buran
Phoenix, AZ 85008
(800) 228-5150

CORNERSTONE INN & SUITES
4301 n. 24th St.
Phoenix, AZ 85016
(602) 954-9220

**CRESCENT HOTEL AT KOLL
CENTER**
2620 W. Dunlap Ave.
Phoenix, AZ 85021
(800) 423-4126

**CROWN STERLING SUITES
BILTMORE**
2630 E. Camelback
Phoenix, AZ 85016
(800) 433-4600

DAYS INN PHOENIX-CAMELBACK
502 W. Camelback Rd.
Phoenix, AZ 85013
(800) 325-2525

DESERT ROSE MOTEL
3424 E. Van Buren
Phoenix, AZ 85008
(602) 275-4421

**DOUBLETREE SUITES AT THE
PHOENIX GATEWAY CENTER**
320 N. 44 St.
Phoenix, AZ 85008
(800) 528-0444

**EMBASSY SUITES HOTEL
PHOENIX WESTSIDE**
3210 N.W. Grand Ave.
Phoenix, AZ 85017
(800) EMBASSEY

**EMBASSY SUITES/THOMAS ROAD/
AIRPORT WEST**
2333 E. Thomas
Phoenix, AZ 85016
(800) EMBASSEY

FOUNTAIN SUITES HOTEL
2577 W. Greenway Rd.
Phoenix, AZ 85023
(800) 527-7715

HILTON SUITES-PHOENIX
10 E. Thomas Rd.
Phoenix, AZ 85012
(800) HILTONS

HOLIDAY INN NORTH CENTRAL
4321 N. Central Ave.
Phoenix, AZ 85012
(602) 277-6671

HOTEL WESTCOURT
10220 N. Metro Pkwy. E.
Phoenix, AZ 85051
(800) 858-1033

PHOENIX

Continued

HYATT REGENCY PHOENIX
122 N. Second St.
Phoenix, AZ 85004
(800) 233-1234

INN SUITES PHOENIX/CENTRAL HOTEL
3101 N. 32nd St.
Phoenix, AZ 85018
(800) 842-4242

LEXINGTON HOTEL & CITY SQUARE SPORTS CLUB
100 W. Clarendon
Phoenix, AZ 85013
(800) 272-2439

LOS OLIVOS EXECUTIVE HOTEL
202 E. Mc.Dowell Rd.
Phoenix, AZ 85004
(800) 776-5560

MARICOPA MANOR B&B INN
P.O. Box 7186
Phoenix, AZ 85011
(800) 274-6302

METRO CENTER COURTYARD BY MARRIOTT HOTEL
10220 N. Metro Pkwy. E.
Phoenix, AZ 85051
(800) 321-2211

MOTEL 6
2323 E. Van Buran
Phoenix, AZ 85006
(800) 267-7511

OMNI ADAMS HOTEL
111 N. Central Ave.
Phoenix, AZ 85004
(800) 359-7253

ORANGE ARBOR APT/EXEC. SUITES
3535 W. Camelback Rd.
Phoenix, AZ 85019
(800) 359-7253

PHOENIX AIRPORT DAYS INN & CONVENTION CENTER
3333 E. Van Buran
Phoenix, AZ 85008
(800) 528-8191

PHOENIX AIRPORT HILTON
2435 S. 42nd St.
Phoenix, AZ 85034
(800) HILTONS

POINTE AT SQUAW PEAK
7677 N. 16th St.
Phoenix, AZ 85020
(800) 528-0428

POINTE HILTON AT TAPATIO CLIFFS, THE
11111 N. 7th St.
Phoenix, AZ 85020
(800) 528-0428

POINTE HILTON RESORT ON SOUTH MOUNTAIN, THE
7777 S. Pointe Pkwy.
Phoenix, AZ 85044
(800) 528-0421

PREMIER INNS METRO CENTER
10402 Black Canyon Mountain
Phoenix, AZ 85051
(800) 786-6835

PYRAMID INN
3307 E. Van Buran
Phoenix, AZ 85008
(602) 275-3691

QUALITY HOTEL PARK CENTRAL
3600 N. Central Ave.
Phoenix, AZ 85013
(800) HOTEL

QUALITY INN / AIRPORT
3541 E. Van Buran
Phoenix, AZ 85008
(800) 228-5151

QUALITY INN-SOUTH / MOUNTAIN
5121 E. La Puente Ave.
Phoenix, AZ 85044
(800) 562-3332

RADDISON HOTEL MIDTOWN-PHX
401 Clarendon Ave.
Phoenix, AZ 85051
(800) 527-3467

RAMADA INN METRO CENTER
12027 N. 28th Dr.
Phoenix, AZ 85029
(800) 228-2828 / 164 Units

RITZ-CARLTON PHOENIX, THE
2401 E. Camelback Rd.
Phoenix, AZ 85016
(800) 228-2828

RODEWAY INN AIRPORT WEST
1202 S. 24th St.
Phoenix, AZ 85034
(602) 273-1211

RODEWAY INN GRAND
3400 Grand Ave.
Phoenix, AZ 85017
(800) 228-2000

ROYAL PALMS INN
5200 E. Camelback Rd.
Phoenix, AZ 85018
(602) 840-3610

ROYAL SUITES
10421 N. 33rd. Ave.
Phoenix, AZ 85051
(602) 942-1000

SAN CARLOS HOTEL
202 N. Central Ave.
Phoenix, AZ 85004
(800) 528-5446

SHERATON GREENWAY INN
2510 W. Greenway Rd.
Phoenix, AZ 85023
(602) 993-0800

**SIERRA GRANDE MOTEL /
EXECUTIVE SUITES**
2645 E. Cactus
Phoenix, AZ 85032
(602) 867-4644

**WESTWAYS PRIVATE BOUTIQUE
RESORT INN**
P.O. Box 41624
Phoenix, AZ 85080
(800) 528-0483

WIGWAM, THE
300 E. Indian School Rd.
Litchfeild Park, AZ 85340
(800) 327-0396

WOOLEY SUITES HOTEL
3211 E. Pinchot Ave.
Phoenix, AZ 85018
(800) 321-9491

PINE

POPULATION: N/A

WINBRENNER'S B&B
38 Pinecreek Rd
Pine, AZ 85544
(602) 476-3843

PINETOP-LAKESIDE

POPULATION: 7,500

BEST WESTERN INN OF PINETOP
P.O. Box 1006
Pinetop-Lakeside, AZ 85935
(800) 528-1234

BONANZA MOTEL
P.O. Box 358
Pinetop-Lakeside, AZ 85935
(602) 367-4440

DOUBLE B LODGE
P.O. Box 747
Pinetop-Lakeside, AZ 85935
(602) 367-2747

ECONO LODGE OF PINETOP
Hwy. 260 & Billy Creek Rd.
Pinetop-Lakeside, AZ 85935
(602) 367-3636

HILLTOP MOTEL
577 E. White Mountain Blvd.
Pinetop-Lakeside, AZ 85935
(602) 367-4451

LAKESIDE INN
P.O. Box 1130-D
Pinetop-Lakeside, AZ 85935
(800) 843-4792

MEADOW VIEW LODGE
P.O. Box 325
Pinetop-Lakeside, AZ 85935
(602) 367-4642

MOUNTAIN HACIENDA LODGE
P.O. Box 713
Pinetop-Lakeside, AZ 85935
(602) 367-4146

SIERRA SPRINGS RANCH
HC62 Box 32100
Pinetop-Lakeside, AZ 85935
(602) 275-8514

WHISPERING PINES RESORT
P.O. Box 1043
Pinetop-Lakeside, AZ 85935
(602) 367-4386

PRESCOTT

POPULATION: 25,000

BEST WESTERN PRESCOTTNIAN
1317 E. Gurley St.
Prescott, AZ 86301
(602) 445-3096

COMFORT INN
1290 White Spar Rd.
Prescott, AZ 86303
(602) 778-5770

**COTTAGES AT PRESCOTT
COUNTRY INN**
502 Montezumza Rd.
Prescott, AZ 86303
(602) 445-7991

HASSAYAMPA INN
122 E. Gurley St.
Prescott, AZ 86301
(602) 778-9434

PINE VIEW MOTEL
500 Copper Basin Rd.
Prescott, AZ 86303
(602) 445-4660

PRESCOTT PINES INN B&B
901 White Spar Rd.
Prescott, AZ 86303
(800) 541-5374

**SHERATON RESORT &
CONFERENCE CENTER**
1500 Hwy. 69
Prescott, AZ 86301
(800) 445-4848

SUPER 8 MOTEL
1105 E. Sheldon Rd.
Prescott, AZ 86301
(800) 800-8000

WHEEL INN MOTEL
333 S. Montezuma
Prescott, AZ 86303
(602) 778-7346

PRESCOTT VALLEY
POPULATION: 10,000

PRESCOTT VALLEY MOTEL
8390 E. Hwy. 69
Prescott Valley, AZ 86312
(602) 772-9412

RIO RICO
POPULATION: 2,203

**RIO RICO RESORT &
COUNTRY CLUB**
1069 Camino Caralampi
Rio Rico, AZ 85648
(800) 288-4746

SAFFORD
POPULATION: 7,271

BEST WESTERN DESERT INN
1391 Thatcher Blvd.
Safford, AZ 85546
(800) 528-1234

COMFORT INN OF SAFFORD
1528 W. Thatcher Blvd.
Safford, AZ 85546
(800) 228-5150

SANDIA MOTEL
520 E. Hwy. 70
Safford, AZ 85546
(800) 578-2151

**TOWN HOUSE MOTEL &
DINING ROOM**
225 Hwy. 70 E.
Safford, AZ 85546
(602) 438-3474

SALOME
POPULATION: 1,700

SHEFFLER'S MOTEL
AZ Hwy. 60 Midway Los Angeles-
Grand Canyon
Salome, AZ 85348
(602) 859-3801

SASABE
POPULATION: 1,700

**RANCHO DE LA OSA
GUEST/DUDE RANCH**
P.O. Box 1
Sasabe, AZ 85633
(800) 872-6240

SCOTTSDALE
POPULATION: 125,335

ABC RESORT SUITES
P.O. Box 1
Scottsdale, AZ 85251
(602) 994-0375

**ABODE APARTMENT HOTEL OF
SCOTTSDALE**
3635 N. 68 St.
Scottsdale, AZ 85251
(602) 945-3544

**BEST WESTERN PAPAGO INN &
RESORT HOTEL**
7017 E. McDowell Rd.
Scottsdale, AZ 85257
(800) 528-1234

**BEST WESTERN THUNDERBIRD
SUITES**
7515 E. Butherus Dr.
Scottsdale, AZ 85260
(800) 334-1977

CAMELVIEW-A RADISSON RESORT
7601 E. Indian Bend Rd.
Scottsdale, AZ 85250
(602) 945-3544

**COURTYARD BY MARRIOTT
(Scottsdale/Mayo Clinic)**
13444 E. Shea Blvd.
Scottsdale, AZ 85259
(800) 321-2211

**DAYS INN SCOTTSDALE FASHION
SQUARE RESORT**
4710 N. Scottsdale Rd.
Scottsdale, AZ 85251
(602) 947-5411

EL CHORRO LODGE
5550 E. Lincoln Dr.
Scottsdale, AZ 85251
(602) 948-5170

FAIRFIELD INN SCOTTSDALE
13440 N. Scottsdale Rd.
Scottsdale, AZ 85254
(800) 228-2800

**HOLIDAY IN HOTEL & CONFER-
ENCE CENTER AT SCOTTSDALE
MALL**
7353 E. Indian School Rd.
Scottsdale, AZ 85251
(800) 695-6995

HOLIDAY INN SCOTTSDALE
5101 N. Scottsdale Rd.
Scottsdale, AZ 85250
(800) Holiday

**HOSPITALITY SUITE RESORT
SCOTTSDALE**
409 N. Scottsdale Rd.
Scottsdale, AZ 85257
(800) 445-5115

HYATT REGENCY SCOTTSDALE
7500 E. Doubletree Ranch Rd.
Scottsdale, AZ 85258
(602) 991-3388

JOHN GARDINER'S TENNIS RANCH
5700 E. McDonald Dr.
Scottsdale, AZ 85253
(800) 224-2051

**MARRIOTT'S CAMELBACK RESORT
GOLF CLUB & SPA**
5402 E. Lincoln Dr.
Scottsdale, AZ 85253
(800) 242-2635

MARRIOTT'S MOUNTAIN SHADOWS
5641 E. Lincoln Dr.
Scottsdale, AZ 85253
(800) 228-9290

**ORANGE TREE GOLF & CONFER-
ENCE RESORT**
10601 N. 56th St.
Scottsdale, AZ 85254
(800) 228-0386

PHOENICIAN, THE
5000 E. Camelback Rd.
Scottsdale, AZ 85251
(800) 888-8234

**RAMADA HOTEL VALLEY HO
RESORT**
6850 Main St.
Scottsdale, AZ 85251
(800) 321-4952

RED LION'S LA POSADA RESORT
4949 E. Lion's Dr.
Scottsdale, AZ 85253
(800) 547-8010

REGAL MCCORMICK RANCH
7401 N. Scottsdale Rd.
Scottsdale, AZ 85253
(800) 243-1332

REGISTRY RESORT, THE
7171 N. Scottsdale Rd.
Scottsdale, AZ 85253
(800) 247-9810

SAFARI RESORT
4611 N. Scottsdale Rd.
Scottsdale, AZ 85251
(602) 945-0721

**SCOTTSDALE/CAMELBACK
RESORT & SPA**
6302 E. Camelback
Scottsdale, AZ 85251
(602) 947-3300

**SCOTTSDALE CONFERENCE
RESORT**
7700 E. McCormick Pkwy.
Scottsdale, AZ 85253
(800) 528-0293

**SCOTTSDALE EMBASSY SUITES
RESORT HOTEL**
5001 N. Scottsdale Rd.
Scottsdale, AZ 85250
(800) 528-1456

SCOTTSDALE HILTON
6333 N. Scottsdale Rd.
Scottsdale, AZ 85253
(800) 528-3119

**SCOTTSDALE INN AT ELDORADO
PARK**
7707 E. McDowell Rd.
Scottsdale, AZ 85257
(800) 238-8851

SCOTTSDALE PIMA SUITES
7330 N. Pima Rd.
Scottsdale, AZ 85258
(800) 344-0262

SCOTTSDALE
Continued

SCOTTSDALE PLAZA RESORT, THE
7200 N. Scottsdale Rd.
Scottsdale, AZ 85253
(800) 832-2025

SCOTTSDALE PRINCESS
7575 E. Princess Dr.
Scottsdale, AZ 85255
(800) 344-0262

**SCOTTSDALE RESORT HOTEL
APARTMENTS**
7601 E. 2nd. St.
Scottsdale, AZ 85251
(602) 947-7244

SCOTTSDALE'S FIFTH AVENUE INN
6935 Fifth Ave.
Scottsdale, AZ 85251
(800) 528-7396

SHANGRILA RESORT
6237 N. 59 Pl.
Scottsdale, AZ 85253
(602) 948-5930

SMOKE TREE RESORT
7101 E. Lincoln Dr.
Scottsdale, AZ 85253
(602) 948-7660

**STOUFFER COTTONWOODS RE-
SORT**
6160 N. Scottsdale Rd.
Scottsdale, AZ 85253
(602) 948-5930

SUNBURST RESORT HOTEL
4925 N. Scottsdale Rd.
Scottsdale, AZ 85251
(800) 528-7867

**WYNDHAM PARADISE VALLEY
RESORT**
5401 N. Scottsdale Rd.
Scottsdale, AZ 85250
(800) 822-4200

SEDONA
POPULATION: 14,000

B&B AT SADDLE ROCK RANCH
255 Rock Ridge Dr.
Sedona, AZ 86336
(602) 282-7640

**BEST WESTERN ARROYO ROBLE
HOTEL**
400 N. Hwy. 89A
Sedona, AZ 86336
(602) 282-4001

BRIAR PATCH INN B&B
Star Rt. 3-Box
1002 Oak Creek Canyon
Sedona, AZ 86336
(602) 282-2342

CASA SEDONA A B&B INN
55 Hozoni Dr.
Sedona, AZ 86336
(800) 525-3756

CANYON PORTAL MOTEL
280 N. Hwy. 89A (P.O. Box 10239)
Sedona, AZ 86336
(800) 542-8484

CANYON VILLA B&B INN
125 Canyon Circle Dr. (P.O. Box 204)
Sedona, AZ 86336
(602) 284-1226

CEDARS RESORT
P.O. Box 292
Sedona, AZ 86336
(602) 282-7010

CIMARRON INN
2991 W. Hwy. 89A (P.O. Box 1589)
Sedona, AZ 86336
(602) 282-9166

COZY CACTUS B&B
80 Canyon Cr. Dr.
Sedona, AZ 86336
(800) 788-2082

DON HOEL'S CABINS
9440 N. Hwy. 89A
Sedona, AZ 86336
(800) 292-4635

ENCHANTMENT RESORT
525 Boynton Canyon Rd.
Sedona, AZ 86336
(602) 282-2900

GARLAND'S OAK CREEK LODGE
P.O. Box 152
Sedona, AZ 86336
(602) 282-3343

GRAHAM B&B INN
150 Canyon Circle Dr.
Sedona, AZ 86336
(602) 284-1425

INN AT BELL ROCK, THE
6246 Hwy. 179
Sedona, AZ 86336
(602) 282-4161

JUNIPINE CREEKHOUSE RESORT
8351 N. Hwy. 89A (Oakcreek Canyon)
Sedona, AZ 86336
(800) 742-PINE

KENNEDY HOUSE B&B
HC 30 Box 785K
Sedona, AZ 86336
(602) 282-1624

LANTERN LIGHT B&B INN
3085 W. Hwy.89A
Sedona, AZ 86336
(602) 282-3419

L'AUBERGE DE SEDONA RESORT
301 L'Auberge Lane-Uptown
Sedona, AZ 86336
(800) 272-6777

LA VISTA MOTEL
500 N. Hwy. 89A
Sedona, AZ 86336
(602) 282-7301

LOS ABRIGADOS
160 Portal Lane
Sedona, AZ 86336
(800) 521-3131

MATTERHORN MOTOR LODGE
230 Apple Ave.
Sedona, AZ 86336
(602) 282-7176

OAK CREEK TERRACE RESORT
4548 N. Hwy. 89A
Sedona, AZ 86336
(800) 224-2229

POCO DIABLO RESORT
1752 S. Hwy. 179
Sedona, AZ 86336
(602) 282-7333

QUALITY INN / KING'S RANSOM
P.O. Box 180
Sedona, AZ 86336
(800) 221-2222

SCOTTSDALE
Continued

RAILROAD INN AT SEDONA, THE
2545 W. Hwy. 89A
Sedona, AZ 86336
(800) 858-7245

RED ROCK LODGE
1 Cottage P.O. Box 537
Sedona, AZ 86336
(602) 282-3591

SEDONA MOTEL
P.O. Box 1450
Sedona, AZ 86336
(602) 282-7187

SKY RANCH LODGE MOTEL
P.O. Box 2579
Sedona, AZ 86336
(602) 282-6400

SUGAR LOAF LODGE
P.O. Box JJ-W. Sedona
Sedona, AZ 86340
(602) 282-9451

SHOW LOW
POPULATION: 6,000

B/W PAINT PONY LODGE
581 W. Deuce of Clubs
Show Low, AZ 85901
(602) 587-5773

KIVA MOTEL
261 E. Deuce Of Clubs
Show Low, AZ 85901
(602) 537-4542

THUNDERBIRD MOTEL
1131 E. Deuce Of Clubs
Show Low, AZ 85901
(602) 537-4391

SIERRA VISTA
POPULATION: 34,590

RAMADA INN SIERRA VISTA
2047 S. Hwy. 92
Sierra Vista, AZ 85635
(800) 825-4656

SIERRA SUITES
391 E. Fry Blvd.
Sierra Vista, AZ 85635
(602) 459-4221

SUN CANYON INN
260 N. Canyon Ave.
Show Low, AZ 85635
(800) 822-6966

THUNDER MOUNTAIN INN
1631 S. Hwy. 92
Show Low, AZ 85635
(800) 222-5811

VISTA INN
201 W. Fry Blvd.
Show Low, AZ 85635
(602) 458-6711

SPRINGERVILLE
POPULATION: 1,803

EL JO MOTOR INN
Box 175
Springerville, AZ 85938
(800) 638-6114

REED'S MOTOR LODGE
514 E. Main Hwy. 60
Springerville, AZ 85938
(602) 333-4323

SUN CITY
POPULATION: 42,467

BEST WESTERN INN OF SUN CITY
11201 Grand Ave. (P.O. Box 477)
Sun City, AZ 85351
(800) 528-1234

SURPRISE
POPULATION: 5,305

WINDMILL INN AT SUN CITY WEST
12545 W. Bell Rd.
Surprise, AZ 85374
(800) 527-4747

TEMPE
POPULATION: 144,445

BUTTES, THE
2000 Westcourt Way
Tempe, AZ 85282
(800) 843-1986

EMBASSEY SUITES HOTEL-TEMPE
4400 S. Rural Rd.
Tempe, AZ 85282
(602) 897-7444

FIESTA INN
2100 S. Priest Dr.
Tempe, AZ 85282
(800) 528-6481

HOLIDAY INN-PHOENIX-TEMPE/ ASU
915 E. Apache
Tempe, AZ 85281
(800) 238-5754

INNSUITES HOTEL TEMPE/ PHEONIX AIRPORT
2100 S. Priest Dr.
Tempe, AZ 85283
(800) 841-4242

LA QUINTA MOTOR INN
911 S. 48 St.
Tempe, AZ 85281
(800) 531-5900

QUALITY INNS & SUITES TEMPE/SCOTTSDALE
1635 N. Scottsdale Rd.
Tempe, AZ 85281
(800) 678-8466

RAMADA HOTEL SKY HARBOR
1600 S. 52 St.
Tempe, AZ 85281
(602) 967-6600

RODEWAY INN PHOENIX AIRPORT EAST
1550 S. 52 St.
Tempe, AZ 85281
(602) 967-3000

SHERATON TEMPE MISSION PALMS
60 E. 5 St.
Tempe, AZ 85281
(800) 547-8705

TEMPE/UNIVERSITY TRAVELODGE
1005 E. Apache Blvd.
Tempe, AZ 85281
(800) 255-3050

TOMBSTONE
POPULATION: 1,845

BEST WESTERN LOOKOUT LODGE
Hwy. 80 W. P.O. Box 787
Tombstone, AZ 85638
(800) 528-1234

TORTILLA FLAT
POPULATION: 1,845

APACHE LAKE RESORT & MARINA
P.O. Box 15627
Tortilla Flat, AZ 85638
(602) 467-2511

TUBA CITY
POPULATION: N/A

TUBA MOTEL
Main & Moenave (P.O. Box 247)
Tuba City, AZ 86045
(602) 283-4545

TUBAC
POPULATION: 884

TUBA MOTEL
1 Otero Rd.
Tubac, AZ 85646
(800) 848-7893

TUCSON
POPULATION: 400,000

AIRPORT EMBASSY SUITES HOTEL & CONFERENCE CENTER
7051 S. Tucson Blvd.
Tucson, AZ 85706
(602) 573-0700

ARIZONA INN
2200 E. Elm
Tucson, AZ 85719
(800) 993-1093

BEST WESTERN-A ROYAL SUN INN & SUITES
1015 N. Stone
Tucson, AZ 85705
(800) 352-1212

BEST WESTERN AZTEC INN
102 N. Alvernon Way
Tucson, AZ 85711
(800) 227-6086

BEST WESTERN EXECUTIVE INN
333 W. Drachman
Tucson, AZ 85705
(800) 255-3371

BEST WESTERN INNSUITES HOTEL TUCSON
6201 N. Oracle Rd.
Tucson, AZ 85705
(800) 554-4535

BRIMSTONE BUTTERFLY, THE
940 N. Olson Ave.
Tucson, AZ 85719
(800) 323-9157

CANDELIGHT SUITES
1440 S. Craycroft Rd.
Tucson, AZ 85711
(800) 233-1440

CHATEAU APARTMENT HOTELS
940 N. Olson Ave.
Tucson, AZ 85712
(800) 597-8483

CHATEAU SONATA
550 S. Camino Seco
Tucson, AZ 85710
(800) 597-8483

COMFORT INN TUCSON
715 W. 22 St.
Tucson, AZ 85713
(602) 791-9282

COUNTRY SUITES BY CARLSON, TUCSON
7411 N. Oracle Rd.
Tucson, AZ 85704
(800) 456-4000

DOUBLETREE HOTEL
445 S. Alveron Way
Tucson, AZ 85711
(800) 528-0444

EL PRESIDO B&B
297 Main Ave.
Tucson, AZ 85701
(602) 623-6151

EMBASSY SUITES TUCSON
5335 E. Broadway
Tucson, AZ 85711
(602) 745-2700

HIGHLAND TOWER MOTEL
1919 N. Oracle Rd.
Tucson, AZ 85705
(602) 791-3057

HOTEL PARK TUCSON
5151 Grant Rd.
Tucson, AZ 85712
(800) 257-7275

HOWARD JOHNSON-AIRPORT
1025 E. Benson Hwy.
Tucson, AZ 85713
(800) 446-4656

LA QUINTA TUCSON-WEST
665 N. Freeway
Tucson, AZ 85745
(602) 622-6491

LA POSADA DEL VALLE B&B INN
1640 N. Campbell Ave.
Tucson, AZ 85719
(602) 791-3057

LAZY 8 MOTEL
314 East Benson Hwy.
Tucson, AZ 85713
(602) 622-3336

LAZY K BAR RANCH INC.
8401 N. Scenic Dr.
Tucson, AZ 85743
(800) 321-7018

LODGE ON THE DESERT
306 N. Alvernon Way
Tucson, AZ 85711
(602) 791-3057

LOEWS VENTANA CANYON RESORT
7000 N. Resort Dr.
Tucson, AZ 85715
(800) 233-0888

PARK INN CLUB SANTA RITA
88 E. Broadway Blvd.
Tucson, AZ 85701
(602) 622-4000

TUCSON
Continued

PEPPERTREES B&B INN
724 E. University Blvd.
Tucson, AZ 85719
(800) 348-5763

PLAZA HOTEL & CONFERENCE CENTER
1900 Speedway Blvd.
Tucson, AZ 85719
(800) 843-8052

QUALITY INN UNIVERSITY & CONFERENCE CENTER
1601 N. Oracle Rd.
Tucson, AZ 85705
(602) 622-4000

RADISSON SUITE HOTEL TUCSON
6555 E. Speedway
Tucson, AZ 85710
(800) 333-3333

RAMADA PALO VERDE
5251 S. Julian Drive
Tucson, AZ 85706
(800) 228-2828

RAMADA DOWNTOWN
475 N. Grenada (I-10 & St. Mary)
Tucson, AZ 85701
(800) 228-2828

RESIDENCE INN BY MARRIOTT-TUCSON
644 E. Speedway Blvd.
Tucson, AZ 85710
(800) 331-3131

SAGUARO INN
6161 E. Benson Hwy.
Tucson, AZ 85706
(602) 574-0191

SHERATON EL CONQUISTADOR RESORT & COUNTRY CLUB
10000 N. Oracle Rd.
Tucson, AZ 85737
(602) 742-7000

SMUGGLER'S INN HOTEL
6350 E. Speedway Blvd
Tucson, AZ 85710
(800) 525-8852

TANQUE VERDE GUEST RANCH
14301 E. Speedway
Tucson, AZ 85748
(602) 296-6275

TANQUE VERDE INN
7007 E. Tanque Verde Rd.
Tucson, AZ 85715
(602) 298-2300

TUCSON HILTON
7600 E. Broadway
Tucson, AZ 85710
(602) 721-5600

TUCSON NATIONAL GOLF & RACQUET CLUB
2727 W. Club Dr.
Tucson, AZ 85741
(800) 528-4856

VENTANA CANYON GOLF & RACQUET CLUB
6200 N. Clubhouse Lane
Tucson, AZ 85715
(800) 828-5701

VILLA SERENAS RENTAL RESORT (Apartments)
8111 E. Broadway
Tucson, AZ 85710
(800) 677-6761

VISCOUNT SUITE HOTEL
4855 E. Broadway
Tucson, AZ 85741
(602) 745-6500

VISTA DEL SOL MOTEL
1458 W. Miracle Mile
Tucson, AZ 85705
(800) 528-4856

WAYWARD WINDS LODGE
707 W. Miracle Mile
Tucson, AZ 85741
(602) 791-7526

WESTIN LA PALOMA
3800 E. Sunrise Dr.
Tucson, AZ 85718
(800) 876-DOVE

WESTWARD LOOK RESORT
245 E. Ina Rd.
Tucson, AZ 85704
(800) 528-4856

WHITE STALLION RANCH
9251 W. Twin Peaks Rd.
Tucson, AZ 85743
(800) 782-5546

WINDMILL INN AT ST. PHILIP'S PLAZA
4250 Campbell Ave.
Tucson, AZ 85718
(800) 547-4747

WICKENBURG
POPULATION: 5,000

AMERICINN MOTEL
P.O. Box 1359
Wickenburg, AZ 85358
(602) 684-5467

BEST WESTERN RANCHO GRANDE MOTEL
293 Wickenburg Way
Wickenburg, AZ 85358
(602) 684-5445

FLYING RANCH-21,000 ACRE DUDE & CATTLE RANCH
2801 W. Wickenburg Way
Wickenburg, AZ 85358
(602) 684-2690

GARDEN CITY RESORT
P.O. Box 70
Wickenburg, AZ 85358
(602) 684-2334

RANCHO DE LOS CABALLEROS
P.O. Box 1148
Wickenburg, AZ 85358
(602) 684-5484

WICKENBURG INN TENNIS & GUEST RANCH
P.O. Box P Hwy. 89
Wickenburg, AZ 85358
(602) 684-7811

WESTERNER MOTEL
680 West Wickenburg Way
Wickenburg, AZ 85358
(602) 684-2493

WILLCOX
POPULATION: 3,900

ARIZONA SUNSET MOTEL
340 S. Haskell
Willcox, AZ 85643
(602) 384-4177

WILLCOX
Continued

BEST WESTERN PLAZA INN
1100 W. Rex Allen Dr.
Willcox, AZ 85643
(800) 262-2645

COMFORT INN
724 N. Bissbee Ave.
Willcox, AZ 85643
(800) 221-2222

DESERT BREEZE MOTEL
556 N. Haskell Ave.
Willcox, AZ 85643
(602) 384-4636

ROYAL WESTERN LODGE
590 Haskell Ave.
Willcox, AZ 85643
(206) 384-2266

WILLIAMS
POPULATION: 2,525

ARIZONA SUNSET MOTEL
620 W. Bill Williams Ave.
Williams, AZ 86046
(800) 745-4415

BUTLER MOTEL
437 W. Bil Williams Ave.
Williams, AZ 86046
(620) 635-4341

CANYON MOTEL
Old Easy Hwy. 66
Williams, AZ 86046
(602) 635-9371

COMFORT INN
911 W. Bill Williams Ave.
Williams, AZ 86046
(800) 228-5150

DOWNTOWNER MOTEL, THE
201 E. Bill Williams Ave.
Williams, AZ 86046
(800) 742-8871

ECONOLODGE
710 W. Bill Williams Ave.
Williams, AZ 86046
(800) 733-4814

EL RANCHO MOTEL
617 E. Bill Williams Ave.
Williams, AZ 86046
(800) 228-2370

FRIENDSHIP INN
302 E. Bill Williams Ave.
Williams, AZ 86046
(800) 882-7666

GRAND CANYON INN
P.O. Box 702
Williams, AZ 86046
(602) 635-9203

GRAND CANYON KOA
N. AZ Hwy. 64
Williams, AZ 86046
(602) 635-2307

GRAND MOTEL
234 E. Bill Williams Ave.
Williams, AZ 86046
(602) 635-4601

HYLANDER MOTEL
533 W. Bill Williams Ave.
Williams, AZ 86046
(602) 625-2541

MOUNTAIN SIDE INN, THE
642 E. Bill Williams Ave.
Williams, AZ 86046
(800) 462-9381

NORRIS MOTEL
1001 W. Bill Williams Ave.
Williams, AZ 86046
(800) 341-8000

PATIO MOTEL
128 E. Bill Williams Ave.
Williams, AZ 86046
(602) 635-4791

QUALITY INN MOUNTAIN RANCH RESORT
Route 1, Box 35
Williams, AZ 86046
(800) 221-2222

RODEWAY INN
750 N. Grand Canyon Blvd.
Williams, AZ 86046
(602) 635-9127

WESTERNER MOTEL
530 W. Bill Williams Ave.
Williams, AZ 86046
(602) 635-4312

WILLIAMS COURTESY INN
334 E. Bill Williams Ave.
Williams, AZ 86046
(602) 635-2619

WILLIAMS MOTEL
321 E. Bill Williams Ave.
Williams, AZ 86046
(602) 635-4512

WINSLOW
POPULATION: 10,700

EASY 8 MOTEL
1000 E. 3rd. St.
Winslow, AZ 86047
(800) 877-4813

MOTEL 10 INN
725 W. 3rd. St.
Winslow, AZ 86047
(800) 525-0404

YUMA
POPULATION: 50,755

BEST WESTERN CHILTON INN & CONFERENCE
300 E. 32. St.
Yuma, AZ 85364
(800) 528-1234

BEST WESTERN CORONADO MOTOR HOTEL 49
233 4th Ave.
Yuma, AZ 85364
(800) 528-1234

BEST WESTERN SUITES HOTEL YUMA
1450 Castle Dome Ave.
Yuma, AZ 85364
(602) 783-8341

CARAVAN OASIS MOTEL
10574 Fortuna Rd.
Yuma, AZ 85365
(602) 342-1292

CORCOVADO MOTEL
2607 S. Fourth Ave.
Yuma, AZ 85364
(602) 344-2988

DESERT GROVE RESORT MOTEL
3500 S. 4th Ave.
Yuma, AZ 85364
(602) 726-1400

HOLIDAY INN EXPRESS
3181 South 4th Ave.
Yuma, AZ 85364
(800) HOLIDAY

INTERSTATE 8 INN
2730 S. 4th Ave.
Yuma, AZ 85364
(800) 821-7465

LA FUENTE TRAVELODGE
1513 E. 16th St.
Yuma, AZ 85364
(800) 255-3050

PALMS INN, THE
2655 S. Fourth Ave.
Yuma, AZ 85364
(602) 344-4570

PARK INN SUITES
2600 S. 4th. Ave.
Yuma, AZ 85364
(602) 726-4830

REGALODGE
344 S. Fourth Ave.
Yuma, AZ 85364
(800) 777-4571

TORCH LITE LODGE
2501 S. Fourth Ave.
Yuma, AZ 85364
(602) 344-1600

YUMA CABANA MOTOR HOTEL
2151 Fourth Ave.
Yuma, AZ 85364
(800) 874-0811

YUMA INN MOTEL
260 S. 4th Ave.
Yuma, AZ 85364
(602) 782-4592

EXCURSIONS

NORTHWEST ARIZONA

Grand Canyon National Park

I can't think of a more incredible place to explore than the **Grand Canyon**. For the last two billion years, nature has chipped away for us one of the seven wonders of the world. If you're a first time visitor, you'll be taken aback by the sheer size and beauty that this location has to offer. The canyon is approximately a mile deep and stretches 277 miles long.

P.O Box 129
Grand Canyon, AZ 86023
(602) 638-7888

Lowell Observatory

If you're one of the thousands of people who have taken up stargazing with the use of a personal telescope, you won't want to miss the **Lowell Observatory**, the famous vantage point that led to the discovery of the planet Pluto. You can tour the observatory during the day and participate in one of their stargazing groups in the evening.

1400 W. Mars Hill Rd.
Flagstaff, AZ 85009
(602) 774-2096

Sedona - Oak Creek

Oak Creek Canyon has attracted some of the most prolific landscape photographers from all parts of the world. Ansel Adams, one of our country's most talented, is famous for his incomparable portfolios of this part of the world. The magnificent red hues that blend along the mouth of the Canyon are absolutely spectacular. Try to book a Jeep Tour.

Once you reach Sedona, go shopping in the tastefully decorated Tlaquepaque center, travel along rows of boutiques, and purchase indigenous art in one of the many galleries that you'll find throughout the city.

P.O Box 478 (Chamber of Commerce)
Sedona, AZ 86336
(602) 282-7722

National Monuments

Some of our earlier civilizations lived along vast stretches of intriguing landscapes. When you see the symmetrical cone that the **Sunset Crater** volcano formed nine centuries ago, you'll be amazed. It's been estimated that an 800 Sq. Ft. area was covered by the volcano and that the present sides of it stand at 1,000 feet tall.

You'll find over eight hundred cliff dwellings worth exploring between **Walnut Canyon National Park** and the **Wupatki National Monument.**

Sunset Crater Volcano
National Park
Route 3, Box 149
Flagstaff, AZ 86004
(602) 527-7042

Walnut Canyon
National Monument
Route 3, Box 149
Flagstaff, AZ 86004
(602) 526-3367

Wupatki National
Monument
Route 3, Box 149
Flagstaff, AZ 86004
(602) 527-7040

Flagstaff

The **San Francisco Peaks**, which stand up to 12,600 feet above sea level, make up the highest point in Arizona and should not be missed. If you're a hiker or a mountain biker, make sure you take a chair-lift ride to the top of the mountain. It's an attraction you won't want to miss, and even better, is just one of many that you'll find around the city of Flagstaff.

If your artistic palette is searching for something fresh and new, you can satisfy your appetite by attendng one of the many exquisite performances held at **Northern Arizona University.** Concerts, plays, and other interesting attractions are a part of the school's annual agenda.

Shoppers will find a good variety of stores to probe through and purchase interesting items.

Museum of Northern Arizona

If you want to know more about this part of the country, the **Museum of Northern Arizona** is a gold mine of information. Some of the topics of interest include an introduction to the native peoples and their history, an in-depth look at the region's geology, its past, current, and future history, and a fine display of Southwestern artifacts you'll only find in this part of the country.

3001 N. Fort Valley Rd.
Flagstaff, AZ 86001
(602) 774-5211

Fishing

Flagstaff and **Williams** offer serene, beautiful fishing locations in comfortable settings. Some of the more notable lakes are:

• Ashusrt
• Cataract
• J.D. Dam
• Kaibab
• Kinnikinick
• Long, Soldier, and Soldier Annex Lakes
• Morman Lake
• Upper & Lower Lake Mary

Peach Springs

This area is situated in the southwestern part of the northwest region of the state. It's home to the **Hualapai Indian Reservation**, a hidden paradise waiting for you to discover. Some call it "Hidden Hawaii" for its magnificent waterfalls, lush foliage, flowing orchards, and breathtaking trails!

The occupants require all visitors to make a reservation in a advance of a visit.

Grand Canyon Chamber of Commerce
P.O. Box 3007
Grand Canyon, AZ 86023
(602) 638-2901

NORTHEAST ARIZONA

Canyon De Chelly National Park

You'll find over 100 miles of canyons in this beautiful part of the state. Sand-stone walls stand a mere 25 feet from some of the canyons' heads but at times extend upwards to over 1,000 feet. Prehistoric sites are located throughout the region with splendid views of unique cliff dwellings.

You need to be in the company of an authorized guide to walk, horseback, or ride the canyons. Hollywood has spent millions of dollars making movies on location here for some of its most popular westerns. A guided tour is geared specifically for that interest.

P.O. Box 588
Chinle, AZ 86503
(602) 674-5436

Four Corners Monument

This monument is situated on a spot that intersects Arizona, Utah, Colorado, and New Mexico. You can find it off U.S. 160, east of Monument Valley.

Navajo National Monument

Arizona has a rich heritage that extends back to A.D. 1250. Three of the most prized ruins of the Anasazi culture are located in the state, but none compares to the majestic beauty that can be found at **Keet Seel**, the largest of the ruins and the one that has stood through time in the best condition. If you would like to visit Keet Seel, you'll need to make a reservation with one of the hiking or horseback tours that are available in the area.

The **Betatakin Ruin** is another great location to consider while you're in the area. It's not as far as Keet Seel and it offers spectacular sights for photographers and history buffs alike.

HC 71, Box 3
Tonalea, AZ 86044
(602) 672-2366

Petrified Forest National Park

This 100,000-acre park is an exhibition of wonderment and beauty This forest was once an ancient swampland. Through the process of mineralization, these towering trees transformed into beautiful objects of rocks and rare stones.

The **Painted Desert** is another interesting attraction that is a part of the park. It's a landscape that draws its name from the multicolored sediments that lay over the terrain. The colored hues that shine in the morning dew are unforgettable and make for a beautiful area to practice your photography skills.

P.O. Box 2217
Petrified Forest, AZ 86028
(602) 524-6228

Lake Powell

You'll find more shoreline along **Lake Powell** than in the entire state of California! It's a mecca for vacationers from far and wide to unwind and do the things that make going away fun and special. You can go fishing, scuba diving, water skiing, jet skiing, and more! Enjoy your favorite BBQ meals in one of the many picnic areas and then spend the rest of the day playing and relaxating.

ARA Leisure Services
P.O. Box 56909 (85079)
Phoenix, AZ 85016
(602) 468-6786

Meteor Crater's Museum of Astrogeology

Approximately 49,000 years have passed since this massive meteor hit our planet and left a bowl-like figure 100 feet in diameter, 570 feet deep, and close to a mile from one side to the other. NASA felt that the terrain was so much like the moon that they had their Apollo astronauts use it as a training site. The largest meteorite ever found is on display and is one of many attractions you'll find along the self-guided tour that the museum ofers.

P.O. Box 2217
Petrified Forest, AZ 86028
(602) 524-6228

CENTRAL AND EASTERN ARIZONA

Lyman Lake State Park

This incredible state park is a beautiful place to roam and relax. Its natural beauty attracts thousands of visitors each year.

(602) 337-4441
10 miles south of St. Johns
and east of U.S. 191

Apache/Sitgreaves National Forest

Walk through the **Coronado Trail** and you'll be sidestepping mature aspen, fir, spruce, and pine trees. At certain points, such as **Hannigan Meadow**, the altitude reaches heights over 9,000 feet, so if you're thinking about setting up camp, you'd best bring along some warm clothing for the many cold evenings you'll encounter

P.O. Box 640
Springerville, AZ 85938
(602) 333-4301

Tonto National Forest

You won't find a greater gathering of native ponderosa pine trees on our planet. Zane Grey, the well-known Western novelist, named this area the *Tonto Rim*. The area runs along two major forests that stretch between east and centralArizona.

P.O. Box 5348
Phoenix, AZ 85010
(602) 225-5200

Tonto Natural Bridge State Park

The world's largest travertine bridge is located here. Visit **Pine Creek Falls.**

P.O. Box 5348
Phoenix, AZ 85010
(602) 225-5200

CENTRAL ARIZONA

Sharlot Hall Museum

This museum has preserved some memorable artifacts from its rich pioneer history. You'll view the Bashford home that was first built in 1880, review historical archives, and gaze at the territorial governor's residence. If you happen to be in town during the month of June, you can participate in the annual**Territorial Days and Folk Art Fair.**

415 W. Gurley St.
Prescott, AZ 86301
(602) 445-3122

Prescott National Forest

The **Prescott National Forest** is a haven for people who love the outdoors and are always ready to explore a new piece of territory You can enjoy waking up in the early morning to watch the sun rise above the morning dew and have its rays refracted within the waters of a serene lake. The camp grounds and picnic areas are comfortably set and smartly thought-out. You can go hiking, biking, horseback riding, canoeing, fishing, and much more!

If you're an artist, you will surely find this area a source of inspiration for future work. If you recently bought your favorite author's latest release and you've been waiting for the perfect moment to crack open the cover, the Prescott National Forest is filled with places that will offer you the peace and quiet you've been searching for.

344 S. Cortez
Prescott, AZ 86303
(602) 445-1762

Phippen Museum of Western Art

If you've developed an eye for southwestern art, you may have heard of George Phippen, a Prescott native who is well known for his sculptures and paintings. Each year, he puts together a fabulous exhibition that covers the cultural mainstream of western art.

4701 Hwy. 89 North
Prescott, AZ 86301
(602)-778-1385

Arcosanti

Combining ecology and architecture into a meaningful structure, the **Arcosanti** prototype shelter brings together 5,000 people to examine their daily algorithms. It was architect Paolo Soleri's insight that first discovered this thought as a new way of life for people to live, and for scientists to study the relationships between human groups and their physical and social environments. Daily visits are welcomed, seminars, and workshops are offered, and many splendid musical performances are held throughout the year.

I-17 at Cordes Junction
Mayor, AZ 86333
(602) 632-7135

Montezuma Castle National Monument

Built inside an alcove, five-stories high, and connected to the face of a soaring rock structure, this unbelievable cliff dwelling will have you standing in wonderment from the first moment you view it!

An informative visitors center richly displays the culture and the people that occupied this part of the country hundreds of years ago. It's a fascinating story For example, between 1200-1300A.D., a well-crafted source of transportation was built to direct water to workers through a clever network of ditches. This "Montezuma Well" provided clean water through a colorful limestone sink.

P.O. Box 219
Camp Verde, AZ 86322
(602) 567-3322

Bradshaw Mountains

This part of the country offers a glimpse into a much publicized character that we've all grown accustomed to watching through the magical process of motion pictures ... the outlaw. Many *real* outlaws hid in these mountains from the law. It makes for an interesting piece of nostalgia.

(602) 267-7246

CENTRAL/CENTRAL-SOUTH ARIZONA

South Mountain Park

This gargantuan park covers 16,000 acres of natural desert terrain, making it the largest municipal park in the world. The park is filled with spectacular trails that will lead you to beautiful locations of wondering land structures. It's a landscape and nature photographer's dream world.

Get your family together, pack some sandwiches, and head to the park for a great picnic — and to think, it's all in close proximity to the city of Phoenix.

5245 S. Fifth St.
Phoenix, AZ 85040
(602) 268-0068

Papago Park

Papago Park is closely located to **South Mountain Park** and should serve as an enticing attraction for everyone in your family. Many people enjoy walking through the **Phoenix Zoo**, followed by a walk in the nearby **Botanical Gardens**. An 18-hole golf course is also featured for those of you who can't hold of much longer.

Either way, this is a very attractive location to unwind and enjoy life the way it's supposed to be enjoyed ... without compromise!

5245 S. Fifth St.
Phoenix, AZ 85040
(602) 268-0068

Superstition Mountains

This legendary location is filled with colorful descriptions of the **Lost Dutchman Mine**. You can walk the trails, go horseback riding, and even search for that infamous ... Lost Dutchman Mine. This park has become the nation's most sought-after wilderness location.

Phoenix City Parks & Recreation
2333 N. Central Ave.
Phoenix, AZ 85004
(602) 262-6861

Casa Grande Ruins National Monument

This interesting relic rises up to four stories above its desert foundation. The *Hohokam Indians*, a tribe of people who vanished into the pages of history, are believed responsible for the building of this structure centuries ago.

Archaeological evidence shows that this was once an important dwelling used for both an observatory and a lookout point.

1100 Ruins Dr.
Coolidge, AZ 85228
(602) 723-3172

Phoenix Art Museum

You'll be exposed to many talented artists both old and new in this fascinating museum, which features major traveling attractions from a list of other notable museums throughout the year. You'll be exposed to a grand collection of 19th-century and 20th-century art in the form of paintings, costumes, miniaturizations, and other interesting artifacts.

1625 N. Central Ave.
Coolidge, AZ 85004
(602) 257-1222

Heard Museum

This nationally recognized museum features magnificent native artwork by the area's most notable masters. If you happen to be in town during the month of March, call the museum to find out when they're going to be putting on their annual **Guild Indian Fair and Market**. If your house is decorated in a southwestern, country, or Indian motif, you'll find beautiful pieces you may want to buy for your home.

22 E. Monte Vista Rd.
Coolidge, AZ 85004
(602) 252-8848

Taliesin West

Frank Lloyd Wright was always a step ahead of his fellow architects. His work has long been admired for its simplicity, functionality and aesthetic appeal. Frank established **Taliesin West** as both a school and a studio. This newly established National Landmark has attracted a wide audience that flys in from all over the world to see this ingenious work of art.

(602) 860-2700

Gila River Indian Reservation

This reservation brings together 20 tribes in one location. You can enjoy the **Gila River Arts & Crafts Center** for its wide selection of authentic indian artifacts. If you would like to attend one of their annual shows, you'll need to call them for scheduled dates, but you do have the option of visiting their local museum and park. If you're hungry, the reservation has a restaurant that features NativeAmerican food.

Tempe Chamber of Commerce
60 E. Fifth St, #3
Tempe, AZ 85281
(602) 967-7891

Saguaro National Monument

This monument maintains Saguaro cacti, which are only indigenous to parts of Arizona and Mexico. You can hike along miles of unspoiled trails that run along the desert's vast landscape and mountaintops.

Tempe Chamber of Commerce
60 E. Fifth St, #3
Tempe, AZ 85281
(602) 967-7891

Biosphere 2

You can find this unique building about 37 miles north of Tucson. It's a three-acre enclosed structure that is being used as an experiment to see how we can improve our own biosphere outside this rarefied bubble.

P.O. Box 612
Mt. Lemmon, AZ 85619
(602) 576-1400

Colossal Cave

This "colossal cave" may possibly be the largest dry cavern in the world. It was used as a hiding place for outlaws during the Wild West days of the 1800's. It's also believed that Indians used this cavern as a unique hiding place too. The cave is so large that certain parts of it have still not been charted to this day

P.O. Box D-7
Vail, AZ 85641
(602) 647-7275

Arizona-Sonora Desert Museum

This fantastic museum is a great attraction for all age groups. It allows you to peek at a select group of desert animals and flora and view the way they live and grow in their natural environments. Some of the exhibits are built to allow you to view certain animals underground. It's a facinating way to study a world that we don't normally get to see.

2021 N. Kinney Rd.
Tucson, AZ 85743
(602) 883-1380

WEST/SOUTHWEST ARIZONA

Hoover Dam

At a height of 726 feet, this incredible concrete mass is the largest dam in the western hemisphere. The dam supplies more than 4 billion kilowatt-hours of electricity to California, Nevada, and Arizona. If you would like to learn more about its history and the engineering aspects that went into its creation, the dam ofers guided tours that talk about these subjects and more. When you cross the state line into Nevada, don't expect to gamble in Boulder City: it's the one town in Nevada where gambling is illegal!

Bureau of Reclamation
Lower Colorado Project Dam Office
P.O. Box 60400
Boulder City, NV 89006-0400
(702) 293-8367

Lake Mead National Recreation Area

Lake Mead extends out of the Colorado River and is the largest "man-made" lake in the country. It stretches 105 miles long with a shoreline covering 822 miles. You'll find people picnicking, camping, boating, water-skiing, sailing, and virtually everything that's possible in and around water. You'll also find plenty of commercial establishments that will rent you diferent types of watercraft.

602 Nevada Hwy.
Boulder City, NV 89005
(702) 293-8920

Havasu National Wildlife Refuge

This national wildlife refuge is home to some of the most spectacular birds and animals in the country. On a lucky day, you'll get to see stately bald eagles and majestic peregrine falcons flying high above the ground while waiting for the perfect moment to come charging down for their prey.

This area is yet another popular attraction for boaters and water sports enthusiasts. You'll also find a variety of camping enclaves that are accessible only by boat.

Lake Havasu State Park
Windsor Beach, (in Lake Havasu City, off SR. 95)
(602) 855-7851

SOUTHERN ARIZONA

Cabeza Prieta National Wildlife Refuge
You'll find an abundance of beautiful wildlife throughout this interesting refuge. It's a bird-watchers paradise and one of the few places in the country where you will see bighorn sheep in the wild.

Ajo District Chamber Of Commerce
321 Taladro, P.O. Box 507
Ajo, AZ 85321
(702) 387-7742

Organ Pipe Cactus National Monument
This scenic desert landscape features more than 500 square miles of rare organ pipe cactus. Some of these cacti can rise more than 20 feet tall! You can view the many beautiful arrays of desert flora that this national monument has to ofer from several looping roads.

Route 1, Box 100
Ajo, AZ 85321
(702) 387-6849

Kitt Peak National Observatory
This astronomical observatory features state-of-the-art equipment that features eighteen telescopes of various sizes and configurations, some of which you'll find startling in size. It is unquestionably one of the most important locations for the field of astronomy today. The observatory houses a beautiful visitors center and a great museum that will take you through all of the various equipment and some of the celestial discoveries that have been made with them.

P.O. Box 26732
Tucson, AZ 85726
(702) 322-3350

ARIZONA INDEX

LEGEND

Public = **P**
Semi-private = **SP**
Private = *Italics*
Municipal = **M**
Military = **Mil.**
9-hole = **9H**
Executive = **E**

La Paloma Country Club, 65
Legend Golf Club, The, 33 /P
Leisure World Country Club, 62
Los Caballeros Golf Club, 34 /SP

Maryvale Municipal Golf Course, 34 /M
Mesa Country Club, 62
Mesa View Golf Course, 66
McCormick Ranch Golf Club, 35 /P
Mesa Del Sol Golf & Tennis Club, 59 /P
Moon Valley Country Club, 62
Mt. Graham Golf Course, 24 /M

Hidden Cove Golf Course, 66 /9H

Oakcreek Country Club, The, 22 /SP
Ocotillo Golf Course, 35 /P
Orange Tree Golf Resort, 36 /P
Oro Valley Country Club, 65

Paco Diablo Resort, 61 / 9H
Palm Brook Country Club, 62
Palo Verde Golf Course, 64 /9H
Papago Municipal Golf Course, 36 /M
Pardise Valley Country Club, 63
Payson Golf Course, 24 /P
Pebble Brook Golf Course, 63
Pepperwood Public Golf Course, 64 /9H
Phoenician, The, 37 /SP
Phoenix Country Club, 63
Pima Country Club, 37 /P
Pinetop Country Club, 65
Pinetop Country Club, 65 /9H
Pinnacle Peak Country Club, 63
Pointe Golf Club, The, 38 /P
Pointe Golf Club On Lookout Mountain,
    The, 38 /SP
Presscott Country Club, 58 /SP
Pueblo Del Sol Golf Course, 21 /P
Pueblo El Mirage Country Club, 39 /P

Quail Creek Country Club, 65
Queens Bay Country Club, 64

Randolph Golf Course, 51 /P
Red Mountain Ranch Country Club, 39
    /SP
Rio Verde Country Club, 63
Rio Rico Golf Course, 56 /SP

Rio Salado Golf Course, 64 /9H
Riverview Golf Club, 64
Riverview Municipal Golf Course, 64 /9H
Roadhaven Golf Course, 64 /9H
Rolling Hills Country Club, 65
Royal Palms Golf Course, 64 /9H

Saddlebrook Country Club, 65
San Ignacio Golf Club, 52 /P
San Marcos Country Club, 40 /SP
Scottsdale Country Club, 40 /SP
Sedona Golf Resort, 23 /P
Shalimar Public Country Club, 64 /9H
Sheraton 9-Hole Golf Course, 66 /9H
Show Low Country Club, 47 /P
Silverbell Golf Course, 52 /P
Silver Creek Golf Club, 47 /SP
Skyline Country Club, 65
Snow Flake Municipal Golf, 48 /M
Stardust Golf Course, 63
Starr Pass Golf Club, 53 /SP
Stonecreek, The Golf Club, 41 /SP
Superstition Springs Golf Club, 41 /P
Sun City Country Club, 63
Sun City Vistoso, 53 /SP

Tatum Ranch Golf Club, 42 /P
Thunderbird Country Club, 42 /P
Tom Weiskopf's Foothills Golf, 43 /SP
Tournament Players Club, 43 /P
Troon Golf & Country Club, 63
Troon North Golf Club, 44 /SP
Tubac Golf Resort, 57 /SP
Tucson Country Club, 65
Tucson Estates Vagabond, 65
Tucson National Golf & Conference
    Resort, 54 /SP
Turquoise Valley Golf & RV Park, 61 /9H

Union Hills Country Club, 63

Valle Vista Country Club, 46 /SP
Valley Club, 64 /9H
Ventana Canyon Golf Club, 65
View Point Golf Resort, 64 /9H
Village Of Oakcreek Club, 23 /SP
Villa De Paz Golf Course, 44 /P
Villa Monterey Golf Club, 64 /9H

Valle Vista Country Club, 46 /SP
Valley Club, 64 /9H
Ventana Canyon Golf Club, 65
View Point Golf Resort, 64 /9H
Village Of Oakcreek Club, 23 /SP
Villa De Paz Golf Course, 44 /P
Villa Monterey Golf Club, 64 /9H

Westbrook Village Country Club, 45 /SP
White Mountain Country Club, 65
Wickenburg Country Club, 63
Wigwam, The, 45 /SP
Willowbrook Golf Course, 66

Yuma Golf & Country Club, 66

NEVADA
THE SILVER STATE

NEVADA/COUNTIES AND CITIES

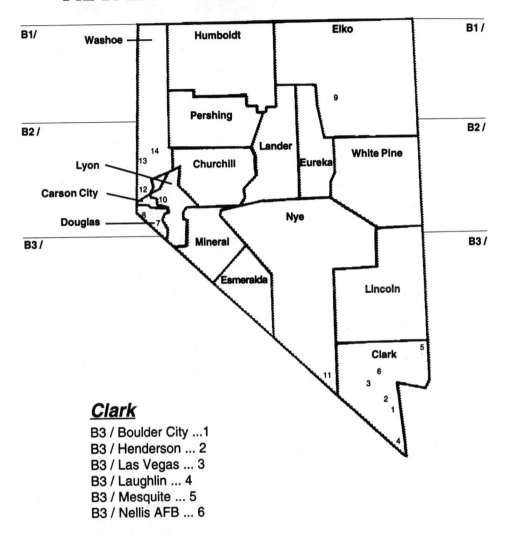

Clark

B3 / Boulder City ...1
B3 / Henderson ... 2
B3 / Las Vegas ... 3
B3 / Laughlin ... 4
B3 / Mesquite ... 5
B3 / Nellis AFB ... 6

Douglas

B2 / Gardnerville ... 7
B2 / Stateline ... 8

Elko

B1 / Elko ... 9

Lyon

B2 / Dayton ... 10

Nye

B3 / Panrump ... 11

Washoe

B2 / Incline Village ... 12
B2 / Reno ... 13
B2 / Sparks ... 14

CLARK COUNTY

ANGEL PARK GOLF CLUB

100 South Ramport, Las Vegas, NV 89128 / (702) 254-4653

BASIC INFORMATION

Course Type: Public
Year Built: 1989
Architect: Arnold Palmer
Local Pro: Craig Smith

Course: Mountain Course (18 / Par 71)
Holes: 36

Back : 6,722 yds. Rating: 72.4 Slope: 128
Middle: 6,235 yds. Rating: 70.3 Slope: 117
Ladies: 5,164 yds. Rating: 69.9 Slope: 119

Tee Time: 30 days in advance.
Price: $50 - $78

Credit Cards:	■	Restaurant:	■
Driving Range:	■	Lounge:	■
Practice Green:	■	Meeting Rooms:	■
Locker Room:	■	Tennis:	
Rental Clubs:	■	Swimming:	
Walkers:		Jogging Trails:	
Snack Bar:	■	Boating:	

COURSE DESCRIPTION

Leave it to the "King" to design the most sought after golf course in the area. It was voted #1 by local readers of the **Review Journal**, a well respected local newspaper.

As tough as the course may be for some, it does offer you a generous amount of room to work the ball from the tees. The fairways are subtly contoured and are tastefully accentuated with mounds running along their sides. The front-nine favors a draw while the back-nine favors a fade, yet they both offer equally challenging hole designs.

You'll find another splendid championship course and an 18-hole putting course to choose from as well.

DIRECTIONS

Take Hwy. 15 north to Hwy. 95 and proceed north to the Summerlin Pkwy. Follow the signs to the course.

BLACK MOUNTAIN GOLF & COUNTRY CLUB

500 East Greenway Rd., Henderson, NV 89015 / (702) 565-7933

BASIC INFORMATION

Course Type: Semi-private
Year Built: 1956
Architect: Bob Baldock
Local Pro: Mark A. Yelenich

Course: N/A
Holes: 18 / Par 72

Back: 6,541 yds. Rating: 71.2 Slope: 123
Middle: 6,223 yds. Rating: 69.8 Slope: 120
Ladies: 5,478 yds. Rating: 71.6 Slope: 125

Tee Time: 7 days in advance.
Price: $25 - $40

Credit Cards:	■	Restaurant:	
Driving Range:	■	Lounge:	
Practice Green:	■	Meeting Rooms:	
Locker Room:		Tennis:	
Rental Clubs:	■	Swimming:	
Walkers:	■	Jogging Trails:	
Snack Bar:	■	Boating:	

COURSE DESCRIPTION

This course has a gentle way of creeping up on a player with many different surprises. At first sight, the fairways seem to be level and straightforward, but the reality is that the course is made up of gently rolling terrain, comprised with undulations that will often place your ball on a difficult lie, making it hard to hit your following shot with enough clubhead-speed for distance and accuracy.

The fairways are lined with numerous sand-traps and hazards that lead to severely undulating greens.

Winds are often a factor during the winter and early spring.

DIRECTIONS

Go southeast on U.S. 93-95 "Boulder Hwy." to Greenway Rd. in Henderson. Turn right and go straight for about a mile to the course.

BOULDER CITY GOLF COURSE

#1 Clubhouse Dr., Boulder City, NV 89005 / (702) 293-9236

BASIC INFORMATION

Course Type: Municipal
Year Built: 1972
Architect: Gary Casper
Local Pro: Gale Parcell

Course: N/A
Holes: 18 / Par 72

Back: 6,561 yds. Rating: 70.2 Slope: 110
Middle: 6,132 yds. Rating: 68.3 Slope: 106
Ladies: 5,566 yds. Rating: 70.7 Slope: 113

Tee Time: 7 days in advance.
Price: $23 - $31

Credit Cards:		Restaurant:	
Driving Range:	■	Lounge:	■
Practice Green:	■	Meeting Rooms:	■
Locker Room:		Tennis:	
Rental Clubs:	■	Swimming:	
Walkers:		Jogging Trails:	
Snack Bar:	■	Boating:	

COURSE DESCRIPTION

If you haven't had a chance to play golf in a while, you may want to consider using this course as a platform to work on your game.

The majority of the holes play straight from tee-to-green and feature wide fairways that will allow you to grab your driver out of the bag as often as you wish.

The flexibility of the course makes it an admirable attraction for local players. If you like playing golf aggressively, the course is certainly set up for that sort of play, but if you don't have the ability to hit the ball long, a smartly-planned strategic approach will still allow you many opportunities for par or better.

DIRECTIONS

Take Hwy. 93 south towards Phoenix and make a right on Buchanan Blvd. The course will be 1 mile on your right.

CRAIG RANCH GOLF COURSE

628 West Craig Rd., N. Las Vegas, NV 89030 / (702) 642-9700

BASIC INFORMATION

Course Type: Public
Year Built: 1962
Architect: N/A
Local Pro: Sam Camerano

Course: N/A
Holes: 18 / Par 72

Back: 6,001 yds. Rating: 66.8 Slope: 105
Middle: 5,432 yds. Rating: 64.6 Slope: N/A
Ladies: 5,221 yds. Rating: 67.4 Slope: N/A

Tee Time: 7 days in advance.
Price: $12

Credit Cards:		Restaurant:	
Driving Range:	■	Lounge:	
Practice Green:	■	Meeting Rooms:	
Locker Room:		Tennis:	
Rental Clubs:	■	Swimming:	
Walkers:	■	Jogging Trails:	
Snack Bar:	■	Boating:	

COURSE DESCRIPTION

A good "short-game" – the ability to play well from a distance of 100 yards from the hole – is the single most important aspect of the game. That is what distinguishes a single handicapper from all the rest.

The *Craig Ranch Golf Course* is designed with over 7,000 trees spread over a distance of only 6,001 yards from the back-tees. You'll have to navigate your ball between tight fairways, desert rough, and twelve parallel fairways. The combination of these elements makes this the perfect place to fine-tune your short-game at the beginning of the season. Accuracy is a must!

DIRECTIONS

Three miles west of I-15 in N. Las Vegas. Five miles east of Hwy. 91 on Craig Rd. exit.

CLARK COUNTY

DESERT INN HOTEL & COUNTRY CLUB
3145 Las Vegas Blvd. S., Las Vegas, NV 89109 / (702) 733-4288

BASIC INFORMATION

Course Type: Semi-private
Year Built: 1952
Architect: Lawrence Huges
Local Pro: Dave Johnson

Course: N/A
Holes: 18 / Par 72

Back: 7,074 yds. Rating: 74.4 Slope: 134
Middle: 6,581 yds. Rating: 72.0 Slope: 129
Ladies: 5,809 yds. Rating: 72.7 Slope: 115

Tee Time: 365 days in advance.
Price: $50 - $150

Credit Cards:	■	Restaurant:	■
Driving Range:	■	Lounge:	■
Practice Green:	■	Meeting Rooms:	■
Locker Room:	■	Tennis:	■
Rental Clubs:	■	Swimming:	■
Walkers:		Jogging Trails:	■
Snack Bar:	■	Boating:	

COURSE DESCRIPTION

This course is consistently rated one of the top 75 resort attractions in the country by **Golf Digest** magazine. It's one of three host courses for the Las Vegas Senior Classic (Senior PGA Tour) and the Desert Inn International (LPGA Tour).

Strategically set bunkers, mounds, and water hazards combine inventively between mature elm and pine trees. You'll find a good combination of doglegs mixed with straight holes that evenly support both a draw or a fade. A good round consists of hitting the ball well off the tee.

The closing four holes on the front side post the greatest combined challenge and should be played cautiously.

DIRECTIONS
Located in the heart of the Las Vegas Strip.

DESERT ROSE GOLF COURSE
5483 Clubhouse Dr., Las Vegas, NV 89122 / (702) 431-4653

BASIC INFORMATION

Course Type: Public
Year Built: 1962
Architect: N/A
Local Pro: Rusty Postlewait

Course: N/A
Holes: 18 / Par 71

Back : 6,511 yds. Rating: 70.5 Slope: 112
Middle: 6,135 yds. Rating: 68.7 Slope: 108
Ladies: 5,458 yds. Rating: 69.6 Slope: 115

Tee Time: 3-7 days in advance.
Price: $15 - $39

Credit Cards:	■	Restaurant:	■
Driving Range:	■	Lounge:	■
Practice Green:	■	Meeting Rooms:	
Locker Room:		Tennis:	
Rental Clubs:	■	Swimming:	
Walkers:	■	Jogging Trails:	
Snack Bar:	■	Boating:	

COURSE DESCRIPTION

Traditionally designed, this links-styled course is moderately challenging for average players.

The fairways are tightly constructed and demand a large measure of accuracy off the tees, but you needn't worry about having to hit the ball a far distance, because the course is only 6,511 yards – a comfortable distance for many types of players.

Some of the par-5's are reachable in two, making them an integral and exciting part of the game.

DIRECTIONS
Take I-95 south to the Charleston Ave. Make a left at the first light and a right on Nellis Blvd. At the intersection of Nellis and Sahara, make a left followed by a right onto Winterwood. The course will be three blocks straight to the clubhouse.

EMERALD RIVER GOLF COURSE

1155 Casino Dr., Laughlin, NV 89029 / (702) 298-0061

BASIC INFORMATION

Course Type: Public
Year Built: 1990
Architect: Tom Clark
Local Pro: None

Course: N/A
Holes: 18 / Par 72

Back: 6,809 yds. Rating: 73.6 Slope: 144
Middle: 6,296 yds. Rating: 70.7 Slope: 136
Ladies: 5,205 yds. Rating: 71.3 Slope: 129

Tee Time: 7 days in advance.
Price: $21 - $40

Credit Cards:	■	Restaurant:	
Driving Range:	■	Lounge:	
Practice Green:	■	Meeting Rooms:	
Locker Room:		Tennis:	
Rental Clubs:	■	Swimming:	
Walkers:		Jogging Trails:	
Snack Bar:		Boating:	

COURSE DESCRIPTION

If your handicap is above a single digit, play from one of the two middle tees instead (the second is rated at 69.1 with a slope of 131), for this is the hardest rated course in Nevada, and the 8th toughest in the Southwest region of the country.

The fairways have many difficult elements that come into play both off the tee and on your approach shots. Many of them slope from one side to the other and feature sandtraps, waste areas, and hills. Level lies are few and far apart.

Give up distance for accuracy; if you miss the fairway, your ball will often trickle onto the desert.

DIRECTIONS

Take Casino Dr. straight to the course. It's the only course in the city of Laughlin.

LAS VEGAS GOLF CLUB

4349 Vegas Dr., Las Vegas, NV 89108 / (702) 646-3003

BASIC INFORMATION

Course Type: Municipal
Year Built: 1950's
Architect: N/A
Local Pro: Tom Carlson

Course: N/A
Holes: 18 / Par 72

Back : 6,631 yds. Rating: 71.8 Slope: 117
Middle: 6,337 yds. Rating: 70.3 Slope: 114
Ladies: 5,715 yds. Rating: 71.2 Slope: 113

Tee Time: 7 days in advance.
Price: $20 - $37

Credit Cards:	■	Restaurant:	■
Driving Range:	■	Lounge:	■
Practice Green:	■	Meeting Rooms:	■
Locker Room:		Tennis:	
Rental Clubs:	■	Swimming:	
Walkers:	■	Jogging Trails:	
Snack Bar:	■	Boating:	

COURSE DESCRIPTION

The *Las Vegas Golf Club* is the only Municipal course in Las Vegas.

It's a traditional layout with a well balanced set of holes that will appeal to many different types of golfers. Generally speaking, the course is not terribly difficult for better players, but the average player will undoubtedly find it complementary in style, and ultimately be happy to have played it. Perhaps that explains why this is one of the busiest courses in Las Vegas.

You'll find a nice mixture of trees on the front-nine and more of an open field on the back-nine.

DIRECTIONS

Take Hwy. 95 north to Decatur Rd. and further north to Washington St. Make a right, heading east, and look for the course on your right.

LEGACY GOLF CLUB

130 Par Excellence Dr., Henderson, NV 89014 / (702) 897-2187

BASIC INFORMATION

Course Type: Public
Year Built: 1989
Architect: Arthur Hills
Local Pro: Dave Barnhart

Course: N/A
Holes: 18 / Par 72

Back: 7,233 yds. Rating: 74.9 Slope: 136
Middle: 6,744 yds. Rating: 72.1 Slope: 128
Ladies: 6,211 yds. Rating: 71.0 Slope: 120

Tee Time: 30 day in advance.
Price: $40 - $90

Credit Cards: ■   Restaurant: ■
Driving Range: ■   Lounge: ■
Practice Green: ■   Meeting Rooms:
Locker Room: ■   Tennis:
Rental Clubs: ■   Swimming:
Walkers: Jogging Trails:
Snack Bar: ■   Boating:

COURSE DESCRIPTION

The *Legacy* is a Scottish links style design that has hosted the local U.S. Open Qualifying during the last four years, the Southern Nevada Amateur Championship between two of those years, and the Nevada Match Play Championship in 1993.

Like all traditional courses of this kind, the open architecture lends itself to the forces of the wind, which can often make a dramatic change to the overall length of the course. During a windy day, you'll need to play your ball on a lower trajectory to keep it on line.

DIRECTIONS

Go south on Hwy. 95 to the Lake Mead exit. Make a right at the stop light, and another right 5 miles further down on Green Valley Pkwy. Drive 2 miles until you come to a four-way-intersection. Make a right and look for the course on your left.

LOS PRADOS COUNTRY CLUB

5150 Los Prados Circle, Las Vegas, NV 89130 / (702) 645-5696

BASIC INFORMATION

Course Type: Semi-public
Year Built: 1987
Architect: N/A
Local Pro: Keith Flatt

Course: N/A
Holes: 18 / par 70

Back : 5,358 yds. Rating: 65.0 Slope: 107
Middle: 4,937 yds. Rating: 62.0 Slope: 101
Ladies: 4,474 yds. Rating: 64.4 Slope: 104

Tee Time: 3 days in advance.
Price: $20 - $35

Credit Cards: ■   Restaurant: ■
Driving Range: Lounge: ■
Practice Green: ■   Meeting Rooms: ■
Locker Room: ■   Tennis:
Rental Clubs: ■   Swimming:
Walkers: ■   Jogging Trails:
Snack Bar: ■   Boating:

COURSE DESCRIPTION

If you're short on distance or new to the game, you may want to consider playing the *Los Prados Country Club* course.

The layout was built around a housing development that features narrow fairways snaking along a path among the area's neighborhood. Thus, the fairways are narrow, and the greens are small ... a perfect combination for accuracy.

Obviously, if you're an above average player, you won't get much use out of this course, unless you choose to limit your playing partner and yourself to a game that would only allow you ... say, three clubs.

DIRECTIONS

Take I-15 north to I-9395 north until you get to Loan Mountain Rd. Make a right and proceed for about a 1/2 mile to the course. It will be on your right.

CLARK COUNTY

PAINTED DESERT GOLF COURSE
5555 Painted Mirage Way, Las Vegas, NV 89129 / (702) 645-2880

BASIC INFORMATION

Course Type: Public
Year Built: 1987
Architect: Jay Morrish
Local Pro: Bruce Applin

Course: N/A
Holes: 18 / Par 72

Back : 6,840 yds. Rating: 73.7 Slope: 136
Middle: 6,623 yds. Rating: 71.0 Slope: 128
Ladies: 5,711 yds. Rating: 72.7 Slope: 120

Tee Time: 7 days in advance.
Price: $48 - $85

Credit Cards:	■	Restaurant:	
Driving Range:	■	Lounge:	■
Practice Green:	■	Meeting Rooms:	
Locker Room:		Tennis:	
Rental Clubs:	■	Swimming:	
Walkers:	■	Jogging Trails:	
Snack Bar:	■	Boating:	

COURSE DESCRIPTION

Since 1987, when this course was first completed, people have been praising this target design for its avant garde principles. Today, these signature courses have become retreats for golfers to enjoy from all parts of the globe.

The back-tees are set up exclusively for single-digit handicappers. You have to have a good solid array of shots to play well here. If you're a double-digit handicapper, play the course from the middle-tees, for they will offer you the most amount of fun in combination with a thoughtful challenge.

DIRECTIONS

Take Hwy. 95 north to Ann Rd. and make a left. Look for the course down the first driveway on your left.

PEPPERMILL PALMS GOLF COURSE & RESORT
1137 Mesquite Blvd., Mesquite, NV 89024 / (800) 621-0187

BASIC INFORMATION

Course Type: Public
Year Built: 1989
Architect: William S. Hull
Local Pro: Dan Sommers

Course: N/A
Holes: 18 / Par 72

Back: 7,022 yds. Rating: 74.9 Slope: 137
Middle: 6,284 yds. Rating: 71.7 Slope: 130
Ladies: 5,162 yds. Rating: 72.0 Slope: 120

Tee Time: 7 - 28 days in advance.
Price: $30 - $65

Credit Cards:	■	Restaurant:	■
Driving Range:	■	Lounge:	■
Practice Green:	■	Meeting Rooms:	■
Locker Room:	■	Tennis:	■
Rental Clubs:	■	Swimming:	■
Walkers:		Jogging Trails:	
Snack Bar:	■	Boating:	■

COURSE DESCRIPTION

You're going to feel as though you've played two entirely different courses by the time you sink your last putt on the 18th green.

The flat terrain of the front-nine features fairways that wind around 27 acres of water and palm trees. If your handicap is above a single digit, play the course from the middle tees. The back nine is set on a hilly terrain that features many elevated tee shots. One of the most exciting moments for most golfers is directly attributed to the tee shot from the 15th hole. It features an elevation change of 115 ft. to the fairway below. The entire course is over-seeded in September.

DIRECTIONS

Go north on I-15 from Las Vegas (77 miles) to Exit 122. Turn right and make your first left onto Hillside Dr. Follow the road to the course. It will be on your right.

CLARK COUNTY

ROYAL KENFIELD COUNTRY CLUB

1 Showboat Circle Dr., Henderson, NV 89014 / (702) 434-9000

BASIC INFORMATION

Course Type: Public
Year Built: 1958 / 1991
Architect: Hubert Green & Robert Cupp ('91)
Local Pro: Carroll Peterson

Course: N/A
Holes: 18 / Par 72

Back : 7,053 yds. Rating: 75.2 Slope: 135
Middle: 6,513 yds. Rating: 72.2 Slope: 129
Ladies: 5,372 yds. Rating: 71.3 Slope: 125

Tee Time: 7-30 days in advance.
Price: $25 - $75

Credit Cards:	■	Restaurant:	■
Driving Range:	■	Lounge:	■
Practice Green:	■	Meeting Rooms:	■
Locker Room:	■	Tennis:	■
Rental Clubs:	■	Swimming:	■
Walkers:		Jogging Trails:	
Snack Bar:	■	Boating:	

COURSE DESCRIPTION

The Royal Kenfield Country Club is the hardest course in Nevada, yet it does offer great golf for nonprofessionals who want to play it for fun, rather than have the layout take control of them from tee-to-green.

You can't say enough about this course. It's truly one of the finest in the area. It's a traditional design made for better players that can work a ball in many different directions while hitting it long at the same time. Strict course management is mandatory for a good score.

DIRECTORY

Take I-15 north to Lake Mead Blvd. Make a left at Green Valley Pkwy. and look for the course on your right.

SAHARA COUNTRY CLUB

1911 E. Desert Inn Rd., Las Vegas, NV 89109 / (702) 796-0013

BASIC INFORMATION

Course Type: Public
Year Built: 1961
Architect: Bert Stamps
Local Pro: Bruce McNee

Course: N/A
Holes: 18 / Par 72

Back : 6,815 yds. Rating: 73.2 Slope: 123
Middle: 6,418 yds. Rating: 71.1 Slope: 119
Ladies: 5,741 yds. Rating: 70.7 Slope: 114

Tee Time: 21 days in advance.
Price: $50 - $85

Credit Cards:	■	Restaurant:	■
Driving Range:	■	Lounge:	■
Practice Green:	■	Meeting Rooms:	■
Locker Room:	■	Tennis:	
Rental Clubs:	■	Swimming:	
Walkers:		Jogging Trails:	
Snack Bar:	■	Boating:	

COURSE DESCRIPTION

The *Sahara Country Club* is a thinking man's golf course with many clever holes.

Distance and accuracy need to be coupled with proper course management to score well. The fairways are moderately wide and feature a healthy abundance of trees and strategically placed traps that often come into play.

This is only one of five courses in the U.S. that has a Rangemaster Computerized Distance Caddie on all of their carts. Like the saying goes, "You have to see it, to believe it!"

DIRECTIONS

From the Las Vegas Strip, go east on Desert Inn Rd. for about ten minutes. The course will be on your right side.

CLARK / DOUGLAS COUNTIES

SUN CITY SUMMERLIN GOLF COURSE
9201 Del Web Blvd., Las Vegas, NV 89134 / (702) 363-4373

BASIC INFORMATION

Course Type: Semi-private
Year Built: 1989
Architect: Nash Accociates / Billy Casper
Local Pro: John Spatz

Course: N/A
Holes: 18 / Par 27

Back : 6,840 yds. Rating: 72.3 Slope: 127
Middle: 6,340 yds. Rating: 69.8 Slope: 124
Ladies: 5,500 yds. Rating: 71.5 Slope: 124

Tee Time: 7 days in advance.
Price: $35 - $85

Credit Cards:	■	Restaurant:	■
Driving Range:	■	Lounge:	
Practice Green:	■	Meeting Rooms:	
Locker Room:		Tennis:	
Rental Clubs:	■	Swimming:	
Walkers:		Jogging Trails:	
Snack Bar:	■	Boating:	

COURSE DESCRIPTION

You'll find a nice unification of hole designs throughout the layout of the *Sun City Summerlin Course*.

Everyone should easily find their particular brand of golf from one of their three tees. From the back, you'll need to be long and accurate to make par or better. The middle-tees are a shotmakers' paradise as the course forsakes distance for accuracy, yet every shot needs to be played just right for a clear approach shot to the green. The same can be said from the ladies tees.

If you're in the area, take the time to play this course; you won't be disappointed.

DIRECTIONS

Take U.S. 95 north to Lake Head Blvd. Go west to Del Webb Blvd. and look for the course on your right.

CARSON VALLEY GOLF COURSE
1027 Riverview Dr., Gardnerville, NV 89410 / (702) 265-3181

BASIC INFORMATION

Course Type: Public
Year Built: 1965
Architect: Red Swift
Local Pro: Janelle Freeman

Course: N/A
Holes: 18 / Par 71

Back: 5,759 yds. Rating: 67.0 Slope: N/A
Middle: N/A   Rating: N/A Slope: N/A
Ladies: 5,283 yds. Rating: 69.0 Slope: N/A

Tee Time: 7 days in advance.
Price: $18

Credit Cards:		Restaurant:	■
Driving Range:	■	Lounge:	■
Practice Green:	■	Meeting Rooms:	
Locker Room:		Tennis:	
Rental Clubs:	■	Swimming:	
Walkers:	■	Jogging Trails:	
Snack Bar:		Boating:	

COURSE DESCRIPTION

Although this course plays short, it still presents a formidable challenge with many interesting holes. You'll have to hit your drives accurately to land your ball safely on the tight fairways and away from the many mature cottonwood trees that can deflect and interfere with the direction of your ball's flight.

The 15th hole, a par-5, stretches 425 yds., and is the hardest rated hole on the course. You'll need to hit both your drive and your approach shots accurately between the Carson river, which hugs the right side, and an irrigation canal that runs along the full length of the left side and down to the front of the green.

DIRECTIONS

Take Hwy. 395 south of Gardnerville and turn right on Riverview Dr.

EDGEWOOD TAHOE GOLF COURSE

P.O. Box 5400, Stateline, NV 89449 / (702) 588-3566

BASIC INFORMATION

Course Type: Public
Year Built: N/A
Architect: N/A
Local Pro: Lou Eiguren

Course: N/A
Holes: 18 / Par 72

Back: 7,491 yds. Rating: 76.0 Slope: 139
Middle: 6,544 yds. Rating: 70.8 Slope: 128
Ladies: 5,749 yds. Rating: 71.2 Slope: 130

Tee Time: 14 days in advance.
Price: $125

Credit Cards:	■	Restaurant:	■
Driving Range:	■	Lounge:	■
Practice Green:	■	Meeting Rooms:	■
Locker Room:	■	Tennis:	
Rental Clubs:	■	Swimming:	
Walkers:	■	Jogging Trails:	
Snack Bar:	■	Boating:	■

COURSE DESCRIPTION

The *Edgewood Tahoe Golf Course* is home to the Isuzu Celebrity Golf Championship and has hosted the 1985 U.S. Senior Open.

You'll find the terrain flat with sudden undulations and few surprises. The appearance of wide fairways hides the fact that this is a very serious course with highly demanding qualities. Every shot needs to be played to a strategic point that will set you up for your following shot. If you ever played a game of pool, you'll know exactly what I mean.

Stunning views of Lake Tahoe come into view on the last three finishing holes.

DIRECTIONS

Take Hwy. 50 north to Lake Parkway and make a left at the light (heading west). The Edgewood gate will be on your right.

RUBY VIEW GOLF COURSE

2100 Ruby View Dr., Elko, NV 89801 / (702) 738-6212

BASIC INFORMATION

Course Type: Public
Year Built: 1968
Architect: Jack Snyder
Local Pro: Rick Longhurst

Course: N/A
Holes: 18 / Par 72

Back : 6,928 yds. Rating: N/A   Slope: N/A
Middle: 6,718 yds. Rating: 70.5 Slope: 118
Ladies: 5,958 yds. Rating: 72.5 Slope: 123

Tee Time: 7 days in advance.
Price: $18 - $26

Credit Cards:	■	Restaurant:	■
Driving Range:	■	Lounge:	■
Practice Green:	■	Meeting Rooms:	
Locker Room:		Tennis:	
Rental Clubs:	■	Swimming:	
Walkers:	■	Jogging Trails:	
Snack Bar:	■	Boating:	

COURSE DESCRIPTION

The Ruby Mountains are absolutely astonishing to look at, and to have a tremendously thoughtful golf course to play at the same time makes this golfing experience an even more splendid occasion.

Oddly enough, for a description such as the one above, you'll find that the course plays rather flat. It's a wonderful layout that features two great stretches of nine holes, with the front playing a little more difficult than the back. The shapes of the holes will call you to play your best draw more often than a fade. The greens are big with subtle undulations.

DIRECTIONS

Take I-80 west to Elko and merge onto Exit 5 or Idaho St. Make a right at Convention Way, and look for the course on your right.

DAYTON VALLEY COUNTRY CLUB
51 Palmer Dr., Dayton, NV 89403 / (702) 246-7888

BASIC INFORMATION

Course Type: Semi-private
Year Built: 1990
Architect: Arnold Palmer
Local Pro: Tom Duncan

Course: N/A
Holes: 18 / Par 72

Back : 7,218 yds. Rating: 72.9 Slope: 136
Middle: 6,637 yds. Rating: 70.1 Slope: 130
Ladies: 5,897 yds. Rating: 67.2 Slope: 124

Tee Time: 14 days in advance.
Price: $25 - $55

Credit Cards:	■	Restaurant:	■
Driving Range:	■	Lounge:	■
Practice Green:	■	Meeting Rooms:	
Locker Room:	■	Tennis:	
Rental Clubs:	■	Swimming:	
Walkers:		Jogging Trails:	
Snack Bar:	■	Boating:	■

COURSE DESCRIPTION

Dayton Valley Country Club is undoubtedly one of the finest in all of Nevada.

Arnold Palmer did a wonderful job in designing a course that is suitable for both professionals and amateurs alike.

It's already hosted a State Open and a U.S. Amateur Qualifier. At only three years of age, that's both an accomplishment to the staff and an even greater complement to the course.

Having the ability to work the ball in both directions helps a great deal towards scoring low numbers. The layout plays consistently on both nines and should feel relatively the same throughout.

DIRECTIONS

Take Hwy. 50 east from Carson City to Dayton and make a right on Palmer Road. The course straight ahead.

CALVADA COUNTRY CLUB
P.O. Box 220, Panrump, NV 89041 / (702) 727-4653

BASIC INFORMATION

Course Type: Semi-private
Year Built: 1978
Architect: William Bell
Local Pro: Tom Storey / Dir. : Bill Cummings

Course: Calvada Valley (18 / Par 72)
Holes: 36

Back : 7,025 yds. Rating: 73.2 Slope: 124
Middle: 6,538 yds. Rating: 70.9 Slope: 117
Ladies: 5,948 yds. Rating: 74.3 Slope: 123

Tee Time: 3 days in advance.
Price: $30 - $33

Credit Cards:	■	Restaurant:	
Driving Range:	■	Lounge:	■
Practice Green:	■	Meeting Rooms:	
Locker Room:	■	Tennis:	
Rental Clubs:	■	Swimming:	
Walkers:		Jogging Trails:	
Snack Bar:	■	Boating:	

COURSE DESCRIPTION

This lushly landscaped course sits like an oasis in the far reaches of the desert. Although it plays quite long from the back-tees, it's not as treacherous as the total yardage indicated on the scorecard. Anyway, you always have the option of playing from the middle-tees, which reduces the length of the course by 487 yards.

The front-nine is set up flatter and wider along the fairways, and is the easier half of the course. Filled with undulations and contours, the back-nine shifts the action of play onto a nice rolling terrain.

DIRECTIONS

Take Hwy. 160 and turn left at the waterfall entrance on Calvada Blvd. Go 2-miles and turn right on Mt. Charleston. Look for the course on your left.

WASHOE COUNTY

INCLINE VILLAGE GOLF RESORT
955 Fairway Blvd., Incline Village, NV 89452 / (702) 832-1162

BASIC INFORMATION

Course Type: Public
Year Built: 1964
Architect: Robert Trent Jones Sr.
Local Pro: John Hughes

Course: Championship (18 / Par 72)
Holes: 36

Back : 6,915 yds. Rating: 72.6 Slope: 129
Middle: 6,446 yds. Rating: 70.5 Slope: 124
Ladies: 5,350 yds. Rating: 70.3 Slope: 126

Tee Time: Any day in advance.
Price: $85 / incudes green fees and cart.

Credit Cards:	■	Restaurant:	■
Driving Range:	■	Lounge:	■
Practice Green:	■	Meeting Rooms:	■
Locker Room:	■	Tennis:	■
Rental Clubs:	■	Swimming:	
Walkers:	■	Jogging Trails:	
Snack Bar:	■	Boating:	■

COURSE DESCRIPTION

The *Incline Village* Championship course was designed by Robert Trent Jones, Sr. who once described the course as "... an example of the ideal mountain golf course."

Carved out of the ponderosa pines in the mountains around Lake Tahoe, each shot presents a challenge framed by towering trees, majestic mountain backgrounds and many other fabulous views. Although the course measures 6,910 yds., your ball should travel farther at the course elevation of 6,500 feet.

You'll need to pull-off some fancy shots to play a low scoring round.

DIRECTIONS

From Reno, take Hwy. 395 to Hwy. 431 and make a right. Make a left on Country Club Dr. and a right at Fairway Blvd. Look for the course on your left.

LAKE RIDGE GOLF COURSE
1200 Razorback Rd., Reno, NV 89509 / (702) 825-2200

BASIC INFORMATION

Course Type: Public
Year Built: 1969
Architect: Robert Trent Jones, Jr. & Sr.
Local Pro: Paul Lane

Course: N/A
Holes: 18 / Par 72

Back : 6,703 yds. Rating: 70.8 Slope: 127
Middle: 6,140 yds. Rating: 68.3 Slope: 123
Ladies: 5,159 yds. Rating: 64.0 Slope: 114

Tee Time: 7 days in advance.
Price: $36 - $60

Credit Cards:	■	Restaurant:	■
Driving Range:	■	Lounge:	■
Practice Green:	■	Meeting Rooms:	
Locker Room:	■	Tennis:	
Rental Clubs:	■	Swimming:	
Walkers:	■	Jogging Trails:	
Snack Bar:	■	Boating:	

COURSE DESCRIPTION

This is one of the most beautiful golf courses in Reno. Robert Trent Jones, Jr. and Sr. have done a wonderful job in making this layout blend perfectly with its surroundings and at the same time offering a remarkable challenge for both the professional and novice golfer alike.

The signature 15th hole is the most outstanding design on the course. It's an island green par-3, measuring 226 yds., with a vertical drop of 120 feet. From the tee, you're looking down at the magnificent putting green that sits on a beautiful lake featuring gorgeous estate homes along its borders, and a picturesque view of the mountains in the horizon.

DIRECTIONS

Take I-80 east to Virginia St, south to McCarran St., and right to Plumas. Look for the course on Razorback Rd. on your right.

WASHOE COUNTY

NORTHGATE GOLF CLUB
1111 Clubhouse Dr., Las Vegas, NV 89523 / (702) 747-7577

BASIC INFORMATION

Course Type: Public
Year Built: 1988
Architect: Brad Benz
Local Pro: Don Boyle

Course: N/A
Holes: 18 / Par 72

Back: 6,966 yds. Rating: 72.3 Slope: 131
Middle: 6,411 yds. Rating: 69.8 Slope: 126
Ladies: 5,521 yds. Rating: 70.2 Slope: 127

Tee Time: 7 days in advance.
Price: $26 - $37 including cart.

Credit Cards:	■	Restaurant:	
Driving Range:	■	Lounge:	■
Practice Green:	■	Meeting Rooms:	
Locker Room:	■	Tennis:	
Rental Clubs:	■	Swimming:	
Walkers:	■	Jogging Trails:	
Snack Bar:	■	Boating:	

COURSE DESCRIPTION

If you're a golfing purist that enjoys playing the game the way it was originally designed, or a player searching for something a little more "European," you owe it to yourself to play this course.

Deep in the heart of the Aigla Desert, **Northgate Golf Club** was the first course in the state of Nevada to host a U.S. Open Local Qualifier in 1988 & 1989. The course features 32 sand-bunkers and 11 grass bunkers scattered throughout its playing field in strategic spots that are often surprising. You'll be playing your approach shots to fast and undulating demanding greens.

DIRECTIONS

Take I-80 to Exit 10 and go right to Mae Ave., left for two miles to Aveneida DeLanda, right to Beaumont, and left to the entrance.

ROSEWOOD LAKES GOLF COURSE
6800 Pembroke Dr., Reno, NV 89502 / (702) 857-2892

BASIC INFORMATION

Course Type: Municipal
Year Built: 1990
Architect: Brad Benz
Local Pro: Mike Mazzaferri

Course: N/A
Holes: 18 / Par 72

Back: 6,693 yds. Rating: 71.1 Slope: 127
Middle: 6,104 yds. Rating: 68.5 Slope: 123
Ladies: 5,481 yds. Rating: 69.3 Slope: 120

Tee Time: 7 days in advance.
Price: $11.00 - $23.00

Credit Cards:	■	Restaurant:	
Driving Range:	■	Lounge:	
Practice Green:	■	Meeting Rooms:	
Locker Room:	■	Tennis:	
Rental Clubs:	■	Swimming:	
Walkers:	■	Jogging Trails:	
Snack Bar:	■	Boating:	

COURSE DESCRIPTION

Rosewood Lakes Golf Course is spread over 160 acres of land with 60 of those acres federally protected for 45 species of birds and waterfowl that use these lands for food, water, and shelter.

Like any good links styled course, the open architecture lends itself to the wide variety of wind patterns that make it difficult to determine the proper way to shape a shot for best results. If such is the case, try playing a knock-down shot with a less lofted iron and a three quarter swing. This will keep the ball below the wind, allowing it a greater chance of holding its line to the pin.

Keep your eyes open for coyote!

DIRECTIONS

Take Hwy. 80 east to McCarren. Go south and turn left on Pembroke.

WASHOE COUNTY

SIERRA SAGE GOLF COURSE

6355 Silver Lake Blvd., Reno, NV 89506 / (702) 972-1564

BASIC INFORMATION

Course Type: Municipal
Year Built: 1960
Architect: John Benson and Moana Nursery
Local Pro: Mike Mitchell

Course: N/A
Holes: 18 / Par 72

Back : 6,623 yds. Rating: 69.3 Slope: 120
Middle: 6,207 yds. Rating: 67.9 Slope: 118
Ladies: 5,573 yds. Rating: 70.1 Slope: 113

Tee Time: 7 days in advance.
Price: $14 - $22

Credit Cards:	Restaurant:	
Driving Range: ■	Lounge:	
Practice Green: ■	Meeting Rooms:	
Locker Room:	Tennis:	
Rental Clubs: ■	Swimming:	
Walkers: ■	Jogging Trails:	
Snack Bar: ■	Boating:	

COURSE DESCRIPTION

This course is fairly flat and features fairways that are accentuated with sagebrush along their sides and towards the mostly medium sized greens. Walkers will enjoy the benefits of playing the game the way it was originally intended to be played.

Some of the par-5's are reachable in two, and may end up giving you an eagle if you're on your game, but if the wind makes its presence known, all of the par-5's (as well as some of the par-4's) are next to impossible for the average golfer.

Water comes into play from the tees on four holes.

DIRECTIONS

Take Hwy. 395 north from Reno and exit on Stead Blvd. and turn right. Go down to the lights and turn left on Silver Lake Blvd. Look for the course on your right.

WASHOE COUNTY GOLF COURSE

2601 South Arlington St., Reno, NV 89505 / (702) 785-4286

BASIC INFORMATION

Course Type: Public
Year Built: 1936
Architect: N/A
Local Pro: Barney Bell

Course: N/A
Holes: 18 / Par 72

Back : 6,695 yds. Rating: 70.0 Slope: 119
Middle: 6,485 yds. Rating: N/A Slope: 116
Ladies: 5,973 yds. Rating: 72.4 Slope: 120

Tee Time: 7 days in advance.
Price: $12 - $14

Credit Cards:	Restaurant: ■	
Driving Range: ■	Lounge:	
Practice Green: ■	Meeting Rooms: ■	
Locker Room: ■	Tennis: ■	
Rental Clubs: ■	Swimming:	
Walkers: ■	Jogging Trails:	
Snack Bar: ■	Boating:	

COURSE DESCRIPTION

The greatest enjoyment of playing this course is that it gives you a chance to see what it was like to play golf in an earlier time. Think about a time when all clubs had forged-blades and the balls that were used didn't fly as far and as accurately as they do today.

You'll find fairways wide open and surrounded by trees. You can hit your drives long, yet it isn't always the best way to control these holes. Most of your approach shots will be played to small undulating greens. You'll need to finesse some your shots close to the cup to play well here.

DIRECTIONS

Take Hwy. 395 to South Arlington St. Look for the course on your right side.

WILDCREEK GOLF COURSE
3500 Sullivan Lane, Sparks, NV 89431 / (702) 673-3100

BASIC INFORMATION

Course Type: Public
Year Built: 1978
Architect: Phelps & Benz
Local Pro: Fred Elliott

Course: N/A
Holes: 18 / Par 72

Back : 6,932 yds. Rating: 72.1 Slope: 132
Middle: 6,244 yds. Rating: 69.1 Slope: 124
Ladies: 5,415 yds. Rating: 70.5 Slope: 120

Tee Time: 3 days in advance.
Price: $26 - $39

Credit Cards: ■   Restaurant: ■
Driving Range: ■   Lounge: ■
Practice Green: ■   Meeting Rooms: ■
Locker Room: ■   Tennis:
Rental Clubs: ■   Swimming:
Walkers: ■   Jogging Trails:
Snack Bar: ■   Boating:

COURSE DESCRIPTION

The *Wildcreek Golf Course* features a beautiful layout with no two holes playing alike. By the time you step off the 18th green, you'll surely have played every club in your bag. The rolling terrain is hugged by numerous trees flowing on both sides of the fairways along a wandering creek and six lakes that vary in size.

The 5th-hole (par-4/389 yards) is the number one handicap hole. You'll need to hit your tee-shot between 220-240 yards to a tight landing area. This will leave you approximately 140-160 yards to the green which features a lake in front and a creek to the right of it. Good luck!

DIRECTIONS

Coming west on "80," go north on US-395 and go right off the W. McCarren exit. Make a left on Sullivan Lane to the course.

NEVADA
ALTERNATIVE COURSES

Clark
Private

Canyon Gate Country Club
2001 Cayon Gate Dr.
Las Vegas, NV 89117
(702) 363-0481

Las Vegas Country Club
3000 Joe W. Brown Dr.
Las Vegas, NV 89109

Shadow Creek Golf Club
5400 Losee Rd.
Las Vegas, NV 89030
(702) 399-0747

Spanish Trail Country Club
5050 Spanish Trail Lane
Las Vegas, NV 89113
(702) 364-0357

Sunrise Golf Club
5500 East Flamingo Rd.
Las Vegas, NV 89122
(702) 456-3160

Tournament Players Club At Summerlin
1700 Village Center Circle
Las Vegas, NV 89134
(702) 256-0222

Washoe
Private

Hidden Valley Country Club
3575 East Hidden Valley Dr.
Reno, NV 89502
(702) 857-4735

Clark
Military

Nellis AFB Golf Course
200 Kinsley Dr. (Bldg. 7-1619)
Nellis AFB, NV 89191
(702) 652-2602

WHERE TO STAY IN NEVADA

ALAMO
POPULATION: N/A

MEADOW LANE MOTEL
U.S. Hwy. 93
Alamo, NV 89001
(702) 725-3371

AUSTIN
POPULATION: N/A

LINCOLN MOTEL
28 Main St., P.O. Box 134
Austin, NV 89310
(702) 725-3371

MOUNTAIN MOTEL
Hwy. 50, P.O. Box 91
Austin, NV 89310
(702) 964-2471

PONY CANYON MOTEL
Hwy. 50, P.O. Box 86
Austin, NV 89310
(702) 964-2605

BAKER
POPULATION: N/A

BORDER INN
Hwy's 50 & 6. P.O. Box 30
Baker, NV 89311
(702) 234-7300

SILVERJACK MOTEL
Main St., P.O. Box 166
Baker, NV 89311
(702) 234-7323

BATTLE MOUNTAIN
POPULATION: N/A

BEL COURT MOTEL
292 E. Front St.
Battle Mountain, NV 89820
(702) 635-2569

BEST WESTERN-BIG CHIEF MOTEL
434 W. Front St.
Battle Mountain, NV 89820
(800) 528-1234

COLT SERVICE CENTER
650 W. Foront St.
Battle Mountain, NV 89820
(800) 343-0085

HO MOTEL
150 W. Front St.
Battle Mountain, NV 89820
(702) 635-5101

NEVADA HOTEL
36 E. Front St.
Battle Mountain, NV 89820
(702) 635-2453

OWL MOTEL
8 E. Front St.
Battle Mountain, NV 89820
(702) 635-5155

BEATTY
POPULATION: N/A

BURRO INN
Hwy. 95 S., P.O. Box 7
Beatty, NV 89003
(800) 843-2078

BEATTY

Continued

EL PORTEL MOTEL
301 Main St., P.O. Box 626
Beatty, NV 89003
(800) 742-7762

EXCHANGE CLUB OF BEATTY
604 Main St., P.O. Box 97
Beatty, NV 89003
(702) 553-2368

PHOENIX INN
Hwy. 95 & 1st., P.O. Box 503
Beatty, NV 89003
(800) 845-7401

STAGECOACH HOTEL & CASINO
State Rt. 95, P.O. Box 856
Beatty, NV 89003
(800) 4BIG-WIN

BOULDER CITY

POPULATION: N/A

**BEST WESTERN
LIGHTHOUSE INN & RESORT**
110 Ville Dr.
Boulder City, NV 89005
(702) 293-6444

BOULDER DAM HOTEL
1305 Arizona St.
Boulder City, NV 89005
(702) 293-1808

DESERT INN OF BOULDER CITY
800 Nevada Hwy.
Boulder City, NV 89005
(702) 293-1808

EL RANCHO BOULDER MOTEL
725 Nevada Hwy.
Boulder City, NV 89005
(702) 293-2827

FLAMINGO INN MOTEL
804 Nevada Hwy.
Boulder City, NV 89005
(702) 293-3565

GOLD STRIKE INN & CASINO
U.S. Hwy. 93
Boulder City, NV 89005
(702) 293-5000

LAKE MEAD MARINA
(Seven Crown Resorts)
322 Lakeshore Rd.
Boulder City, NV 89005-1214
(800) 752-9669

NEVADA INN
1009 Nevada Hwy.
Boulder City, NV 89005
(800) 638-8890

SANDS MOTEL
809 Nevada Hwy.
Boulder City, NV 89005
(702) 293-2589

STARVIEW MOTEL
1017 Nevada Hwy.
Boulder City, NV 89005
(702) 293-1658

SUPER 8 MOTEL
704 Nevada Hwy.
Boulder City, NV 89005
(702) 293-8888

CAL-NEV-ARI
POPULATION: N/A

BLUE SKY MOTEL
1 Spirit Mountain Lane
Cal-Nev-Ari, NV 89039
(702) 297-9289

CALIENTE
POPULATION: N/A

CALIENTE HOT SPRINGS MOTEL
Hwy. 93 N., P.O. Box 216
Caliente, NV 89008
(800) 266-4468

MIDWAY MOTEL
P.O. Box 113
Caliente, NV 89008
(702) 726-3199

RAINBOW CANYON MOTEL
884 A St., P.O. Box 278
Caliente, NV 89008
(702) 726-3291

SHADY MOTEL
450 Front St., P.O. Box 186
Caliente, NV 89008
(702) 726-3106

CARLIN
POPULATION: N/A

CAVELIER MOTEL
10th & Hwy. 40
Carlin, NV 89822
(702) 754-6311

CARSON CITY
POPULATION: N/A

BEST WESTERN - TRAILSIDE INN
1300 N. Carson St.
Carson City, NV 89701
(702) 883-7300

CARSON MOTOR LODGE
1421 N. Carson St.
Carson City, NV 89701
(702) 882-3572

CARSON STATION HOTEL/CASINO
900 S. Carson St., P.O. Box 1966
Carson City, NV 89701
(800) 528-1234

CITY CENTER MOTEL
800 N. Carson St.
Carson City, NV 89701
(702) 883-5535

DAYS INN
3103 N. Carson St.
Carson City, NV 89701
(702) 883-3343

DEER RUN RANCH BED & BREAKFAST
5440 Eastlake Blvd.
Carson City, NV 89704
(702) 882-3643

DESERT HILLS MOTEL
1010 S. Carson St.
Carson City, NV 89701
(800) NEVADA-1

DOWNTOWNER MOTEL
801 N. Carson St.
Carson City, NV 89701
(702) 882-1333

CARSON CITY
Continued

FORTY-NINER MOTEL
2450 N. Carson St.
Carson City, NV 89701
(702) 882-1123

FRONTIER MOTEL
1718 N. Carson St.
Carson City, NV 89701
(702) 882-1377

HARDMAN HOUSE MOTOR INN
917 N. Carson St.
Carson City, NV 89701
(702) 882-7744

MILL HOUSE INN
3251 S. Carson St.
Carson City, NV 89701
(702) 882-2715

MOTEL ORLEANS
2731 S. Carson St.
Carson City, NV 89701
(702) 882-2007

MOTEL 6
2749 S. Carson St.
Carson City, NV 89701
(702) 885-7710

NUGGET MOTEL
651 N. Stewart St.
Carson City, NV 89701
(702) 882-7711

ORMSBY HOUSE HOTEL/CASINO
600 S. Carson St., P.O. Box 1890
Carson City, NV 89702
(702) 882-1890

PIONEER MOTEL
907 S. Carson St.
Carson City, NV 89701
(702) 882-3046

PLAZA MOTEL
805 S. Plaza St.
Carson City, NV 89701
(702) 882-3046

ROUND HOUSE INN
1400 N. Carson St.
Carson City, NV 89701
(702) 882-3446

ROYAL CREST INN
1930 N. Carson St.
Carson City, NV 89701
(702) 882-1785

SIERRA SAGE MOTEL
801 S. Carson St.
Carson City, NV 89701
(702) 882-1419

SIERRRA VISTA MOTEL
711 S. Plaza St.
Carson City, NV 89701
(702) 883-9500

SILVER QUEEN INN
201 W. Caroline
Carson City, NV 89701
(800) NEVADA-1

SUPER 8 MOTEL
2829 S. Carson St.
Carson City, NV 89701
(800) 800-8000

WARREN INN
1850 N. Carson St.
Carson City, NV 89701
(800) 331-7700

WESTERNER INN
555 N. Stewart St.
Carson City, NV 89701
(702) 883-6565

COTTONWOOD COVE
POPULATION: N/A

COTTONWOOD COVE RESORT & MARINA
1000 Cottonwood Cove Rd.
Cottonwood, NV 89046
(702) 297-1464

DENIO
POPULATION: N/A

DENIO JUNCTION HOTEL
Denio Junction
Denio, NV 89822
(702) 754-6311

ELKO
POPULATION: N/A

BEST WESTERN-MARQUIS MOTOR INN
837 Idaho St.
Elko, NV 89801
(800) 528-1234

BEST WESTERN-RED LION MOTOR INN
2050 Idaho St.
Elko, NV 89801
(800) 528-1234

CENTRE MOTEL
475 Third St.
Elko, NV 89801
(702) 738-3226

EL NEVA MOTEL
736 Idaho St.
Elko, NV 89801
(800) 521-9999

ELKO MOTEL
1243 Idaho St.
Elko, NV 89801
(702) 738-4433

ESQUIRE MOTOR LODGE
505 Idaho St.
Elko, NV 89801
(702) 738-3157

GOLDRUSH INN
1930 Idaho St.
Elko, NV 89801
(702) 738-8787

HOLIDAY INN
3015 Idaho St.
Elko, NV 89801
(800) Hoiday

HOLIDAY MOTEL
1276 Idaho St.
Elko, NV 89801
(702) 738-7187

KEY 7 MOTEL
650 W. Idaho St.
Elko, NV 89801
(702) 738-8081

LOUIS MOTEL
2100 W. Idaho St., P.O. Box 86
Elko, NV 89801
(702) 738-3536

MANOR MOTOR LODGE
185 Idaho St.
Elko, NV 89801
(702) 738-3515

ELKO
Continued

MID-TOWN MOTEL
294 Idaho St.
Elko, NV 89801
(702) 738-3515

MOTEL 6
3021 Idaho St.
Elko, NV 89801
(702) 738-4337

NATIONAL 9 EL NEVA MOTEL
736 Idaho St.
Elko, NV 89801
(800) 348-0850

NATIONAL 9 TOPPERS MOTEL
1500 Idaho St.
Elko, NV 89801
(800) 348-0850

NELSON MOTEL
1003 Idaho St.
Elko, NV 89801
(702) 738-5527

OK-7 MOTEL
291 Idaho St.
Elko, NV 89801
(702) 738-4644

RED LION INN & CASINO
2065 Idaho St.
Elko, NV 89801
(800) 545-0044

RODEWAY INN
1349 Idaho St.
Elko, NV 89801
(800) 424-4777

SHILO INN - ELKO
2401 Mountain City Hwy.
Elko, NV 89801
(800) 222-2244

STAMPEDE 7 MOTEL
129 W. Idaho St.
Elko, NV 89801
(702) 738-8471

STAR LITE MOTEL
411 10th St.
Elko, NV 89801
(702) 738-8018

MOTEL 6
3021 Idaho St.
Elko, NV 89801
(702) 738-4337

STOCKMAN'S HOTEL
340 Commercial St., P.O. Box 270
Elko, NV 89801
(800) 648-2345

SUPER 8 MOTEL - ELKO
1755 Idaho St.
Elko, NV 89801
(800) 800-8000

THUNDERBIRD MOTEL
345 Idaho St.
Elko, NV 89801
(702) 738-7115

TOWNE HOUSE MOTEL
500 W. Oak
Elko, NV 89801
(702) 738-7269

TRAVELERS MOTEL
1181 Idaho St.
Elko, NV 89801
(702) 738-4048

WESTWARD 7 MOTEL
728 W. Idaho St.
Elko, NV 89801
(702) 738-9293

ELY
POPULATION: N/A

BEST WESTERN - MAIN MOTEL
1101 Aultman St.
Ely, NV 89301
(800) 528-1234

BEST WESTERN-PARK VUE MOTEL
930 Aultman St.
Ely, NV 89301
(800) 528-1234

BRISTLECONE MOTEL
700 Ave. I
Ely, NV 89301
(702) 289-8838

COPPER QUEEN HOTEL & CASINO
700 Ave. I
Ely, NV 89301
(702) 289-4884

DESER-EST MOTOR LODGE
1425 Aultman St.
Ely, NV 89301
(702) 289-4321

EL RANCHO MOTEL
1400 Aultman St.
Ely, NV 89301
(702) 289-3644

ELY & PLAZA HOTELS
700 Ave. I
Ely, NV 89301
(702) 289-9900

FIRESIDE INN
HC 33, Box 33400, McGill Hwy.
Ely, NV 89301
(800) 732-8288

FOUR SEVENS MOTEL
500 High St.
Ely, NV 89301
(702) 289-6958

GRAND CENTRAL MOTEL
1498 Lyons Ave., P.O. Box 1136
Ely, NV 89301
(702) 289-6868

GREAT BASIN INN
701 Ave. F
Ely, NV 89301
(702) 289-4468

HOTEL NEVADA
501 Aultman St., Box 209
Ely, NV 89301
(702) 289-6665

IDLE INN MOTEL
150 Fourth St., P.O. Box 426
Ely, NV 89301
(702) 289-4411

JAILHOUSE MOTEL
Fifth & High St.
Ely, NV 89301
(702) 289-3033

MOTEL 6
770 Ave. O
Ely, NV 89301
(702) 289-6671

RUSTIC INN
1555 Aultman St., P.O. Box 603
Ely, NV 89301
(702) 289-4404

ELY
Continued

STEPTOE VALLEY INN B&B
220 E. 11th St., P.O. Box 151110
East Ely, NV 89315-1110
(702) 289-8687

SURE REST MOTEL
1550 High St.
Ely, NV 89301
(702) 289-2512

TOWN & COUNTRY
710 Ave. G, P.O. Box 1171
Ely, NV 89301
(702) 289-8224

TRAILSIDE MOTEL
1020 Ave. F, Box 452
Ely, NV 89315
(702) 289-3038

WHITE PINE MOTEL
1301 Aultman St., P.O. Box 603
Ely, NV 89301
(702) 289-3800

EUREKA
POPULATION: N/A

COLONNADE HOTEL
Clark & Monroe St., P.O. Box 228
Eureka, NV 89316
(702) 237-9988

EUREKA MOTEL
10289 Main St., P.O. Box 26
Eureka, NV 89316
(702) 237-5247

PARSONAGE HOUSE COTTAGE
Corner of Spring & Bateman,
P.O. Box 99
Eureka, NV 89316
(702) 237-5756

RUBY HILL MOTEL
P.O. Box 281
Eureka, NV 89316
(702) 237-5539

SUNDOWN LODGE
Main St., P.O. Box 324
Eureka, NV 89316
(702) 237-5334

FALLON
POPULATION: N/A

BEST WESTERN - BONANZA INN & CASINO
855 W. Williams Ave.
Fallon, NV 89406
(800) 528-1234

COMFORT INN
1830 W. Williams Ave.
Fallon, NV 89406
(800) 221-2222

DAYS INN
60 S. Allen Rd.
Fallon, NV 89406
(702) 423-7021

ECONOLODGE/OASIS LODGE
70 E. Williams Ave.
Fallon, NV 89406
(800) 424-4777

FALLON LODGE
390 W. Williams Ave.
Fallon, NV 89406
(702) 423-4648

LARIAT MOTEL
850 W. Williams Ave., P.O. Box 649
Fallon, NV 89406
(702) 423-3181

NEVADA BELLE MOTEL
25 N. Taylor
Fallon, NV 89406
(702) 423-4648

RANCH MOTEL
1705 S. Taylor
Fallon, NV 89406
(702) 423-2277

VALUE INN
180 W. Williams Ave.
Fallon, NV 89406
(702) 423-5151

WESTERN HOTEL
120 S. Maine
Fallon, NV 89406
(702) 423-2589

WESTERN MOTEL
125 S. Carson St.
Fallon, NV 89406
(702) 423-5118

FERNLEY
POPULATION: N/A

FERNLY SUPER MOTEL
1350 W. Newlands Dr.
Fernley, NV 89408
(800) 800-8000

LAHONTAN MOTEL
135 E. Main St., P.O. Box 11
Fernley, NV 89408
(702) 575-2744

REST RANCHO MOTEL
325 Main St., P.O. Box 727
Fernley, NV 89408
(702) 575-4452

STARLITE MOTEL
300 W. Main St., Box 2007
Fernley, NV 89408
(702) 575-24444

TRUCK INN
485 Truck Inn Way
Fernley, NV 89408
(702) 351-1000

GABBS
POPULATION: N/A

GABBS MOTEL
100 S. Main St., P.O. Box 15
Gabbs, NV 89409
(702) 285-4068

GARDENVILLE
POPULATION: N/A

NENZEL MANSION B&B, THE
1431 Ezell
Gardenville, NV 89410
(702) 782-7644

OVERLAND HOTEL
691 S. Main
Gardenville, NV 89410
(702) 782-2138

GARDENVILLE
Continued

SIERRA MOTEL
1501 Hwy. 395
Gardenville, NV 89410
(702) 782-5145

SIERRA SPIRIT RANCH
3000 Pinenut Rd.
Gardenville, NV 89410
(702) 782-7011

TOPAZ LODGE & CASINO
1979 U.S. 395 S, P.O. Box 187
Gardenville, NV 89410
(800) 962-0732

VILLAGE MOTEL
1383 Hwy. 395 N.
Gardenville, NV 89410
(702) 782-2624

WESTENER MOTEL
1353 Hwy. 95, P.O. Box 335
Gardenville, NV 89410
(702) 782-3602

GENOA
POPULATION: N/A

GENOA HOUSE INN B&B
180 Nixon St., P.O. Box 141
Genoa, NV 89411
(702) 782-7075

WALLEY'S HOT SPRINGS RESORT
2001 Foothill Rd., P.O. Box 26
Genoa, NV 89411
(702) 782-8155

GERLACH
POPULATION: N/A

BRUNO'S COUNTRY CLUB
300 Main St., P.O. Box 70
Gerlach, NV 89412
(702) 557-2220

GLENDALE
POPULATION: N/A

GLENDALE SERVICE INC.
I-15 Hwy. 168,
Glendale, NV 89025
(702) 864-2277

GOLDFIELD
POPULATION: N/A

SANTA FE SALOON & MOTEL
Fourth & Pearl, P.O. Box 483
Goldfield, NV 89019
(702) 485-3431

HAWTHORNE
POPULATION: N/A

ANCHOR MOTEL
965 Sierra Way, P.O. Box 1245
Hawthorne, NV 89415
(702) 945-2573

BEST WESTERN - DESERT LODGE
1402 E. Fifth St., P.O. Box 1816
Hawthorne, NV 89415
(800528-1234

CLIFF HOUSE LAKESIDE RESORT
1 Cliff House Rd.
Hawthorne, NV 89415
(702) 945-2444

COVERED WAGON MOTEL
1322 Fifth St. & Hwy. 95
P.O. Box 544
Hawthorne, NV 89415
(702) 945-2253

EL CAPTAIN LODGE & CASINO
540 F St., P.O. Box 1000
Hawthorne, NV 89415
(702) 945-3321

HAWTHORNE MOTEL
720 Sierra Hwy. 95
Hawthorne, NV 89415
(702) 945-2544

HOLIDAY LODGE
Fifth 7 J St., P.O. Box 836
Hawthorne, NV 89415
(702) 945-3316

MONARCH MOTEL
1291 E. Fifth St., P.O. Box 1816
Hawthorne, NV 89415
(702) 945-3117

ROCKET MOTEL
694 Sierra Way, P.O. Box 1702
Hawthorne, NV 89415
(702) 945-2143

SAND & SAGE LODGE
1301 E. Fifth St., P.O. Box 2325
Hawthorne, NV 89415
(702) 945-3352

WRIGHT MOTEL
W. Fifth & I St., P.O. Box 1031
Hawthorne, NV 89415
(702) 945-2213

HENDERSON
POPULATION: N/A

BEST WESTERN-LAKE MEAD HOTEL
85 W. Lake Mead Dr.
Henderson, NV 89015
(800) 446-2944

BOBY MOTEL
2100 S. Boulder Hwy.
Henderson, NV 89015
(702) 565-9711

INGLES MOTEL
1636 Boulder Hwy.
Henderson, NV 89015
(702) 565-7929

OUTPOST MOTEL
1104 N. Boulder Hwy.
Henderson, NV 89015
(702) 565-2664

RAILROAD PASS HOTEL & CASINO
2100 Boulder Hwy.
Henderson, NV 89015
(800) 654-0877

SKY MOTEL
1713 N. Boulder Hwy.
Henderson, NV 89015
(702) 565-1534

TOWNHOUSE MOTOR LODGE
43 Water St.
Henderson, NV 89015
(702) 565-3111

INDIAN SPRINGS
POPULATION: N/A

INDIAN SPRINGS HOTEL & CASINO
U.S. 95
Indian Springs, NV 89018
(702) 384-7449

JACKPOT
POPULATION: N/A

BARTON'S CLUB 93
Hwy. 93, P.O. Box 523
Jackpot, NV 89825
(702) 755-2341

**CACTUS PETE'S HOTEL/CASINO/
HORSHU**
Hwy. 93, P.O. Box 508
Jackpot, NV 89825
(800) 821-1103

FOUR JACKS HOTEL-CASINO
Hwy. 93, P.O. Box 468
Jackpot, NV 89825
(702) 755-2491

JEAN
POPULATION: N/A

GOLD STRIKE HOTEL & CASINO
1 Main St., P.O. Box 19278
Jean, NV 89109
(800) 634-1359

**NEVADA LANDING HOTEL & CA-
SINO**
P.O. Box 19278
Jean, NV 89019
(800) 634-1359

PRIMADDONA HOTEL & CASINO
I-15 Stateline, P.O. Box 93718
Jean, NV 89193-3718
(800) 367-7383

WHISKEY PETE'S HOTEL / CASINO
I-15, P.O. Box 93718
Jean, NV 89193-3718
(800) 367-PETE

LAKE TAHOE-NORTH
(Crystal Bay & Incline Village)

POPULATION: N/A

A BELLA PROPERTIES
805 Tahow Blvd., P.O. Box 5365
Lake Tahoe, NV 89450
(800) GO-TAHOE

ALL SEASONS RESORT
807 Alder Ave., P.O. Box 4286
Lake Tahoe, NV 89450
(800) 322-4331

**CAL NEVA LODGE RESORT HOTEL
Spa & Casino**
2 Stateline Rd., P.O. Box 368
Incline Village, NV 89402
(800) CAL-NEVA

CLUB TAHOE RESORT
914 Northwood Blvd., P.O. Box 7440
Incline Village, NV 89452
(800) 527-5154

CRYSTAL BAY MOTEL
24 Hwy. 28, P.O. Box 254
Incline Village, NV 89402
(800) 45-TAHOE

HAUS BRAVARIA B&B
593-Dyer Circle, P.O. Box 3308
Incline Village, NV 89450
(800) GO-TAHOE

**HYATT REGENCY LAKE TAHOE
RESORT & CASINO**
11 Country Club Dr. at Lakeshore Blvd.
P.O. Box 3239
Incline Village, NV 89450-3239
(800) 233-1234

INN & INCLINE & CONDOS
1003 Tahoe Blvd., P.O. Box 4545
Incline Village, NV 89450
(800) 824-6391

LAKE TAHOE-SOUTH
(Glenbrook, Stateline, Zephyr Cove)

POPULATION: N/A

CAESARS TAHOE
55 Hwy. 50, P.O. Box 5800
Stateline, NV 89449
(800) BE-LUCKY

GLENBROOK RESORTS
2070 Pray Meadow Rd., P.O. Box 300
Glenbrook, NV 89413
(702) 749-5663

**HARRAH'S LAKE TAHOE HOTEL
CASINO**
Hwy. 50, P.O. Box 8
Stateline, NV 89449
(702) 588-6611

HARVEY'S RESORT HOTEL & CASINO
Hwy. 50 & Statline Ave., P.O. Box 128
Stateline, NV 89449
(800) 824-6391

HORIZON CASINO RESORT
P.O. Box C
Lake Tahoe, NV 89449
(800) 322-7723

LAKESIDE INN & CASINO
Hwy. 50 at Kingsbury Grade,
P.O. Box 5640
Stateline, NV 89449
(800) 624-7980

RIDGE TAHOE, THE
400 Ridge Club Dr., P.O. Box 5790
Stateline, NV 89449
(702) 588-3553

ZEPHYR COVE RESORT
760 Hwy. 50, P.O. Box 830
Zephyr Cove, NV 89448
(702) 588-6644

LAS VEGAS
POPULATION: N/A

AIRPORT INN
5100 Paradise Rd.
Las Vegas, NV 89119
(800) 634-6439

ALADDIN HOTEL & CASINO
3667 Las Vegas Blvd.,
P.O. Box 93958
Las Vegas, NV 89114
(800) 634-3424

ALEXIS PARK RESORT
375 E. Harmon Ave.
Las Vegas, NV 89109
(800) 453-8000

LAS VEGAS
Continued

AMBASSADOR EAST MOTEL
916 E. Fremont St.
Las Vegas, NV 89101
(800) 634-6703

APACHE MOTEL
407 S. Main St.
Las Vegas, NV 89101
(702) 382-7606

ARIZONA CHARLIE'S HOTEL & CASINO
740 S. Decatur Blvd.
Las Vegas, NV 89107
(800) 342-2695

BALLY'S CASINO RESORT
3645 Las Vegas Blvd., S.
Las Vegas, NV 89109
(800) 634-3434

BARBARY COAST HOTEL & CASINO
3595 Las Vegas Blvd. S.
P.O. Box 19030
Las Vegas, NV 89132
(800) 634-6755

BARCELONA HOTEL & CASINO
5011 E. Craig Rd.
Las Vegas, NV 89115
(800) 223-6330

BEST WESTERN - MAIN STREET INN
1000 N. Main St.
Las Vegas, NV 89101
(800) 851-1414

BEST WESTERN - MARDI GRAS INN
3500 Paradise Rd.
Las Vegas, NV 89109
(800) 732-6501

BEST WESTERN - MARINA INN
1322 E. Fremont St.
Las Vegas, NV 89101
(800) 356-5329

BEST WESTERN - MACARRAN INN
4970 Paradise Rd.
Las Vegas, NV 89119
(800) 626-7575

BEST WESTERN - NELLIS MOTOR INN
5330 E. Craig Rd.
Las Vegas, NV 89115
(800) 528-1234

BEST WESTERN - PARKVIEW INN
905 Las Vedgas Blvd. N.
Las Vegas, NV 89101
(800) 548-6122

BINION'S HORSESHOE HOTEL & CASINO
128 E. Fremont, P.O. Box 520
Las Vegas, NV 89125
(800) 622-6468

BLAIR HOUSE HOTEL
344 E. Desert Inn Rd.
Las Vegas, NV 89109
(800) 553-9111

BLUE ANGEL MOTEL
2110 E. Fremont St.
Las Vegas, NV 89101
(702) 386-9500

BOARDWALK HOTEL / CASINO
3750 Las Vegas Blvd. S.
Las Vegas, NV 89109
(800) 635-4581

BONANZA LODGE
1808 E. Fremont St.
Las Vegas, NV 89101
(702) 382-3990

BOULEVARD MOTEL
525 Las Vegas Blvd. S.
Las Vegas, NV 89101
(702) 384-6090

BOURBON STREET HOTEL & CASINO
120 E. Flamingo Rd.
Las Vegas, NV 89109
(800) 634-6956

BRANDING IRON MOTEL
2519 Las Vegas Blvd. N.
Las Vegas, NV 89030
(702) 642-6618

BUDGET INN
301 S. Main St.
Las Vegas, NV 89101
(702) 385-5560

CAESARS PALACE
3570 Las Vegas Blvd. S.
Las Vegas, NV 89109
(800) 634-6661

CALIFORNIA HOTEL CASINO & RV PARK
12 Ogdon St., P.O. Box 630
Las Vegas, NV 89101
(800) 634-6505

CAPRI MOTEL
3245 E. Fremont St.
Las Vegas, NV 89104
(702) 457-1429

CARRIAGE HOUSE, THE
105 E. Harmon Ave.
Las Vegas, NV 89109
(800) 777-1700

CASA BLANCA INN
1801 Las Vegas Blvd.
Las Vegas, NV 89104
(702) 735-4050

CASA MALAGA HOTEL
4615 Las Vegas Blvd. S.
Las Vegas, NV 89101
(702) 635-4581

CENTER STRIP INN
3688 Las Vegas Blvd. S.
Las Vegas, NV 89109
(800) 777-7737

CIMMARON MOTEL
3680 Boulder Hwy.
Las Vegas, NV 89121
(702) 451-4131

CIRCUS CIRCUS HOTEL & CASINO
2880 Las Vegas Blvd. S.,
P.O. Box 630
Las Vegas, NV 89114-4967
(800) 634-3450

CITY CENTER MOTEL
700 E. Fremont St.
Las Vegas, NV 89101
(702) 382-4766

COMET MOTEL
3565 Boulder Hwy.
Las Vegas, NV 89121
(702) 457-4218

COMFORT INN
211 E. Flamingo Rd.
Las Vegas, NV 89109
(702) 733-7800

LAS VEGAS
Continued

COMFORT INN-SOUTH
5075 Koval Lane
Las Vegas, NV 89119
(702) 736-3600

CONTINENTAL HOTEL & CASINO
4100 Paradise Rd.
Las Vegas, NV 89109
(800) 634-6641

CONVENTION CENTER LODGE
79 Convention Center Dr.
Las Vegas, NV 89109
(702) 735-1315

CONVENTION INN MOTEL
735 E. Desert Inn Rd.
Las Vegas, NV 89121
(800) 845-5564

CREST BUDGET INN
207 N. Sixth St.
Las Vegas, NV 89101
(800) 777-1817

DAISY MOTEL
415 S. Main St.
Las Vegas, NV 89101
(702) 382-0707

DAYS INN CENTER STRIP
3265 Las Vegas Blvd. S.
Las Vegas, NV 89109
(800) 828-8032

DAYS INN DOWNTOWN
707 E. Fremont St.
Las Vegas, NV 89101
(800) 325-2344

DEL MAR RESORT MOTEL
1411 Las Vegas Blvd. S.
Las Vegas, NV 89104
(702) 384-5775

DESERT HILLS MOTEL
2121 E. Fremont St.
Las Vegas, NV 89101
(702) 384-8060

DESERT INN HOTEL & CASINO
3145 Las Vegas Blvd. S.
Las Vegas, NV 89109
(800) 634-6906

DESERT MOON MOTEL
1701 E. Fremont St.
Las Vegas, NV 89101
(702) 382-5535

DESERT PARADISE MOTEL
465 E. Desert Inn Motel
Las Vegas, NV 89109
(800) 634-6635

DESERT ROSE MOTEL
3774 Las Vegas Blvd. S.
Las Vegas, NV 89109
(702) 739-6739

DESERT STAR MOTEL
1210 Las Vegas Blvd. S.
Las Vegas, NV 89104
(702) 384-7172

DI 500
505 E. Desert Inn Rd.
Las Vegas, NV 89109
(702) 735-3160

DIAMOND INN MOTEL
4605 Las Vegas Blvd., S.
Las Vegas, NV 89109
(702) 736-2565

DOMINO MOTEL
1621 S. Main S.
Las Vegas, NV 89104
(702) 384-6000

DOWNTOWNER MOTEL
129 N. Eighth St.
Las Vegas, NV 89101
(800) 777-2566

ECONO INN
3939 Las Vegas Blvd. S.
Las Vegas, NV 89119
(800) 3634-6727

ECONO LODGE
1150 Las Vegas Blvd. S.
Las Vegas, NV 89104
(800) 634-6979

ECONO LODGE DOWNTOWN
520 S. Casino Center Blvd.
Las Vegas, NV 89101
(800) 223-7706

EL CID HOTEL
233 S. Sixth St.
Las Vegas, NV 89101
(702) 384-4696

EL CORTEZ HOTEL
600 E. Fremont St., P.O. Box 680
Las Vegas, NV 89125
(800) 634-6703

EL MIRADOR MOTEL
2310 Las Vegas Blvd. S.
Las Vegas, NV 89104
(702) 384-6570

EL MOROCCO MOTEL
2975 Las Vegas Blvd. S.
Las Vegas, NV 89109
(702) 735-7145

EMERALD SPRINGS INN
325 E. Flamingo Rd.
Las Vegas, NV 89109
(702) 732-7889

EXCALIBUR HOTEL/CASINO
3850 Las Vegas Blvd. S.
P.O. Box 96778
Las Vegas, NV 89109-4300
(800) 3937-7777

E-Z 8 MOTEL
5201 S. Industrial Rd.
Las Vegas, NV 89118
(800) 32-MOTEL

FAIRFIELD INN BY MARRIOTT
3850 Paradise Rd.
Las Vegas, NV 89109
(800) 228-2800

FERGUSONS MOTEL
1028 E. Fremont St.
Las Vegas, NV 89101
(800) 933-STAY

FEZ MOTEL
4213 S. Las Vegas Blvd. S.
Las Vegas, NV 89119
(702) 736-6014

FISHERS ARVIDA MOTEL
1208 Fremont St.
Las Vegas, NV 89104
(702) 382-8131

FITZGERALDS CASINO HOTEL
301 E. Fremont St.
Las Vegas, NV 89101
(800) 274-5825

LAS VEGAS
Continued

FLAMINGO HILTON LAS VEGAS
3555 Las Vegas Blvd. S.
Las Vegas, NV 89109
(800) 732-2111

49ER MOTEL
3045 E. Fremont St.
Las Vegas, NV 89104
(702) 457-5754

FOUR QUEENS HOTEL & CASINO
202 E. Fremont St., P.O. Box 940
Las Vegas, NV 89125-0940
(800) 634-6045

**FREMONT HOTEL & CASINO,
SAM BOYD'S**
200 E. Fremont St., P.O. Box 940
Las Vegas, NV 89125-0940
(800) 634-6460

FRONTIER HOTEL & CASINO
3120 Las Vegas Blvd. S.
Las Vegas, NV 89109
(800) 421-7806

FULL MOON MOTEL
3769 Las Vegas Blvd. S.
Las Vegas, NV 89109
(702) 736-0055

FUN CITY MOTEL
2233 Las Vegas Blvd. S.
Las Vegas, NV 89104
(702) 731-3155

GABLES MOTEL
1301 E. Fremont St.
Las Vegas, NV 89101
(702) 384-1637

GATEWAY MOTEL
928 Las Vegas Blvd.
Las Vegas, NV 89101
(702) 382-2146

GATEWOOD MOTEL
3075 E. Fremont St.
Las Vegas, NV 89104
(702) 457-3660

GLASS POOL INN
4613 Las Vegas Blvd. S.
Las Vegas, NV 89119
(800) 527-7118

GOLD COAST HOTEL & CASINO
4000 W. Flamingo Rd.
P.O. Box 80750
Las Vegas, NV 89103
(800) 331-5334

GOLD SPIKE HOTEL & CASINO
400 E. Ogdon
Las Vegas, NV 89101
(800) 634-6703

GOLDEN CITY MOTEL
3410 Boulder Hwy.
Las Vegas, NV 89121
(800) 457-4373

GOLDEN GATE HOTEL
1 E. Fremont St.
Las Vegas, NV 89101
(702) 384-8204

GOLDEN INN MOTEL
120 Las Vegas Blvd. N.
Las Vegas, NV 89101
(800) 384-8204

GOLDEN NUGGET HOTEL & CASINO
129 E. Fremont St., P.O. Box 610
Las Vegas, NV 89125
(800) 634-3454

GOLDEN WEST MOTEL
1414 Las Vegas Blvd. S.
Las Vegas, NV 89104
(800) 634-6981

GRAND FLAMINGO
100 Winnick Ave.
Las Vegas, NV 89109
(800) 634-6981

HACIENDA RESORT HOTEL & CASINO
3950 Las Vegas Blvd. S.
P.O. Box 98506
Las Vegas, NV 89193
(800) 634-6655

HARRAH'S CASINO HOTEL
3475 Las Vegas Blvd. S.
Las Vegas, NV 89109
(800) 392-9002

HIELEAH MOTEL
1924 E. Fremont St.
Las Vegas, NV 89101
(702) 384-7834

HIGH HAT REGENCY MOTEL
1300 Las Vegas Blvd. S.
Las Vegas, NV 89104
(702) 382-8080

HITCHIN' POST CAMPER PARK & MOTEL
3640 Las Vegas Blvd. N.
Las Vegas, NV 89115
(702) 644-1043

HOLIDAY HOUSE
2211 Las Vegas Blvd. S.
Las Vegas, NV 89101
(702) 732-6464

HOLIDAY MOTEL
2205 Las Vegas Blvd. S.
Las Vegas, NV 89104
(702) 735-6464

HOLIDAY ROYAL APARTMENT SUITES
4505 Paradise Rd.
Las Vegas, NV 89109
(800) 732-7676

HOPS MOTEL
3412 Paradise Rd.
Las Vegas, NV 89109
(702) 732-2494

HOTEL NEVADA & CASINO
3111 W. Tropicana Ave.
Las Vegas, NV 89103
(800) 637-5777

HOWARD JOHNSONS HOTEL & CASINO
3111 W. Tropicana Ave.
Las Vegas, NV 89103
(800) 654-2000

IMPERIAL HOTEL
1326 S. Main St.
Las Vegas, NV 89104
(800) 384-8069

IMPERIAL PALACE
3535 Las Vegas Blvd. S.
Las Vegas, NV 89109
(800) 634-6441

JACKPOT MOTELJACKPOT MOTEL
1600 S. Casino Center Blvd.
Las Vegas, NV 89104
(702) 384-7211

LAS VEGAS
Continued

KING ALBERT MOTEL
185 Albert Ave.
Las Vegas, NV 89109
(800) 553-7753

KING 8 HOTEL & GAMBLING HALL
3330 Tropicana Ave.
Las Vegas, NV 89103
(800) 634-3488

KLONDIKE INN
5191 Las Vegas Blvd. S.
Las Vegas, NV 89119
(702) 739-9351

KNOTTY PINE
1900 Las Vegas Blvd. N.
Las Vegas, NV 89030
(702) 642-8300

LA CONCHA MOTEL
2955 Las Vegas Blvd. S.
Las Vegas, NV 89101
(702) 735-1255

LA PALM MOTEL
2512 E. Fremont St.
Las Vegas, NV 89104
(702) 384-5874

KING ALBERT MOTEL
185 Albert Ave.
Las Vegas, NV 89109
(800) 553-7753

LADY LUCK CASINO/HOTEL
206 N. Third St., P.O. Box 1060
Las Vegas, NV 89125
(800) 634-6580

LAMPLIGHTER MOTEL
2805 E. Fremont St.
Las Vegas, NV 89104
(702) 382-8791

LAQUINTA MOTER INN
3782 Las Vegas Blvd. S.
Las Vegas, NV 89109
(800) 531-5900

LAS VEGAS CLUB HOTEL
18 E. Fremont St., P.O. Box 1719
Las Vegas, NV 89125
(800) 634-6532

LAS VEGAS COURTYARD (Marriott)
3275 Paradise Rd.
Las Vegas, NV 89109
(800) 321-2211

LAS VEGAS DOWNTOWN TRAVELODGE
2028 E. Fremont St.
Las Vegas, NV 89101
(800) 255-3050

LAS VEGAS HILTON
3000 Paradise Rd., P.O. Box 93147
Las Vegas, NV 89109
(800) 732-7917

LAS VEGAS INN
1501 W. Sahara Ave.
Las Vegas, NV 89102
(702) 731-3222

LAS VEGAS MOTEL
1200 Fremont St.
Las Vegas, NV 89101
(702) 384-5670

LEE MOTEL
200 S. Eighth st.
Las Vegas, NV 89101
(702) 382-1297

LIBERTY VEGAS MOTEL
2216 E. Fremont St.
Las Vegas, NV 89101
(702) 383-7062

LUCKY CUSS MOTEL
3305 E. Fremont St.
Las Vegas, NV 89104
(702) 457-1929

LUCKY LADY MOTEL
1308 E. Fremont St.
Las Vegas, NV 89101
(702) 385-1093

LUCKY MOTEL
1111 E. Fremont St.
Las Vegas, NV 89101
(702) 384-1311

MAXIM HOTEL/CASINO
160 E. Flamingo Rd.
Las Vegas, NV 89109
(800) 634-6987

MEADOWS INN
525 E. Bonanza Rd.
Las Vegas, NV 89101
(800) 932-1499

MIRAGE, THE
3400 Las Vegas Blvd. S.
P.O. Box 7777
Las Vegas, NV 89177-0777
(800) 627-6667

MONA MARIE MOTEL
3767 Las Vegas Blvd. S.
Las Vegas, NV 89109
(702) 739-6565

MONACO MOTEL
3073 Las Vegas Blvd. S.
Las Vegas, NV 89109
(702) 735-9222

MOTEL 8 MR. DELI
3961 Las Vegas Blvd. S.
Las Vegas, NV 89119
(800) 798-7223

MOTEL 6
4125 Boulder Hwy.
Las Vegas, NV 89121
(702) 457-8051

MOTEL 6
5085 Industrial Rd.
Las Vegas, NV 89118
(702) 739-6747

MOTEL 6
195 E. Tropicana Ave.
Las Vegas, NV 89109
(702) 798-0728

MOTEL REGENCY
700 N. Main St.
Las Vegas, NV 89101
(702) 382-2332

MOULIN ROUGE
900 W. Bonanza Rd.
Las Vegas, NV 89106
(702) 648-5054

NAVADA PALACE HOTEL & CASINO
5255 Boulder Hwy.
Las Vegas, NV 89122
(800) 634-6283

NEW WEST MOTEL
801 Las Vegas Blvd. S.
Las Vegas, NV 89101
(702) 382-3700

LAS VEGAS

Continued

NORMANDIE MOTEL
708 Las Vegas Blvd. S.
P.O. Box 80666
Las Vegas, NV 89180
(702) 382-1002

OASIS MOTEL
1731 Las Vegas Blvd. S.
Las Vegas, NV 89104
(702) 735-6494

OLYMPIAN PALMS RESORT
3890 Swenson Ave.
Las Vegas, NV 89119
(800) 879-7904

PAIR-A-DICE INN
2217 Fremont St.
Las Vegas, NV 89101
(702) 382-6440

PALACE STATION HOTEL/CASINO
2411 W. Sahara Ave., P.O. Box 26448
Las Vegas, NV 89126-0448
(800) 544-2411

PARADISE RESORT INN
4350 Paradise Rd.
Las Vegas, NV 89109
(702) 733-3900

PARADISE ROAD MOTEL
2110 Paradise Rd.
Las Vegas, NV 89104
(702) 735-2780

PLAZA-SUITE HOTEL
4255 S. Paradise Rd.
Las Vegas, NV 89109
(702) 369-4400

PONDEROSA MOTEL
3325 E. Fremont
Las Vegas, NV 89104
(702) 457-0422

QUALITY INN HOTEL & CASINO
377 E. Flamingo Rd.
Las Vegas, NV 89109
(702) 733-7777

QUALITY SUNRISE SUITES
4575 Boulder Hwy.
Las Vegas, NV 89119
(800) 362-4040

QUEEN OF HEARTS HOTEL & CASINO
19 E. Lewis Ave.
Las Vegas, NV 89101
(800) 835-6005

RAINBOW VEGAS HOTEL
401 S. Casino Center Blvd.
Las Vegas, NV 89101
(800) 634-6635

RESIDENCE INN BY MARRIOTT
3225 Paradise Rd.
Las Vegas, NV 89109
(800) 331-3131

RIO SUITE HOTEL & CASINO
3700 Flamingo Rd., P.O. Box 14160
Las Vegas, NV 59114
(800) 888-1808

RIVIERA HOTEL & CASINO
2901 Las Vegas Blvd. S.
Las Vegas, NV 89109
(800) 634-6753

RODEWAY INN
3786 Las Vegas Blvd. S.
Las Vegas, NV 89109
(800) 350-1132

ROULETTE MOTEL
2019 E. Fremont St.
Las Vegas, NV 89101
(702) 384-3597

ROYAL HOTEL/CASINO
99 Convention Center Dr.
Las Vegas, NV 89109
(800) 634-6118

ROYAL OASIS MOTEL
4375 Las Vegas Blvd. S.
Las Vegas, NV 89119
(702) 739-9119

SAFARI MOTEL
2001 E. Fremont St.
Las Vegas, NV 89101
(702) 384-4021

SAHARA HOTEL & CASINO
2535 Las Vegas Blvd. S.
P.O. Box 98503
Las Vegas, NV 89193
(800) 634-6666

ST. TROPEZ SUITE HOTEL
455 E. Harmon Ave.
Las Vegas, NV 89109
(800) 666-5400

SAN REMO CASINO & RESORT HOTEL
115 E. Tropicana Ave.
Las Vegas, NV 89109
(800) 522-7366

SAM'S TOWN HOTEL & GAMBLING HALL
5111 Boulder Hwy.
Las Vegas, NV 89122
(800) 634-6371

SANDS HOTEL & CASINO
3355 Las Vegas Blvd. S.
Las Vegas, NV 89109
(800) 446-4678

SANTA FE HOTEL & CASINO
4949 N. Rancho
Las Vegas, NV 89130
(800) 872-6823

SHALIMAR HOTEL
1401 Las Vegas Blvd. S.
Las Vegas, NV 89104
(702) 338-0301

SHEFFIELD INN HOTEL & RESORT
3970 Paradise Rd.
Las Vegas, NV 89101
(800) 632-4040

SHOWBOAT HOTEL, CASINO & BOWLING CENTER
2800 Fremont St.
Las Vegas, NV 89104
(800) 634-3484

SILVER SANDS MOTEL
4617 Las Vegas Blvd. S.
Las Vegas, NV 89119
(702) 736-2545

SKY RANCH MOTEL
2009 E. Fremont St.
Las Vegas, NV 89101
(702) 382-2846

SOMBRERO MOTEL
4915 Las Vegas Blvd. S.
Las Vegas, NV 89119
(702) 739-6186

LAS VEGAS
Continued

SOMERSET HOUSE
294 Convention Center Dr.
Las Vegas, NV 89109
(702) 735-4411

SPORTSMAN MANOR
5660 Boulder Hwy.
Las Vegas, NV 89112
(702) 458-7071

SQUADRON EXECUTIVE SUITES
5230 E. Craig Rd.
Las Vegas, NV 89115
(702) 644-3300

STAR VIEW MOTEL
1217 E. Fremont St.
Las Vegas, NV 89101
(702) 382-2831

STARDUST RESORT & CASINO
3000 Las Vegas Blvd. S.
Las Vegas, NV 89109
(702) 732-6111

STEVEN MOTEL & APARTMENTS
2112 N. Nellis Blvd.
Las Vegas, NV 89115
(702) 452-8199

SULINDA BY GASLIGHT
2035 Las Vegas Blvd. S.
Las Vegas, NV 89104
(702) 732-2000

SUN HARBOR BUDGET SUITES
4625 Boulder Hwy.
Las Vegas, NV 89121
(800) 752-1501

SUN HARBOR BUDGET SUITES
1500 Stardust Rd.
Las Vegas, NV 89109
(800) 752-1501

SUNBIRD INN
3969 Las Vegas Blvd. S.
Las Vegas, NV 89109
(702) 739-1915

SUNRISE VISTA EXECUTIVE SUITES
3801 E. Charleston Blvd.
Las Vegas, NV 89104
(702) 459-7908

SUPER 8 HOTEL & CASINO
4250 Koval Lane
Las Vegas, NV 89109
(800) 800-8000

SUPER 8 MOTEL
5288 Boulder Hwy.
Las Vegas, NV 89120
(800) 825-0880

SUPER 8 MOTEL
4435 Las Vegas Blvd. N.
Las Vegas, NV 89115
(800) 800-8000

TAHITI MOTEL
3725 Las Vegas Blvd. S.
Las Vegas, NV 89109
(800) 634-6727

TAM O'SHANTER MOTEL
3317 Las Vegas Blvd. S.
Las Vegas, NV 89109
(800) 727-DICE

TIKI MOTEL
4635 Boulder Hwy.
Las Vegas, NV 89121
(702) 451-3376

TOD MOTEL
1508 Las Vegas Blvd. S.
Las Vegas, NV 89104
(702) 477-0022

TOWN HALL CASINO HOTEL
4155 Koval Lane
Las Vegas, NV 89109
(800) 634-6541

TOWN LODGE MOTEL
225 N. Seventh St.
Las Vegas, NV 89101
(702) 386-7988

TOWN PALMS HOTEL
321 S. Casino Center
Las Vegas, NV 89101
(800) 282-2558

TOWNE & COUNTRY MOTEL
2033 E. Fremont St.
Las Vegas, NV 89101
(702) 336-8576

TRAVEL INN MOTEL
217 Las Vegas Blvd. N.
Las Vegas, NV 89101
(702) 384-3040

TRAVELER'S MOTEL
1100 E. Fremont St.
Las Vegas, NV 89101
(702) 384-7121

TRAVELODGE CENTER STRIP
3419 Las Vegas Blvd. S.
Las Vegas, NV 89109
(800) 854-7666

TRAVELODGE LAS VEGAS STRIP
2830 Las Vegas Blvd. S.
Las Vegas, NV 89109
(800) 422-3313

TRAVELODGE SOUTH STRIP
3735 Las Vegas Blvd. S.
Las Vegas, NV 89109
(800) 255-3050

TREASURE ISLAND AT THE MI-RAGE
3300 Las Vegas Blvd. S.
Las Vegas, NV 89109
(800) 627-6667

TROPICANA INN
5150 Duke Ellington Way
Las Vegas, NV 89119
(702) 736-8964

TROPICANA RESORT & CASINO
3801 Las Vegas Blvd. S.
Las Vegas, NV 89109
(800) 468-9494

UNION PLAZA HOTEL/CASINO
1 Main St.
Las Vegas, NV 89101
(800) 634-6575

UPTOWN MOTEL
813 Ogdon
Las Vegas, NV 89101
(800) 382-5257

VACATION VILLAGE HOTEL CA-SINO
6711 Las Vegas Blvd., S.
Las Vegas, NV 89119
(800) 658-5000

VALLEY MOTEL
1313 E. Fremont St.
Las Vegas, NV 89101
(702) 384-6890

LAS VEGAS
Continued

VEGAS WORLD HOTEL & CASINO
2000 Las Vegas Blvd. S.
Las Vegas, NV 89104
(800) 634-6301

VICTORY BUDGET MOTEL
307 S. Main St.
Las Vegas, NV 89101
(702) 384-0260

VILLA INN
255 Las Vegas Blvd. S.
Las Vegas, NV 89101
(702) 382-3878

VILLA ROMA MOTEL
220 Convention Center Dr.
Las Vegas, NV 89109
(800) 634-6535

VISTA MOTEL
209 N. Seventh St.
Las Vegas, NV 89101
(702) 382-4920

WARRAN MOTEL & APARTMENTS
3965 Las Vegas Blvd. S.
Las Vegas, NV 89109
(702) 736-6235

WESTERN HOTEL BINGO PARLOR & CASINO
899 E. Fremont St.
Las Vegas, NV 89101
(800) 634-6703

WESTWARD HO MOTEL/CASINO
2900 Las Vegas Blvd. S.
Las Vegas, NV 89109
(800) 634-6803

WHITE SANDS MOTEL
3889 Las Vegas Blvd. S.
Las Vegas, NV 89119
(702) 736-2515

YUCCA MOTEL
1727 Las Vegas Blvd. S.
Las Vegas, NV 89104
(702) 735-2787

LAUGHLIN
POPULATION: N/A

BAY SHORE INN
1955 W. Casino Dr., P.O. Box 31377
Laughlin, NV 89029
(800) 677-6172

BEST WESTERN - RIVERSIDE RESORT HOTEL & CASINO
1650 Casino Way, P.O. Box 500
Laughlin, NV 89029
(800) 227-3849

COLORADO BELLE HOTEL & CASINO
2100 Casino Dr., P.O. Box 77000
Laughlin, NV 89029
(800) 458-9500

EDGEWATER HOTEL & CASINO
220 Casino Dr., P.O. Box 30707
Laughlin, NV 89028
(800) 677-4837

FLAMINGO HILTON LAUGHLIN
1900 S. Casino Dr., P.O. Box 30630
Laughlin, NV 89028
(800) FLAMINGO

GOLD RIVER GAMBLING HALL & RESORT
2700 S. Casino Dr., P.O. Box 77700
Laughlin, NV 89029-7770
(800) 835-7903

GOLDEN NUGGET LAUGHLIN
2300 S. Casino Dr., P.O. Box 77111
Laughlin, NV 89029
(800) 237-1739

HARRAH'S CASINO HOTEL
2900 S. Casino Dr., P.O. Box 33000
Laughlin, NV 89029
(800) 634-3469

PIONEER HOTEL & GAMBLING HALL
2110 Casino Dr., P.O. Box 29664
Laughlin, NV 89029
(800) 634-3469

RAMADA EXPRESS HOTEL/CASINO
2121 S. Casino Dr., P.O. Box 77771
Laughlin, NV 89029
(800) 2-RAMADA

LOVELOCK
POPULATION: N/A

BEST WESTERN - STURGEON'S
1420 Cornell Ave., P.O. Box 56
Lovelock, NV 89419
(702) 273-2971

BROOKWOOD MOTEL
205 Cornell Ave., P.O. Box 56
Lovelock, NV 89419
(702) 273-2438

CADILLAC INN
1395 Cornell Ave., P.O. Box 988
Lovelock, NV 89419
(702) 273-2798

COVERED WAGON MOTEL
945 Dartmouth Ave.
Lovelock, NV 89419
(702) 273-2339

DESERT HAVEN MOTEL
885 Dartmouth Ave.
Lovelock, NV 89419
(702) 273-2339

LOVELOCK INN
Hwy. 40 W., P.O. Box 757
Lovelock, NV 89419
(702) 273-2937

SAGE MOTEL, THE
1335 Cornell Ave., P.O. Box 988
Lovelock, NV 89419
(702) 273-0444

SUNSET MOTEL
1145 Cornell Ave.
Lovelock, NV 89419
(702) 273-7366

SUPER 10 MOTEL
1145 Cornell Ave., P.O. Box 819
Lovelock, NV 89419
(702) 273-7366

WINDMILL HOTEL & PART LOUNGE
285 Ninth St.
Lovelock, NV 89419
(702) 273-7853

MCDERMITT
POPULATION: N/A

DIAMOND MOTEL
140 U.S. 95, P.O. Box 158
McDermitt, NV 89421
(702) 532-8551

MCDERMITT
Continued

MCDERMITT SERVICE & MOTEL
Hwy. 95, P.O. Box 335
McDermitt, NV 89421
(702) 532-8558

MESQUITE
POPULATION: N/A

DESERT PALMS MOTEL
Mesquite Blvd., P.O. Box 667
Mesquite, NV 89024
(702) 346-5756

HARDY'S DELUXE MOTEL
141 Mesquite Blvd., P.O. Box 239
Mesquite, NV 89024
(702) 346-5502

PEPPERMILL RESORT HOTEL & CASINO
1134 N. Mesquite Blvd., P.O. Box 360
Mesquite, NV 89024
(800) 621-0187

STATE LINE CASINO
490 Mesquite Blvd., P.O. Box 730
Mesquite, NV 89024
(702) 346-5752

VALLEY INN MOTEL
791 W. Mesquite Blvd., P.O. Box 1390
Mesquite, NV 89024
(702) 346-5281

VIRGIN RIVER HOTEL
915 Mesquite Blvd. N., P.O. Box 1620
Mesquite, NV 89024
(800) 346-7721

MINDEN
POPULATION: N/A

CARSON VALLEY INN
1627 Hwy. 395 N.
Minden, NV 89423
(800) 321-6983

HOLIDAY LODGE
1591 Hwy. 395, P.O. Box 848
Minden, NV 89423
(800) 266-2289

MT. CHARLESTON
POPULATION: N/A

MT. CHARLESTON HOTEL
2 Kyle Canyon Rd.
Mt. Charleston, NV 89124
(702) 872-5500

MOUNTAIN CITY
POPULATION: N/A

CHAMBERS HOTEL
P.O. Box 188
Mountain City, NV 89831
(702) 763-6626

MOUNTAIN CITY STEAKHOUSE & CASINO
P.O. Box 102
Mountain City, NV 89831
(702) 763-6617

NORTH LAS VEGAS
POPULATION: N/A

ARROWHEAD MOTEL
2403 Las Vegas Blvd.
North Las Vegas, NV 89830
(702) 399-9043

BARKER MOTEL
2600 Las Vegas Blvd. N.
North Las Vegas, NV 89030
(702) 642-1138

BRANDING IRON MOTEL
2519 Las Vegas Blvd. N.
North Las Vegas, NV 89030
(702) 642-8300

DAYS INN NORTH
3227 Civic Center Dr.
North Las Vegas, NV 89030
(702) 399-3297

MOTEL 5
1645 N. Main St.
North Las Vegas, NV 89101
(702) 649-8984

STARLITE MOTEL
1873 Las Vegas Blvd. N.
North Las Vegas, NV 89030
(702) 642-1750

STRIP 91 MOTEL
2091 Las Vegas Blvd. N.
North Las Vegas, NV 89030
(702) 642-1138

VEGAS CHALET MOTEL
2401 Las Vegas Blvd. N.
North Las Vegas, NV 89030
(702) 642-2115

OLD NEVADA
POPULATION: N/A

BONNIE SPRINGS OLD NEVADA
1 Gunfighter Land
Old Nevada, NV 89004
(702) 875-4400

ORVADA
POPULATION: N/A

ROCK VIEW MOTEL
Hwy. 95 N., P.O. Box 109
Old Nevada, NV 89425
(702) 272-3337

OVERTON
POPULATION: N/A

OVERTON MOTEL
137 N. Main, P.O. Box 577
Overton, NV 89040
(702) 397-2463

PLAZA MOTEL
231 S. Main
Overton, NV 89040
(702) 397-2414

PAHRUMP
POPULATION: N/A

CHARLOTTA INN MOTEL
Hwy 160 S., P.O. Box 157
Pahrump, NV 89041
(702) 727-5445

PAHRUMP
Continued

PAHRUMP STATION - DAYS INN
Hwy 160 Loop Rd., P.O. Box 38
Pahrump, NV 89041
(800) 325-2525

SADDLE WEST HOTEL & CASINO
Hwy 160 S., P.O. Box 234
Pahrump, NV 89041
(800) 522-5953

PARADISE VALLEY
POPULATION: N/A

STONEHOUSE GUEST RANCH
P.O. Box 77
Paradise Valley, NV 89426
(800) 447-6411

PIOCHE
POPULATION: N/A

HARTLY MOTEL
La Cour St., P.O. Box 300
Pioche, NV 89043
(702) 962-5551

HUTCHINGS MOTEL
Hwy. 93, P.O. Box 353
Pioche, NV 89043
(702) 962-5404

RENO
POPULATION: N/A

ADVENTURE INN
3575 S. Virginia St.
Reno, NV 89502
(800) 937-1436

AIRPORT PLAZA HOTEL
1981 Terminal Way
Reno, NV 89502-3255
(800) 648-3525

AMERICANA INN
340 Lake St.
Reno, NV 89501
(702) 786-4422

ASPEN MOTEL
495 Lake St.
Reno, NV 89501
(800) 329-6011

BED & BREAKFAST - SOUTH RENO
136 Andrew Lane
Reno, NV 89511
(702) 849-0772

BEST WESTERN - CONTINENTAL LODGE
1885 S. Virginia St.
Reno, NV 89502
(800) 626-1900

BEST WESTERN - DANIEL'S
Motor Lodge
375 N. Sierra St.
Reno, NV 89501

BIG 8 MOTEL
795 W. Fourth St.
Reno, NV 89503
(702) 329-3420

**BOB CASHELL'S HORSESHOE
CLUB**
222 N. Sierra St.
Reno, NV 89501
(800) 843-7403

BONANZA CASINO & MOTEL
4720 N. Virginia St.
Reno, NV 89506
(702) 323-2724

BONANZA MOTOR INN
215 W. Fourth St.
Reno, NV 89501
(702) 322-8632

CABANA MOTEL
370 West St.
Reno, NV 89501
(702) 786-2977

CAPRI MOTEL
895 N. Virginia St.
Reno, NV 89501
(702) 323-8398

CARRIAGE INN
690 W. Fourth St.
Reno, NV 89503
(702) 329-8848

CASTAWAY INN
525 W. Second St.
Reno, NV 89503
(702) 329-2555

CAVALIER MOTOR LODGE
150 Island Ave.
Reno, NV 89502
(702) 323-1881

CENTER LODGE
200 S. Center St.
Reno, NV 89501
(702) 329-9000

CHEERS HOTEL & CASINO
567 W. Fourth St.
Reno, NV 89503
(702) 322-8181

CIRCUS CIRCUS HOTEL & CASINO
500 N. Sierra St., P.O. Box 5880
Reno, NV 89503
(702) 648-5010

CITY CENTER MOTEL
365 West St.
Reno, NV 89501
(702) 323-8880

CLARION HOTEL CASINO
3800 S. Virginia St., P.O. Box 70130
Reno, NV 89570-0130
(800) 723-6500

COACH INN
500 N. Center St.
Reno, NV 89501
(702) 323-3222

COLONIAL INN HOTEL & CASINO
250 N. Arlington Ave.
Reno, NV 89501
(800) 336-7366

COLONIAL MOTOR INN
232 West St.
Reno, NV 89501
(800) 255-7366

COMSTOCK HOTEL & CASINO
200 West Second St.
Reno, NV 89501
(800) 648-4866

CREST INN
525 West Fourth St.
Reno, NV 89501
(702) 329-9000

RENO
Continued

CROSBY'S LODGE
Sutcliffe Star Route
Reno, NV 89510
(702) 476-0400

DAYS INN
701 E. Seventh St.
Reno, NV 89512
(800) 448-4555

DESERT SUNSET HOTEL
1435 E. Fourth St.
Reno, NV 89512
(702) 329-5300

DONNER INN MOTEL
720 West Fourth St.
Reno, NV 89503
(702) 323-1851

DOWNTOWNER MOTOR LODGE
150 Stevenson St.
Reno, NV 89503
(702) 322-1188

DUTCH WIFE MOTEL
4275 W. Fourth St.
Reno, NV 89503
(702) 747-4701

EASY 8 MOTEL
255 W. Fifth St.
Reno, NV 89503
(702) 322-4588

EL CORTEZ HOTEL
239 W. Second St.
Reno, NV 89501
(702) 322-9161

EL LOBO MOTEL & CAFE
1659 N. Virginia St.
Reno, NV 89503
(702) 323-8309

EL PATIO MOTEL
3495 S. Virginia St.
Reno, NV 89502
(702) 825-6666

EL RAY MOTEL
330 N. Arlington
Reno, NV 89501
(702) 329-6669

EL TAVERN MOTEL
1801 W. Fourth
Reno, NV 89503
(702) 322-4504

ELDORADO HOTEL/CASINO
345 N. Virginia St., P.O. Box 3399
Reno, NV 89501
(800) 648-4597

EVERYBODY'S INN
1756 E. Fourth St.
Reno, NV 89502
(702) 323-6577

EXECUTIVE INN
205 S. Sierra St.
Reno, NV 89501
(800) 849-4545

FANTASY INN
2905 S. Virginia St.
Reno, NV 89502
(702) 662-8812

FARRIS MOTEL
1752 E. Fourth St.
Reno, NV 89501
(702) 322-3190

FIRESIDE INN
205 E. Fourth St.
Reno, NV 89501
(702) 786-1666

FITZGERALDS CASINO/HOTEL
255 N. Virginia St., P.O. Box 1291
Reno, NV 89504
(800) 648-5022

FLAMINGO HILTON RENO
255 N. Sierra St., P.O. Box 1291
Reno, NV 89504
(800) 648-4882

FLAMINGO MOTEL
520 N. Center St.
Reno, NV 89501
(800) FOR-RENO

GATEKEEPER INN
221 W. Fifth St.
Reno, NV 89503
(702) 786-3500

GATEWAY INN COMPLEX
1275 Stardust St.
Reno, NV 89503
(800) 345-2910

GOLD COIN MOTEL
2555 E. Fourth St.
Reno, NV 89512
(702) 323-0237

GOLD DUST WEST CASINO
444 Vine St., P.O. Box 2959
Reno, NV 89503
(702) 323-2211

GOLD KEY MOTEL
445 Lake St.
Reno, NV 89503
(702) 323-0731

GOLDEN WEST MOTOR LODGE
530 N. Virginia St.
Reno, NV 89501
(702) 329-2192

GRAND HOTEL
239 E. Plaza
Reno, NV 89501
(702) 322-2944

HARRAH'S RENO CASINO/HOTEL
219 N. Center St., P.O. Box 10
Reno, NV 89504
(800) 423-1121

HEART O TOWN MOTEL
520 N. Virginia St.
Reno, NV 89501
(702) 322-4066

HI HO MOTOR LODGE
1233 E. Fourth St.
Reno, NV 89512
(702) 323-1583

HO HUM HOTEL
1025 S. Virgina St.
Reno, NV 89502
(702) 322-9630

HOLIDAY HOTEL/CASINO
111 Mill St., P.O. Box 2700
Reno, NV 89504
(800) 648-5431

HOLIDAY INN - CONVENTION CENTER
5851 S. Virginia St.
Reno, NV 89502
(800) 648-5431

HOLIDAY INN - RENO
1000 Sixth St.
Reno, NV 89512
(800) 648-4877

RENO
Continued

HORSESHOE MOTEL
490 Lake St.
Reno, NV 89501
(702) 786-5968

IN TOWN MOTEL
260 W. Fourth St.
Reno, NV 89503
(702) 323-1421

JUNIPER COURT HOTEL
320 Evans Ave.
Reno, NV 89501
(702) 329-7002

KENO MOTEL NO. 1
322 N. Arlington Ave.
Reno, NV 89501
(702) 322-6281

KENO MOTEL NO. 2
331 West St.
Reno, NV 89501
(702) 322-4146

KEY MARTIN LODGE
6950 S. Virginia
Reno, NV 89511
(702) 853-6504

LA QUINTA INN
4001 Market St.
Reno, NV 89502
(800) 531-5900

LAKEMILL LODGE
200 Mill St., P.O. Box 321
Reno, NV 89501
(800) 648-3530

LENOX HOTEL
427 Evans Ave.
Reno, NV 89501
(702) 323-6751

LEO COURT
49 High St.
Reno, NV 89502
(702) 329-1512

LIDO INN
280 W. Fourth St.
Reno, NV 89501
(702) 322-3822

LONGHORM MOTEL
844 S. Virginia St.
Reno, NV 89502
(702) 322-2633

MAJESTIC INN
400 N. Virginia St.
Reno, NV 89501
(702) 322-2868

MARDI GRAS MOTOR LODGE
200 W. Fourth St.
Reno, NV 89505
(702) 329-7470

MARK TWAIN MOTEL
2201 s. Virginia ST.
Reno, NV 89502
(702) 826-2101

MIDTOWN MOTEL
611 W. Second St.
Reno, NV 89503
(702) 323-7178

MINER'S INN
1651 N. Virginia St.
Reno, NV 89506
(800) 626-1900

MOTEL 500
500 S. Center St.
Reno, NV 89501
(702) 786-2777

MOTEL 6 - RENO CENTRAL
866 N. Wells Ave.
Reno, NV 89512
(702) 786-9852

MOTEL 6 - RENO SOUTH
1901 S. Virginia St.
Reno, NV 89502
(702) 827-0255

MOTEL 6 - SOUTH CENTRAL
666 N. Wells Ave.
Reno, NV 89512
(702) 329-8681

MOTEL 6 - RENO WEST
1400 Stardust St.
Reno, NV 89503
(702) 747-7390

MURF'S TIME ZONE MOTEL
448 Lake St.
Reno, NV 89501
(800) 322-4666

NEVADA INN
330 E. Second St.
Reno, NV 89501
(800) 999-9686

OLYMPIC APARTMENT HOTEL
195 W. Second St.
Reno, NV 89501
(702) 323-0726

OX-BOW MOTOR LODGE
941 South Virtginia St.
Reno, NV 89509
(702) 329-1483

OXFORD MOTEL
11 Lake St.
Reno, NV 89501
(800) 648-3044

PARK VILLA APARTMENTS MOTEL
61 S. Park St.
Reno, NV 89502
(702) 322-0983

PEPPERMILL HOTEL CASINO
2707 S. Virginia St.
Reno, NV 89502
(800) 648-6992

PIONEER INN HOTEL/CASINO
221 S. Virginia St.
Reno, NV 89501
(800) 879-8879

PLAZA MOTOR LODGE
11 E. Plaza
Reno, NV 89501
(702) 786-1077

PLAZA RESORT CLUB
121 West St.
Reno, NV 89501
(800) 648-5990

PONDEROSA HOTEL
515 S. Virginia St.
Reno, NV 89501
(800) 228-6820

PONDEROSA LODGE
1400 E. Fourth St.
Reno, NV 89512
(702) 323-1400

PONDEROSA MOTEL
595 Lake St.
Reno, NV 89501
(702) 786-3070

RENO
Continued

R&R LODGE
500 N. Lake St., P.O. Box 751
Reno, NV 89504
(800) 648-3600

RANCH MOTEL
7400 S. Virginia St.
Reno, NV 89511
(702) 851-1129

RANCHO NAVALTO MOTEL
1455 W. Fourth St.
Reno, NV 89503
(702) 324-5000

RANCHO SIERRA MOTEL
411 W. Fourth St.
Reno, NV 89503
(702) 322-2761

REINDEER LODGE
9000 Mt. Rose Hwy.
Reno, NV 89511
(702) 849-9902

RENO 8 MOTEL
1113 E. Fourth St.
Reno, NV 89512
(702) 786-6828

RENO HILTON
2500 E. Second St.
Reno, NV 89595
(800) 648-5080

RENO RAMADA HOTEL CASINO
Sixth & Lake St., P.O. Box 751
Reno, NV 89504
(800) 648-3600

RENO RIVIERA
395 W. First St.
Reno, NV 89503
(800) FOR-RENO

RENO ROYAL PARK N WALK MOTEL
350 West St.
Reno, NV 89501
(702) 323-4477

RENO SPA RESORT CLUB
140 Court St.
Reno, NV 89501
(800) 634-6981

RENO TRAVELODGE DOWNTOWN
655 W. Fourth St.
Reno, NV 89503
(800) 255-3050

RIVER HOUSE MOTOR HOTEL
2 Lake St., P.O. Box 2425
Reno, NV 89505
(702) 329-0036

RIVERBOAT HOTEL & CASINO
34 W. Second St.
Reno, NV 89501
(800) 888-5525

RODEWAY INN
2050 Market St.
Reno, NV 89502
(800) 648-3800

SAGE MOTEL
411 Lake St.
Reno, NV 89501
(702) 329-4084

ST. FRANCIS HOTEL
354 N. Virginia St.
Reno, NV 89501
(702) 323-4161

SANDMAN HOTEL
1755 E. Fourth St.
Reno, NV 89512
(702) 322-0385

SANDS REGENCY HOTEL/CASINO
345 N. Arlington Ave.
Reno, NV 89501
(800) 648-3553

SAVOY MOTOR LODGE
705 N. Virginia St.
Reno, NV 89501
(800) FOR-RENO

SEASONS INN
495 West St.
Reno, NV 89503
(702) 322-6000

7-11 MOTOR LODGE
465 W. Second St.
Reno, NV 89503
(702) 348-8770

777 MOTEL
777 S. Virginia St.
Reno, NV 89501
(702) 786-0405

SHAMROCK INN
505 N. Center St.
Reno, NV 89501
(702) 786-5182

SHOWBOAT INN
660 N. Virginia
Reno, NV 89501
(702) 786-4032

SILVER CHAPPARAL MOTEL
645 S. Virtginia St.
Reno, NV 89501
(800) FOR-RENO

SILVER DOLLAR MOTOR LODGE
817 N. Virginia St.
Reno, NV 89501
(702) 323-6875

SILVER SPUR MOTEL
4335 W. Fourth St.
Reno, NV 89523
(702) 747-4701

SILVER STATE LODGE
1791 W. Fourth St.
Reno, NV 89503
(702) 322-1380

SIX GUN MOTEL
1661 E. Sixth St.
Reno, NV 89512
(800) 648-3074

SPRING HILL INN
1450 Mill St.
Reno, NV 89502
(702) 788-8040

STARDUST LODGE
455 N. Arlington Ave.
Reno, NV 89509
(702) 322-5641

SUNDANCE MOTEL
850 N. Virginia St.
Reno, NV 89501
(702) 329-9248

SUNDOWNER HOTEL CASINO
450 N. Arlington
Reno, NV 89503
(800) 648-5490

TAHOE MOTEL
1650 E. Fourth St.
Reno, NV 89512
(702) 322-1491

RENO
Continued

TOWN HOUSE MOTOR LODGE
303 W. Second St.
Reno, NV 89503
(800) 367-7366

TOWN VIEW MOTOR LODGE
131 W. Third St.
Reno, NV 89501
(702) 329-1560

TOWN SITE MOTEL
250 W. Commercial Row
Reno, NV 89501
(702) 3322-0345

TRUCKEE RIVER LODGE
501 W. First St.
Reno, NV 89503
(800) 635-8950

UNIVERSITY INN
1001 N. Virginia St.
Reno, NV 89557
(702) 323-0321

UPTOWN MOTEL
570 N. Virginia St.
Reno, NV 89501
(702) 323-8906

VAGABOND INN
3131 S. Virinia St.
Reno, NV 89502
(800) 522-1555

VIRGINIAN HOTEL / CASINO
140 N. Virgina St.
Reno, NV 89501
(800) 874-5558

WASHOE INN
75 Pringle Way
Reno, NV 89501
(800) FOR-RENO

WESTERNER MOTEL
4395 W. Fourth St.
Reno, NV 89523
(702) 747-4701

WHITE COURT MOTEL
465 Evans Ave.
Reno, NV 89501
(702) 329-1957

WINDSOR HOTEL
214 West St.
Reno, NV 89501
(702) 323-6171

WONDER LODGE
430 Lake St.
Reno, NV 89501
(702) 786-6840

SEARCHLIGHT
POPULATION: N/A

EL REY LODGE
430 Hobson at I-95
Searchlight, NV 89406
(702) 297-1144

RENTERIA MOTEL
P.O. Box 769
Searchlight, NV 89406
(800) 297-1581

SPARKS
POPULATION: N/A

JOHN ASCUAGA'S NUGGET
1100 Nugget Ave., P.O. Box 797
Sparks, NV 89432-0797
(800) 843-2427

BEST INN, THE
255 N. McCarran Blvd.
Sparks, NV 89431
(702) 358-2222

BLUE FOUNTAIN MOTEL
1950 B St.
Sparks, NV 89431
(800) 367-7366

BRIARWOOD LODGE
1200 C St.
Sparks, NV 89431
(702) 358-7171

EMERALD MOTEL
145 15 St.
Sparks, NV 89431
(702) 358-5930

MCCARRAN HOUSE INN
55 E. Nugget Ave.
Sparks, NV 89431
(800) 3548-5798

MOTEL 6 - RENO EAST
2405 B. St.
Sparks, NV 89431
(702) 358-1080

NENDELS INN OF RENO / SPARKS
60 E. B St.
Sparks, NV 89431
(800) 547-0106

PONY EXPRESS LODGE
2406 Prater Way
Sparks, NV 89431
(702) 358-7110

SAFARI MOTEL
1800 B St.
Sparks, NV 89431
(702) 358-6443

SILVER CLUB HOTEL / CASINO
1040 B St.
Sparks, NV 89431
(800) 648-1137

SUNRISE MOTEL
210 B St.
Sparks, NV 89431
(800) FOR-RENO

THUNDERBIRD REORT CLUB
200 Nichols Blvd.
Sparks, NV 89431
(800) 821-4912

VICTORIAN INN
1555 B St.
Sparks, NV 89431
(702) 331-3203

WAGON TRAIN MOTEL
1662 B St.
Sparks, NV 89431
(702) 358-0468

WESTERN VILLIAGE INN & CASINO
815 E. Nichols Blvd.
Sparks, NV 89431
(800) 648-1170

TONOPAH
POPULATION: N/A

BEST WESTERN - HI-DESERT INN
323 Main St., P.O. Box 351
Tonopah, NV 89049
(800) 528-1234

JIM BUTLER MOTEL
100 Main St., P.O. Box 1352
Tonopah, NV 89049
(800) 635-9455

GOLDEN HILLS MOTEL
826 Erie Main, P.O. Box 906
Tonopah, NV 89049
(702) 482-6238

MIZPAH HOTEL / CASINO
100 Main St., P.O. Box 952
Tonopah, NV 89049
(702) 482-6202

SILVER QUEEN MOTEL
255 Erie Main, P.O. Box 311
Tonopah, NV 89049
(702) 482-6291

SILVER STRIKE MOTEL
N. Main St., P.O. Box 906
Tonopah, NV 89049
(702) 482-6266

STATION HOUSE
1100 Erie Main, P.O. Box 1351
Tonopah, NV 89049
(702) 482-9777

UNIONVILLE
POPULATION: N/A

**OLD PIONEER GARDEN B&B
GUEST RANCH**
Box 79 H-C 64
Unionville, NV 89418-9503
(702) 538-7585

VERDI
POPULATION: N/A

BOOMTOWN HOTEL/CASINO
I-80 at Garson Rd., P.O. Box 399
Verdi, NV 89439-0399
(800) 648-3790

VIRGINIA CITY
POPULATION: N/A

**CHOLLAR MANSION BED &
BREAKFAST**
565 S. D. St., P.O. Box 889
Virginia City, NV 89440
(702) 847-0777

COMSTOCK LODGE
875 S. C. St., P.O. Box 386
Virginia City, NV 89440
(702) 847-0233

GOLD HILL HOTEL
1540 Main St., P.O. Box 710
Virginia City, NV 89440
(702) 847-0111

**EDITH PALMER'S COUNTRY INN
B&B**
46 South B St., P.O. Box 756
Virginia City, NV 89440
(702) 847-0707

SUGAR LOAF MOTEL
416 S C St., P.O. Box 946
Virginia City, NV 89440
(702) 847-0505

VIRGINA CITY MOTEL
675 South C St., P.O. Box 556
Virginia City, NV 89440
(702) 847-0277

WELLS
POPULATION: N/A

BEST WESTERN - SAGE MOTEL
576 Sixth St., P.O. Box 343
Wells, NV 89835
(800) 528-1234

LONE STAR MOTEL
676 Sixth St., P.O. Box 426
Wells, NV 89835
(702) 752-3632

MOTEL 6
I-80 & Hwy. 93, P.O. Box 516
Wells, NV 89835
(702) 752-2116

LONE STAR MOTEL
676 Sixth St., P.O. Box 426
Wells, NV 89835
(702) 752-3632

MOTEL 6
I-80 & Hwy. 93, P.O. Box 516
Wells, NV 89835
(702) 752-2116

MOUNTAIN VIEW MOTEL
134 Sixth St., P.O. Box 732
Wells, NV 89835
(702) 752-3345

OLD WEST INN
456 Sixth St., P.O. Box 79
Wells, NV 89835
(702) 752-3888

OVERLAND HOTEL
P.O. Box 79
Wells, NV 89835
(702) 752-3888

SHARON MOTEL
633 Sixth St., P.O. Box 426
Wells, NV 89835
(702) 752-3232

SHELL CREST MOTEL
575 Sixth St., P.O. Box 426
Wells, NV 89835
(702) 752-3755

WAGON WHEEL
326 Sixth St., P.O. Box 397
Wells, NV 89835
(702) 752-2151

WELLS CHINATOWN
455 S. Humboldt Ave., P.O. Box 96
Wells, NV 89835
(702) 752-2101

WENDOVER
POPULATION: N/A

**NEVADA CROSSING HOTEL/
CASINO**
P.O. Box 2457
Wendover, NV 89883
(800) 537-0207

PEPPERMILL INN & CASINO
680 Wendover Blvd.
Wendover, NV 89883
(800) 648-9660

WENDOVER
Continued

STATE LINE/SILVER SMITH
Hotel Casino
100 Wendover Blvd., P.O. Box 789
Wendover, NV 89883
(800) 848-7300

SUPER 8 MOTEL
1325 Wendover Blvd., P.O. Box 2259
Wendover, NV 89883
(800) 848-8888

WINNEMUCCA
POPULATION: N/A

BEST WESTERN - HOLIDAY MOTEL
670 W. Winnemucca Blvd.
Winnemucca, NV 89445
(800) 633-6435

BEST WESTERN - RED LION
Inn & Casino
741 W. Winnemucca Blvd.
Winnemucca, NV 89445
(800) 633-6435

BULL HEAD MOTEL
500 E. Winnemucca Blvd.
Winnemucca, NV 89445
(702) 623-3636

COZY MOTEL
344 E. Winnemucca Blvd.
Winnemucca, NV 89445
(702) 623-2615

DOWNTOWN MOTEL
251 E. Winnemucca Blvd.
Winnemucca, NV 89445
(702) 623-2394

FRONTIER MOTEL
477 E. Winnemucca Blvd.
Winnemucca, NV 89445
(702) 623-2915

GOLD COUNTRY INN
921 E. Winnemucca Blvd.
Winnemucca, NV 89445
(800) 346-5306

LA VILLA MOTEL
Fourth & Aiken
Winnemucca, NV 89445
(702) 623-2334

MODEL T MOTEL
1122 Winnemucca Blvd.
Winnemucca, NV 89445
(702) 623-1180

NEDA MOTEL
300 W. Winnemucca Blvd.
Winnemucca, NV 89445
(702) 623-3703

NEVADA MOTEL
635 W. Winnemucca Blvd.
Winnemucca, NV 89445
(702) 623-5281

PARK MOTEL
740 W. Winnemucca Blvd.
Winnemucca, NV 89445
(702) 623-2810

PYRENEES MOTEL
714 W. Winnemucca Blvd.
Winnemucca, NV 89445
(800) 238-9754

SCOTT SHADY COURT
400 First St., P.O. Box 670
Winnemucca, NV 89445
(702) 623-3646

STARDUST MOTEL
451 E. Winnemucca Blvd.
Winnemucca, NV 89445
(702) 623-3646

THUNDERBIRD MOTEL
511 E. Winnemucca Blvd.
Winnemucca, NV 89445
(702) 623-3661

TOWN HOUSE MOTEL
375 Monroe
Winnemucca, NV 89445
(702) 623-3620

VAL-U INN
125 E. Winnemucca Blvd.
Winnemucca, NV 89445
(800) 443-7777

WINNERS HOTEL/CASINO
185 W. Winnemucca Blvd.
Winnemucca, NV 89445
(800) 648-4770

RANCH HOUSE MOTEL
311 W. Bridge St.
Yerington, NV 89447
(702) 463-2200

ROBRIC RANCH B&B
Osborne Lane, P.O. Box 2
Yerington, NV 89447
(702) 463-3515

YERINGTON HOTEL APARTMENTS
103 N. West
Yerington, NV 89447
(702) 463-5563

YERINGTON
POPULATION: N/A

CITY CENTER MOTEL
307 N. Main St.
Yerington, NV 89447
(702) 463-2135

HARBOR HOUSE B&B
39 N. Center
Yerington, NV 89447
(702) 463-2991

IN TOWN MOTEL
111 S. Main St.
Yerington, NV 89447
(702) 463-2164

EXCURSIONS

NORTHERN NEVADA

Jarbridge

This is a perfect location for hikers, bikers, campers, fishers, and hunters. Don't forget your camera! The **Jarbridge Wilderness Area** contains approximately 65,000 acres of land filled with outstanding mountain scenery. You'll find eight peaks that rise upwards to 10,000 feet above sea level.

1008 Burley Ave.
Buhl, ID 93316
(208) 543-4129

Northeastern Nevada Museum

Topics include the natural world, Native American art, mining exhibits in miniaturized form, weaponry, and much more!

1515 Idaho St.
Elke, NV 89801
(702) 738-3418

Ruby Mountain Wilderness Area Horseback Rides

You couldn't dream of a better experience on horseback! Guided tours are available for different types of riders, regardless of ability. You can choose to ride anywhere from half-a-day to a week. Bring your camera along and get ready to take some fantastic pictures along the way. Many of the riders bring fishing poles for good fishing between rides.

227 Belloak Court
Elko, NV 89801
(702) 738-7539

Wild Horse State Recreation Area

This extraordinary part of the state is particularly beautiful. The recreation area comprises approximately 120 acres of exceptional land. Horseback riding, fishing, hunting, sight-seeing and photography are the major attractions that motivate people to come here.

Elko, NV 89801
(702) 758-6493

Pershing County Marzen House Museum

This house was built in 1874 on a 3,400-acre spread of land. Many of its original contents are still left as they were over a century ago. You can see Indian artifacts, mining equipment, and more. If you've ever wondered what it must have been like to be an American cowboy during the late 1800's, you may get a little bit closer to answering that question.

P.O. Box 566
Marzen Lane
Lovelock, NV 89419
(702) 273-7213 / (702) 273-2053

Buckaroo Hall Of Fame

There was a time in our history when every child thought about what it would be like to be a cowboy. Out in the vast countryside, working the land, and riding a horse ... does life get any better than this? A whole plethora of memorabilia honoring the American cowboy is on display for public viewing.

P.O. Box 566
Marzen Lane
Lovelock, NV 89419
(702) 273-7213

WESTERN NEVADA

Nevada State Museum

If you'd like to learn more about Nevada's history, this museum is an excellent start. Some of the displays include a full-size model underground mine, exhibits of coin minting equipment, and a look into the state's geology and culture.

600 N. Carson St.
Carson City, NV 89710
(702) 687-4810

Nevada State Railroad Museum

This museum houses a fine collection of over 50 segments of railroad equipment, including two fully restored Virgina & Truckee trains, freight cars, a few passenger cars, and the show stopper of them all, a 1920's Edwards Motor Car If you like railroad paraphernalia, this is the place to go.

2180 S. Carson St.
Carson City, NV 89710
(702) 687-6953

Genoa Courthouse Museum

This museum shows you the Old Douglas County courthouse, which was constructed in 1865. It's an informative look at how Nevada's old justice system worked and how this particular courthouse appeared during that time. Other attractions include a jail house, a blacksmith shop, a kitchen, and a school room. You'll also see a fine exhibit of Washoe Indian artifacts.

P.O. Box 957
Genoa, NV 89411
(702) 782-4325

WALLEY'S HOT SPRINGS RESORT

These hot springs were originally designed in 1862 and later remodeled in 1979. There are six mineral baths to choose from, plus a sauna, a swimming room, and a workout facility.

2001 Foothill Rd.
P.O. Box 26
Genoa, NV 89411
(702) 782-8155

LAKE TAHOE NEVADA STATE PARK

Go swimming, boating, hiking, fishing, camping, mountain biking, and horseback riding at this beautiful park.

2005 Hwy. 28
P.O. Box 8867
Incline Village, NV 89540
(702) 831-0494

M.S. DIXIE CRUISESHIP

The **M.S. Dixie**, built 22 years ago, claims the right to be called Lake Tahoe's original paddlewheeler ship. Breakfast, lunch, and dinner tours are available daily through the scenic waters of Emerald Bay.

760 Hwy. 50
P.O. Box 1667
Zephyr Cove, NV 89448
(702) 588-3508

Ponderosa Ranch

Yes, this is the original ranch of the Western TV series, and both the ranch and the Cartwright home are available to tour. You can explore the grounds and view some spectacular carriages, rare farm equipment, automobiles, guns, and the full western town.

100 Ponderosa Ranch Rd.
Incline Village, NV 89451
(702) 831-0691

Bull Creek Ranch

This is one tour you'll never forget! If any of you enjoyed the silver screen motion picture *City Slickers*, this ranch offers a lot of the same qualities. You can participate in cattle drives, try your luck at roping and cutting, ride the beautiful **Sierra Nevada Mountains** by horseback, and more.

1850 W. Old Hwy. 40
Verdy, NV 89439
(702) 345-7600

Fleishman Planetarium

This is the best planetarium and astronomical museum in Nevada. It's the oldest of its kind, and offers exciting attractions that should keep you and your family happy for the day. The **Star Theater** is a brilliant attraction that shows planetarium shows and Cinema 360 "hemisphere" movies. You'll also find a fabulous Solar System display and other exhibits that are based on astronomy and space science. You can participate in one of the free sky-viewing sessions that are available upon request.

1650 North Virgina St.
Reno, NV 89557
(702) 784-4812

Harold's Club Gun Collection

This is one of the finest collections of guns in the world. In fact, a good assortment of them were used during the days of the turbulent Old West. Handguns, rifles, shotguns, and an additional 500 firearms manufactured between the 13th and 20th century are on display.

1650 North Virgina St.
Reno, NV 89557
(702) 784-4812

National Automobile Museum

Any fine car collector will tell you that this is unquestionably one of the best collections of automobiles in the world. Two hundred antiques, vintage, and special interest vehicles are on display as colorful period pieces. You'll find comprehensive movie presentations, hands-on exhibits, and more.

1650 North Virgina St.
Reno, NV 89557
(702) 784-4812

Wilbur D. May Arboretum And Botanical Gardens

You'll find more than eight acres of lushly landscaped gardens that show of the many beautiful shrubs, trees, and flowering plants. Six hundred species of Nevada plant life are showcased along rows of walking-paths that are a joy to discover

The best time of the year to see these plants in their most attractive form is between the beginning of April and the tail end of May.

1502 Washington St.
Rancho San Raphael Park
Reno, NV 89503
(702) 785-4153

CENTRAL NEVADA

Great Basin National Park

Great Basin National Park measures over 77,000 acres and is Nevada's first national park. You'll find many fascinating areas to explore. One of the trails will lead you into the world's largest and oldest area of bristlecone pine trees.

Baker, NV 89311
(702) 234-7331

Cave Lake State Recreation Area

This is a great place to unwind and take in the beauty of nature. Time holds no restrictions, you are free to do whatever you want. It really doesn't matter what you choose; walking, hiking, biking, fishing, picnicking, etc., are all great options.

P.O. Box 82
Eureka, NV 89316
(702) 728-4467

Hidden Cave

You'll love learning about this captivating archaeological site that provides a glimpse into Nevada's glorious past. Guided tours are available through the Churchill County Museum & Archives.

1050 S. Maine St.
Fallon, NV 89406
(702) 423-3677

Fort Churchill State

Established in 1860, this military fort was the last one of its kind to be active in Nevada. One particular attraction, *The Civil War Enactment*, shouldn't be missed.

Silver Springs, NV 89429
(702) 577-2345

SOUTH-CENTRAL NEVADA

Berlin-Ichthyosaur State Park

Berlin is an old mining town that came into being about the turn of the century You'll find fossils spread all over.

Ichthyosaurs were marine reptile dinosaurs that swam through this area approximately 225 million years ago. Some of their fossil remains are on display for your viewing pleasure.

Route 1, Box 32
Austin, NV 89310
(702) 867-3001

Rhyolite State Historic Site
Beatty Chamber Of Commerce

Bring your camera along to photograph this incredible ghost town that started attracting workers after the turn of the century Its humble remains have been chipped down to a collage of concrete ruins.

P.O. Box 956
Beatty, NV 89003
(702) 553-2424

Pahrump Valley Winery

As you enter this beautiful Mediterranean-style winery you'll instinctively know you're in for something special. You can enjoy a tour of the premises and take part in a gathering of wine tasting — a great way to spend a day.

The best part of the tour is when you discover a new wine, while relaxing and viewing some of the wonderful mountainous landscapes of **Mount Charleston**.

3810 Homestead Rd.
P.O. Box 1540
Pahrump, NV 89041
(800) 368-WINE

Million Dollar Courthouse

How could it be possible that a town would have to pay over a million dollars to build a courthouse that was originally budgeted at $20,000? High interest bonds coupled with an incompetent managerial staf – that's how! Today, the courthouse is fully restored and features historical documents, a jail, ofices, and a unique mining exhibit for your viewing pleasure.

Main St.
P.O. Box 515
Pioche, NV 89043
(702) 962-5207

Spring Valley State Park

Camping is strictly on a first-come, first-serve basis. The park offers splendid trails that you can explore on land or by water. Its an excellent location to relax and take in some inspirational scenery.

Logan Feild Rd.
P.O. Box 326
Tonopah, NV 89049
(702) 482-9676

SOUTHERN NEVADA

Black Canyon River Raft Tours

Be a part of a one day exploration tour by raft that starts at **Hoover Dam** and ends at the gorgeous **Willow Beach Resort and Marina**.

1297 Boulder Hwy.
Boulder City, NV 89005
(702) 293-3776

Ethel M Chocolate Factory & Cactus Garden

Once you take the self-guided tour through this wonderful factory, you'll have visions of being a kid again. It's fun to watch the factory machinery working in a harmonious pattern, as it produces great desert treats.

The factory also showcases two and a half acres of cactus fields. With over 350 species, it is certainly one of the greatest collections of cactus plants in the world.

2 Cactus Garden Dr.
Henderson, NV 89014
(702) 458-8864

Floyd Lamb State Park

If there was a "Hall Of Fame" for state parks, this would be one among an elite grouping. It features everything from mature grown trees, fabulous landscaping, places to fish and hike, horseback riding, and even a horse-drawn carriage tour when weather permits. The Las Vegas Gun Club offers skeet shooting for experts and amateurs alike.

9200 Tule Springs Rd.
Las Vegas, NV 89131
(702) 456-5413

NEVADA INDEX

NEW MEXICO

THE LAND OF ENCHANTMENT

NEW MEXICO/COUNTIES AND CITIES

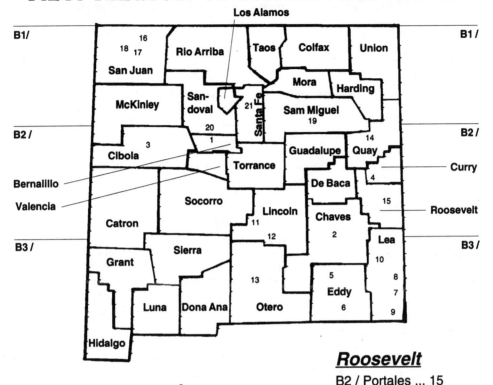

Bernalillo
B2 / Albuquerque ... 1

Chaves
B2 / Roswell ... 2

Cibola
B2 / Grants Milan ... 3

Curry
B2 / Cannon AFB ... 4

Eddy
B3 / Artesia ... 5
B3 / Carlsbad ... 6

Lea
B3 / Eunice ... 7
B3 / Hobbs ... 8
B3 / Jal ... 9
B3 / Lovington ... 10

Lincoln
B2 / Carrizozo ... 11
B2 / Ruidoso ... 12

Otero
B3 / Alamogordo ... 13

Quay
B2 / Tucumcari ... 14

Roosevelt
B2 / Portales ... 15

San Juan
B1 / Aztec ... 16
B1 / Farmington ... 17
B1 / Kirtland ... 18

San Miguel
B1 / Las Vegas ... 19

Sandoval
B1 / Rio Rancho ... 20

Santa Fe
B1 / Santa Fe ... 21

BERNALILLO COUNTY

ARROYO DEL OSO GOLF COURSE

7001 Osuna N.E., Albuquerque, NM 87109 / (505) 884-7505

BASIC INFORMATION

Course Type: Public
Year Built: 1965
Architect: Snyder
Local Pro: Guy Wimberly & Bob Meiering

Course: Champion (18 / Par 72)
Holes: 27

Back: 6,892 yds. Rating: 72.0 Slope: 121
Middle: 6,545 yds. Rating: 70.4 Slope: 116
Ladies: 5,998 yds. Rating: 72.3 Slope: 117

Tee Time: 7 days in advance.
Price: $12.05

Credit Cards:	■	Restaurant:	■
Driving Range:	■	Lounge:	
Practice Green:	■	Meeting Rooms:	■
Locker Room:		Tennis:	
Rental Clubs:	■	Swimming:	
Walkers:	■	Jogging Trails:	
Snack Bar:		Boating:	

COURSE DESCRIPTION

With over 90,000 rounds of golf played here annually, this course is one of the busiest golfing attractions in New Mexico.

Take a look at the price of admission and you'll quickly know why: Seniors (age 62 and over) are admitted at $9.05 and Juniors (age 17 and younger) are admitted at $6.05.

Surprisingly enough, the course features a well-balanced layout that favors neither a fade nor a draw. You should notice a considerable gain in distance off your drives because of the rock bottom terrain that the layout was built upon.

DIRECTIONS

Take I-25 south to I-40 and go east to Louisiana. From this point, go north, until you see the course parking lot at the dead-end of the road.

LADERA GOLF COURSE

3401 Ladera Dr. N.W., Albuquerque, NM 87120 / (505) 836-4449

BASIC INFORMATION

Course Type: Public
Year Built: 1980
Architect: Dick Phelphs
Local Pro: Don Zamora

Course: N/A
Holes: 18 / Par 72

Back : 7,107 yds. Rating: 73.0 Slope: 123
Middle: 6,618 yds. Rating: 71.4 Slope: 119
Ladies: 5,966 yds. Rating: 71.8 Slope: 113

Tee Time: 7 days in advance.
Price: $8.40 - $12.05

Credit Cards:	■	Restaurant:	■
Driving Range:	■	Lounge:	
Practice Green:	■	Meeting Rooms:	
Locker Room:		Tennis:	
Rental Clubs:	■	Swimming:	
Walkers:	■	Jogging Trails:	
Snack Bar:	■	Boating:	

COURSE DESCRIPTION

You'll experience moments of excitement throughout this fabulous course. It offers a beautiful arrangement of holes that work beautifully together.

If you're new to mountain golf, you're going to love the distance your ball will travel in the thin mountain air. That's why the slope rating is only 123. That's unheard of for a venue measuring over 7,000 yards.

The putting greens are extremely large and forgiving, which makes them a pleasure to approach; but once on, they are difficult to read.

DIRECTIONS

Take I-40 and Coors Blvd. north. At the second set of lights, make a left onto Sequioa St. and proceed straight to the course.

LOS ALTOS GOLF COURSE
9717 Cooper N.E., Albuquerque, NM 87123 / (505) 298-1897

BASIC INFORMATION

Course Type: Public
Year Built: 1965
Architect: Red Swift
Local Pro: Janelle Freeman

Course: N/A
Holes: 18 / Par 71

Back: 5,759 yds. Rating: 67.0 Slope: N/A
Middle: N/A Rating: N/A Slope: N/A
Ladies: 5,283 yds. Rating: 69.0 Slope: N/A

Tee Time: 7 days in advance.
Price: $18

Credit Cards: Restaurant: ■
Driving Range: ■   Lounge: ■
Practice Green: ■   Meeting Rooms:
Locker Room: Tennis:
Rental Clubs: ■   Swimming:
Walkers: ■   Jogging Trails:
Snack Bar: Boating:

COURSE DESCRIPTION

Although the course plays short, it still presents a formidable challenge with many interesting holes. You'll have to hit your drives accurately to land your ball safely on the tight fairways and away from the many mature cottonwood trees that can deflect and interfere with the direction of your ball's flight.

The 15th hole, a par-5, stretches 425 yds., and is the hardest rated hole on the course. You'll need to hit both your drive and your approach shots accurately between the Carson River, which hugs the right side, and an irrigation canal that runs along the full length of the left side and down to the front of the green.

DIRECTIONS
Take Hwy. 395 south of Gardnerville and turn right on Riverview Dr.

PARADISE HILLS GOLF CLUB
10035 Country Club Dr. N.W., Albuquerque, NM 87106 / (505) 265-5636

BASIC INFORMATION

Course Type: Public
Year Built: 1964
Architect: William Lawerence
Local Pro: Sam Zimmerly

Course: N/A
Holes: 18 / Par 72

Back: 6,895 yds. Rating: 72.0 Slope: 118
Middle: 6,629 yds. Rating: 70.8 Slope: 116
Ladies: 6,098 yds. Rating: 73.5 Slope: 118

Tee Time: 7 days in advance.
Price: $9 - $24

Credit Cards: ■   Restaurant: ■
Driving Range: ■   Lounge: ■
Practice Green: ■   Meeting Rooms: ■
Locker Room: Tennis:
Rental Clubs: ■   Swimming:
Walkers: ■   Jogging Trails:
Snack Bar: ■   Boating:

COURSE DESCRIPTION

Paradise Hills Golf Club offers a country club feel with public price admission.

The course was remodeled in 1991 and it has never looked better. If you're looking for a course with a friendly atmosphere, this is one you'll want to consider.

The design is straightforward and easily understood and features many mature trees throughout. The only real difference between the back-nine and the front-nine is that the front favors a draw while the back favors a fade.

DIRECTIONS
Take the I-25 west on Paseo Del Norte and turn right on Golf Course Rd. and left on Country Club Lane.

BERNALILLO COUNTY

UNIVERSITY OF NEW MEXICO

University Blvd. S.E., Albuquerque, NM 87131 / (505) 277-4546

BASIC INFORMATION

Course Type: Public
Year Built: 1967
Architect: Robert Lawrence
Local Pro: Henry Sandles

Course: Championship (18 / Par 72)
Holes: 27

Back : 7,248 yds. Rating: 74.7 Slope: 138
Middle: 6,581 yds. Rating: 71.8 Slope: 131
Ladies: 6,031 yds. Rating: 75.1 Slope: 131

Tee Time: Thursday for the following week.
Price: $18 - $20

Credit Cards:	■	Restaurant:	■
Driving Range:	■	Lounge:	■
Practice Green:	■	Meeting Rooms:	■
Locker Room:	■	Tennis:	
Rental Clubs:	■	Swimming:	
Walkers:	■	Jogging Trails:	
Snack Bar:	■	Boating:	

COURSE DESCRIPTION

The course is set on a semi-desert terrain with rolling fairways and very large undulating greens that are nicely bunkered and open to many different pin positions.

The astronomical slope rating seems specifically designed for low handicap players, yet the course does offer a fair challenge for average players if they choose to play from the middle tees. You'll find very few blind shots and forced carries.

This scenic course features beautiful wildlife such as: roadrunners, hawks, owls, rabbits, and even a few coyotes. It's been rated in **Golf Digest's** top 75 courses and was number one in New Mexico's **Golfweek** magazine.

DIRECTIONS

Take the Rio Bravo exit from I-25. Go east and look for the course on your left.

VALLE GRANDE GOLF COURSE

P.O. Box 1736, Bernalillo, NM 87004 / (505) 867-9464

BASIC INFORMATION

Course Type: Semi-private
Year Built: 1990-91
Architect: Ken Killian
Local Pro: Roger Martinez

Course: Tamaya / Coronado (18 / Par 72)
Holes: 27

Back: 6,469 yds. Rating: 72.7 Slope: 123
Middle: 5,922 yds. Rating: 69.9 Slope: 118
Ladies: 4,924yds. Rating: 68.3 Slope: 118

Tee Time: 3 - 7 days in advance.
Price: $20 - $30

Credit Cards:	■	Restaurant:	■
Driving Range:	■	Lounge:	■
Practice Green:	■	Meeting Rooms:	
Locker Room:		Tennis:	
Rental Clubs:	■	Swimming:	
Walkers:	■	Jogging Trails:	
Snack Bar:	■	Boating:	

COURSE DESCRIPTION

The *Valle Grande Golf Course* at Santa Ana Pueblo features 27 holes of suburb links golf along the Sandia mountains. The English translation for Sandia is "Watermelon," which is the color (red) of the mountains in the late afternoon.

One of the most distinctive features of a links style course is the way it blends with its natural surroundings without disturbing the ecosystem in which it was built around. You'll be playing through grass bunkers, mounds, sloping fairways, and undulating greens that are both fast and demanding. The natural cool breezes and stunning views of the mountains are unbeatable.

DIRECTIONS

Take I-25 to Exit 242 and go west to St. Rd. 44. Turn right at Jemez Canyon Rd.

SPRING RIVER GOLF COURSE

1612 W. 8 St., Roswell, NM 88201 / (505) 622-9506

BASIC INFORMATION

Course Type: Municipal
Year Built: N/A
Architect: N/A
Local Pro: Gary Eller

Course: N/A
Holes: 18 / Par 72

Back : 6,488 yds. Rating: 69.0 Slope: 116
Middle: 6,229 yds. Rating: 68.1 Slope: 113
Ladies: 5,419 yds. Rating: 70.5 Slope: 112

Tee Time: 2 days in advance.
Price: $10

Credit Cards:	■	Restaurant:	
Driving Range:	■	Lounge:	
Practice Green:	■	Meeting Rooms:	
Locker Room:		Tennis:	
Rental Clubs:	■	Swimming:	
Walkers:	■	Jogging Trails:	
Snack Bar:	■	Boating:	

COURSE DESCRIPTION

The average slope rating according to the United States Golf Association (USGA) is 113 and that is exactly how this course plays from the middle tees.

Seniors love the way the course plays from the front tees, and better players are up to the test from the back tees which bring both water and sand into play to make things a little more interesting and exciting.

The 14th hole (566 yds./par-5) is the number one handicap hole on the course. A good drive will allow long hitters an Eagle opportunity if they can hit their approach shot over water. Most players prefer to lay up.

DIRECTIONS

From 280 (a north-south Hwy.) turn west at 8th street (by Mc.Donalds) and go straight for 16-blocks to the course.

DOS LAGOS GOLF COURSE

N. 4 St., Anthony, NM 88021 / (505) 882-2830

BASIC INFORMATION

Course Type: Public
Year Built: 1960's
Architect: N/A
Local Pro: Mike Olson

Course: N/A
Holes: 18 / Par 72

Back : 6,424 yds. Rating: 70.4 Slope: 120
Middle: 6,226 yds. Rating: 69.4 Slope: 118
Ladies: 5,658 yds. Rating: 70.6 Slope: 111

Tee Time: 7 days in advance.
Price: $10 - $12

Credit Cards:		Restaurant:	■
Driving Range:	■	Lounge:	■
Practice Green:	■	Meeting Rooms:	■
Locker Room:	■	Tennis:	
Rental Clubs:	■	Swimming:	
Walkers:	■	Jogging Trails:	
Snack Bar:		Boating:	

COURSE DESCRIPTION

This is a wonderful course for shotmakers who are a little short on distance, but use their skills to maneuver the ball around each hole in the least amount of space.

The course is not very long, but it does hold a respectable Rating and Slope for all types of players. Low handicappers can use this course to sharpen up on their iron skills.

The terrain is mostly flat and straightforward. The front-nine is a little bit longer than the back, but you should find both equally challenging.

DIRECTIONS

Take I-10 west to Anthony Town (Exit 162) and make a left, about a half-mile away, at the next Stop sign. Your next available left will take you to the course. Look for it on your left side.

DONA ANA COUNTY

LAS CRUCES COUNTRY CLUB
2700 N. Main State Hwy. 70 E., Las Cruces, NM 88004 / (505) 526-8731

BASIC INFORMATION

Course Type: Semi-private
Year Built: 1928
Architect: Al Valestino (First 6-holes)
Local Pro: Bobby Deeves

Course: N/A
Holes: 18 / Par 72

Back : 6,324 yds. Rating: 69.6 Slope: 118
Middle: 6,094 yds. Rating: 68.5 Slope: 116
Ladies: 5,898 yds. Rating: 71.5 Slope: 112

Tee Time: 3 days in advance.
Price: $14 - $17

Credit Cards: ■   Restaurant: ■
Driving Range: ■   Lounge: ■
Practice Green: ■   Meeting Rooms: ■
Locker Room: Tennis:
Rental Clubs: ■   Swimming: ■
Walkers: ■   Jogging Trails:
Snack Bar: ■   Boating:

COURSE DESCRIPTION
Technically speaking, the *Las Cruces Country Club* is considered to be a private establishment. Yet it is open to the general public to play and experience.

The course was built in 1928 and still retains a little of the original character that has supported its longevity over the years. Like most of the traditional courses across the U.S., this one places accuracy above distance as the formidable challenge. You'll need to drive the ball straight and hit your approach shots to the proper landing areas along the small Bermuda greens.

DIRECTIONS
From I-25, take Hwy. 70 to the Main St. Exit. Go south for about 1 1/2 miles and look for the course on your left.

NEW MEXICO STATE UNIVERSITY GOLF COURSE
Box 3595, Las Cruces, NM 88003 / (505) 646-4131

BASIC INFORMATION

Course Type: Public
Year Built: 1961
Architect: Floyd Farley
Local Pro: Ross Nettles

Course: N/A
Holes: 18 / Par 72

Back : 7,040 yds. Rating: 72.5 Slope: 125
Middle: 6,659 yds. Rating: 70.0 Slope: 122
Ladies: 6,084 yds. Rating: 73.0 Slope: 121

Tee Time: Fri.(for weekdays) / Wed.
Price: $14.70 - $16.80

Credit Cards: ■   Restaurant:
Driving Range: ■   Lounge:
Practice Green: ■   Meeting Rooms:
Locker Room: Tennis:
Rental Clubs: ■   Swimming:
Walkers: ■   Jogging Trails:
Snack Bar: ■   Boating:

COURSE DESCRIPTION

You know you're in for a competitive course when it's owned by a University that has hosted some of the NCAA's most notable amateur golf tournaments.

You need to play the course aggressively if you're going to be playing from the Championship (back) tees. It's a strategically designed layout that features a collection of mature trees that often come into the play of action if you're not hitting your ball well.

The flat terrain of the front nine makes it the easier half of the course. The hilly back nine will often have you playing out of an uneven and difficult lie. This is an excellent challenge for all types of players.

DIRECTIONS
The course is on the southeast intersection of I-25 and University Blvd.

LAKE CARLSBAD GOLF COURSE
901 N. Muscatel, Carlsbad, NM 88220 / (505) 885-5444

BASIC INFORMATION

Course Type: Municipal
Year Built: 1956
Architect: N/A
Local Pro: John Heaton

Course: N/A
Holes: 18 / Par 72

Back : 6,067 yds. Rating: 66.5 Slope: 105
Middle: N/A Rating: N/A Slope: N/A
Ladies: 5,452 yds. Rating: 71.3 Slope: 110

Tee Time: Every Wednesday
Price: $14 - $17

Credit Cards:		Restaurant:	
Driving Range:	■	Lounge:	
Practice Green:	■	Meeting Rooms:	■
Locker Room:		Tennis:	
Rental Clubs:	■	Swimming:	
Walkers:	■	Jogging Trails:	
Snack Bar:	■	Boating:	

COURSE DESCRIPTION

This is certainly not a course that accomplished players will want to play, but if you're one of many high-handicappers, it may be one that will build up your confidence for the many harder courses you'll be playing in the future.

The fairways are generous in size and will allow you plenty of room to work the ball, yet you'll have to watch out for the out-of-bounds areas ... which incidently, are all over the course.

This is not your typical desert links course. What you'll find is a course that runs along a hilly terrain that at times can get rather difficult to hit out of.

DIRECTIONS

Take Hwy. 62 east to Carlsbad N.M. and follow the signs to the course. Make a right on Muscatel Ave. and follow the road straight to the course.

SILVER CITY GOLF CLUB
P.O. Box 1254, Silver City, NM 88062 / (505) 538-5041

BASIC INFORMATION

Course Type: Public
Year Built: 1958
Architect: N/A
Local Pro: Jim Smith

Course: N/A
Holes: 18 / Par 72

Back : 6,237 yds. Rating: 68.2 Slope: 115
Middle: 5,816 yds. Rating: 66.3 Slope: 111
Ladies: 5,240 yds. Rating: 68.9 Slope: 119

Tee Time: "Any ten-minute interval"
Price: $11.50 - $13.75

Credit Cards:		Restaurant:	
Driving Range:		Lounge:	
Practice Green:	■	Meeting Rooms:	
Locker Room:		Tennis:	
Rental Clubs:	■	Swimming:	
Walkers:	■	Jogging Trails:	
Snack Bar:		Boating:	

COURSE DESCRIPTION

If you're not one to take your golf seriously, you'll certainly enjoy the laid-back atmosphere that is associated with th e *Silver City Golf Club*.

If you're a male traveling with a female partner (or vice-versa) between May 28,29, and 30, you may want to compete in the infamous Mr. & Mrs. Tournament. "A total of 60 couples showed up last year," said one staff member, "... and everyone had a ball."

The main objective of this course is to allow high-handicappers a fun place to play without having to be bothered with outrageously difficult holes to bring down their playing spirits.

DIRECTIONS

Take Hwy. 90 south and keep your eyes open for the course on the left.

LEA/LINCOLN COUNTIES

OCOTILLO PARK GOLF COURSE

N. Lovington Hwy. P.O. Box 146, Hobbs, NM 88240 / (505) 397-9297

BASIC INFORMATION

Course Type: Public
Year Built: 1950's - 1960's
Architect: N/A
Local Pro: Doug Lyle

Course: N/A
Holes: 18 / Par 72

Back : 6,816 yds. Rating: 70.5 Slope: 118
Middle: 6,232 yds. Rating: 69.3 Slope: 115
Ladies: 5,245 yds. Rating: 69.0 Slope: 105

Tee Time: 7 days in advance.
Price: $3.50 - $16

Credit Cards:	■	Restaurant:	■
Driving Range:	■	Lounge:	
Practice Green:	■	Meeting Rooms:	■
Locker Room:	■	Tennis:	
Rental Clubs:	■	Swimming:	
Walkers:	■	Jogging Trails:	
Snack Bar:	■	Boating:	

COURSE DESCRIPTION

This ingenious golf course is a little bit tricky at first. You really have to pay attention to the yardage, for it seems as though the course plays longer than the numbers indicated on the scorecard.

The rough around the fairways is kept higher than most courses, making it mandatory to hit accurate drives to well-defined landing areas on the fairways, despite the fact that these fairways are wide. If you can hit a golf ball a long way, it will certainly work to your advantage, but accurate hitters will find it a pleasure to work around the course en route to a par or better.

DIRECTIONS

From Hobbs N.M., go north on Levington Hwy. for about 5 miles towards the Harry McAdams State Park. Look for the course on your left.

CREE MEADOWS COUNTRY CLUB

310 Country Club Dr., Ruidoso, NM 88345 / (505) 257-5815

BASIC INFORMATION

Course Type: Public
Year Built: 1947
Architect: N/A
Local Pro: Kent Beatty

Course: N/A
Holes: 18 / Par 72

Back: 5,952 yds. Rating: 66.2 Slope: 113
Middle: N/A Rating: N/A Slope: N/A
Ladies: 4,775 yds. Rating: 66.4 Slope: 104

Tee Time: 1 day in advance.
Price: $17 - $35

Credit Cards:	■	Restaurant:	■
Driving Range:		Lounge:	■
Practice Green:	■	Meeting Rooms:	■
Locker Room:	■	Tennis:	
Rental Clubs:	■	Swimming:	■
Walkers:	■	Jogging Trails:	
Snack Bar:	■	Boating:	

COURSE DESCRIPTION

The *Cree Meadows Country Club* offers a very playable layout that will open the door to many pars and birdies for beginners and seniors alike. It's a sensational course for people lacking the distance that it takes to play most of the modern-day courses that seem to be popping up all over the country. For this reason and others, the course has become a favorite stop for most of the area's senior citizen golfers.

If you can place your tee shots on the fairways, you should easily get your approach shots close to the pins on most occasions.

DIRECTIONS

Turn north in midtown at the Eagle Dr. stoplight. Make a right on North St. and a left on Country Club Dr.

LINCOLN/LOS ALAMOS COUNTIES

LINKS AT SIERRA BLANCA

105 Sierra Blanca Dr., Ruidoso, NM 88345 / (505) 258-5330

BASIC INFORMATION

Course Type: Public
Year Built: 1990
Architect: Jim Colbert
Local Pro: Jeff Miller

Course: N/A
Holes: 18 / par 72

Back : 7,003 yds. Rating: 72.9 Slope: 136
Middle: 6,505 yds. Rating: 70.7 Slope: 131
Ladies: 5,202 yds. Rating: 68.9 Slope: 111

Tee Time: 14 days in advance.
Price: $24 - $40

Credit Cards:	■	Restaurant:	■
Driving Range:	■	Lounge:	■
Practice Green:	■	Meeting Rooms:	■
Locker Room:		Tennis:	
Rental Clubs:	■	Swimming:	
Walkers:	■	Jogging Trails:	
Snack Bar:	■	Boating:	

COURSE DESCRIPTION

Jim Colbert is one of the most outstanding performers on the Senior PGA Tour. So it comes as no surprise that his taste in architecture is a reflection of his personal philosophy towards golf. This course is a remarkable extension of his thoughts and one you won't want to miss.

The hilly terrain of this layout lends itself perfectly to the overall playability of the course. The back tees demand long accurate drives to well defined landing areas.

DIRECTIONS

Take Hwy. 70 west to "The Inn Of The Mountain Gods" sign and follow the directions to the end. Make a left onto Sudderth St. and a right at the lights. You'll see the following sign: (Ski - Alpo - Hwy. 48).Go right onto Hwy. 48 (Merchant St.) and look for the course on your right.

LOS ALAMOS GOLF COURSE

4250 Diamond Dr., Los Alamos, NM 87544 / (505) 662-8139

BASIC INFORMATION

Course Type: Public
Year Built: 1947
Architect: N/A
Local Pro: Dennis McCloskey

Course: N/A
Holes: 18 / Par 72

Back : 6,440 yds. Rating: 69.7 Slope: 118
Middle: N/A Rating: N/A Slope: N/A
Ladies: 5,499 yds. Rating: 69.8 Slope: 113

Tee Time: Every Wednesday
Price: $14 - $17.50

Credit Cards:	■	Restaurant:	
Driving Range:	■	Lounge:	■
Practice Green:	■	Meeting Rooms:	■
Locker Room:	■	Tennis:	
Rental Clubs:	■	Swimming:	
Walkers:	■	Jogging Trails:	■
Snack Bar:	■	Boating:	

COURSE DESCRIPTION

No one really knows who was responsible for the design of this course, yet there is speculation that the government may have had a part in it. You may find it interesting to know that this was the location in which the "The Bomb" was built during WW II, and so it was more than likely a place for our beloved countrymen to unwind from the pressure of having to perform on a daily basis.

It's not a terribly long layout, but it is a fun challenge if you're up to it. If you're a senior citizen or high-handicapper searching for a short layout, consider playing this course if you're in the area.

DIRECTIONS

Go north from Santa Fe to Hwy. 285. Head west on Hwy. 520 (Trinity Dr.) and make a right on Diamond Dr. You'll see the course directly in front of you.

MCKINLEY/OTERO COUNTIES

GALLUP MUNICIPAL GOLF COURSE
P.O. Box 1477, Gallup, NM 87301 / (505) 863-9224

BASIC INFORMATION

Course Type: Public
Year Built: 1963
Architect: N/A
Local Pro: Alex Albarez

Course: N/A
Holes: 18 / Par 72

Back : 6,531 yds. Rating: 61.9 Slope: 103
Middle: N/A yds. Rating: N/A Slope: N/A
Ladies: 5,538 yds. Rating: 70.2 Slope: 111

Tee Time: 2 days in advance.
Price: $7 - $10

Credit Cards:	■	Restaurant:	
Driving Range:	■	Lounge:	
Practice Green:	■	Meeting Rooms:	
Locker Room:	■	Tennis:	
Rental Clubs:	■	Swimming:	
Walkers:	■	Jogging Trails:	
Snack Bar:	■	Boating:	

COURSE DESCRIPTION

This may not be the most difficult course you ever play, but it does pay tribute to the fact that every course has its own unique characteristics. If you're a beginner or a senior, the simplicity of this course will only work to complement your style of play. The flat terrain that it was built upon lends itself beautifully for walkers to take advantage of.

Although the course is short and the numbers indicated for the "Rating" and "Slope" are on the low end, you still need to have a certain amount of control to get the ball onto the right part of the fairway for good position – especially if you're a 20+ handicapper.

DIRECTIONS

Take I-40 to the Miyamura Pass Exit heading south. Follow the signs to the course.

DESERT LAKES GOLF COURSE
2351 Hamilton Rd., Alamogordo, NM 88310 / (505) 437-0290

BASIC INFORMATION

Course Type: Municipal
Year Built: N/A
Architect: N/A
Local Pro: Grant M. Delpes

Course: N/A
Holes: 18 / Par 72

Back: 6,491 yds. Rating: 69.5 Slope: 114
Middle: 6,192 yds. Rating: 68.2 Slope: 110
Ladies: 5,407 yds. Rating: 69.7 Slope: 115

Tee Time: 7 days in advance.
Price: $10 - $12

Credit Cards:	■	Restaurant:	■
Driving Range:	■	Lounge:	
Practice Green:	■	Meeting Rooms:	
Locker Room:	■	Tennis:	
Rental Clubs:	■	Swimming:	
Walkers:		Jogging Trails:	
Snack Bar:	■	Boating:	

COURSE DESCRIPTION

Desert Lakes Golf Course is located at the base of the Sacramento mountains in south-central New Mexico's Alamogordo township.

You'll find narrow fairways, elevated greens, and six new lakes carved within the course's terrain to keep you guessing before every shot. Double-digit handicappers should have a lot of fun here.

The front nine is 3,312 yards long and is generally flat with elevated greens. The back-nine at 2,955 yards plays along similar lines .

DIRECTIONS

Take Hwy. 54 south and make a right onto Desert Lakes Rd. Look for the course on your right.

SANDOVAL/SAN JUAN COUNTY

COCHITI LAKE GOLF COURSE
5200 Cochitilake Hwy., Cochhitilake, NM 87083 / (505) 465-2230

BASIC INFORMATION

Course Type: Public
Year Built: 1981
Architect: Robert Trent Jones II
Local Pro: Bill Winfeild

Course: N/A
Holes: 18 / Par 72

Back: 6,451 yds. Rating: 70.0 Slope: 119
Middle: 5,996 yds. Rating: 68.3 Slope: 115
Ladies: 5,292 yds. Rating: 71.0 Slope: 117

Tee Time: 7 days in advance.
Price: $17 - $19

Credit Cards:	■	Restaurant:	
Driving Range:	■	Lounge:	
Practice Green:	■	Meeting Rooms:	
Locker Room:		Tennis:	■
Rental Clubs:	■	Swimming:	■
Walkers:	■	Jogging Trails:	
Snack Bar:	■	Boating:	■

COURSE DESCRIPTION

The course is situated between the Jemez and Sangre de Crista mountain ranges, offering scenic beauty and a quiet atmosphere that is both conducive and enjoyable to a good day of golf.

The layout is challenging from start to finish and features two equally playable nine hole sides. It neither favors a fade nor a draw, and the overall length is easily in reach for the great majority of mid-to-high handicap golfers.

The course has been recognized by **Golf Digest** magazine as one of the Top 25 Public Courses in America.

DIRECTIONS

From I-25 take either Exit 259 or Exit 264, proceed on State Hwy. 22 and look for the course on your right.

PINON HILLS GOLF COURSE
2101 Sunrise Pkwy., Farmington, NM 87401 / (505) 326-6066

BASIC INFORMATION

Course Type: Public
Year Built: 1989
Architect: Ken Dye
Local Pro: Tony Montano

Course: N/A
Holes: 18 / Par 72

Back : 7,250 yds. Rating: 73.3 Slope: 130
Middle: 6,239 yds. Rating: 68.7 Slope: 121
Ladies: 5,522 yds. Rating: 71.5 Slope: 134

Tee Time: 7 days in advance.
Price: $11 - $13

Credit Cards:	■	Restaurant:	■
Driving Range:	■	Lounge:	
Practice Green:	■	Meeting Rooms:	
Locker Room:	■	Tennis:	
Rental Clubs:	■	Swimming:	
Walkers:	■	Jogging Trails:	
Snack Bar:	■	Boating:	

COURSE DESCRIPTION

Here is another course situated between the Jemez and Sangre de Crista mountain ranges, featuring both physical beauty and good golf at the same time.

You'll find a consistent layout that is equally challenging from start to finish. It neither favors a fade nor a draw, and the overall length is easily in reach for the great majority of mid-to-high handicap golfers.

The course has been recognized by **Golf Digest** magazine as the best Public course in New Mexico in 1991,1992, and 1993. **Newsweek** also gave it a notable mention, too.

DIRECTIONS

From I-25 take either Exit 259 or Exit 264, proceed on State Hwy. 22 and look for the course on your right.

SAN MIGUEL COUNTY

ANGEL FIRE COUNTRY CLUB
Drawer B, Angel Fire, NM 87710 / (505) 377-2301

BASIC INFORMATION

Course Type: Public
Year Built: N/A
Architect: Paul Ortiz
Local Pro: Chris Stewart

Course: N/A
Holes: 18 / Par 72

Back   : 6,624 yds. Rating: 71.0 Slope: 127
Middle: 6,268 yds. Rating: 69.0 Slope: 122
Ladies: 5,348 yds. Rating: 65.5 Slope: 118

Tee Time: 7 days in advance.
Price: $20 - $35

Credit Cards:	■	Restaurant:	■
Driving Range:	■	Lounge:	■
Practice Green:	■	Meeting Rooms:	■
Locker Room:	■	Tennis:	■
Rental Clubs:	■	Swimming:	■
Walkers:		Jogging Trails:	■
Snack Bar:	■	Boating:	

COURSE DESCRIPTION

This gem of a course will have you hitting your drives both up and down and every which way! Because of the many undulations that are scattered throughout the playing field, you'll often need to hit your approach shots both above and below your feet.

Playing golf in the mountains is always a joy. You'll hit your drives farther and when they finally hit the rock-bottom fairways, they'll also roll further too. You do need to control the ball to get into good position, otherwise your ball will travel deeper into trouble.

The course is open between the months of May and October.

DIRECTIONS

Take I-25 to Santa Fe. At Taos, get onto Hwy. 64 going east to the course. It will be on your right side.

PENDARIES GOLF & COUNTRY CLUB
P.O. Box 820, Rociada, NM 87742 / (505) 425-6018

BASIC INFORMATION

Course Type: Semi-private
Year Built: 1965
Architect: N/A
Local Pro: Tom Neilson

Course: N/A
Holes: 18 / Par 72

Back: 6,128 yds. Rating: 68.4 Slope: 115
Middle: N/A   Rating: N/A Slope: N/A
Ladies: 5,060 yds. Rating: 72.4 Slope: 119

Tee Time: 365 days in advance.
Price: $22 - $26

Credit Cards:	■	Restaurant:	■
Driving Range:		Lounge:	■
Practice Green:	■	Meeting Rooms:	■
Locker Room:	■	Tennis:	■
Rental Clubs:	■	Swimming:	
Walkers:	■	Jogging Trails:	■
Snack Bar:	■	Boating:	

COURSE DESCRIPTION

If you're one of the hundreds of golfers who lack the distance that it takes to tackle some of the longer and more difficult courses that seem to be springing up throughout the country, this course will give you a refreshing breather from the norm.

The thin air will carry your ball a flatteringly long way off the tee and even further along the rock-bottom fairways. The extra 15-20 yards that you'll average will surely boost your confidence to a new level. The many beautiful views combined with the cool mountain air makes this a very attractive place to play.

DIRECTIONS

Leave I-25 at Las Vegas, NM and go north on Hwy. 518 for about 11 miles to Hwy. 105. Go west on Hwy. 105 and look for the course on your left.

NEW MEXICO TECHNICAL GOLF COURSE

#1 Canyon Rd., Socorro, NM 87801 / (505) 835-5335

BASIC INFORMATION

Course Type: Public
Year Built: 1954
Architect: Dr. Jack Workman
Local Pro: Russell Moore

Course: N/A
Holes: 18 / Par 72

Back : 6,550 yds. Rating: 70.9 Slope: 118
Middle: N/A Rating: N/A Slope: N/A
Ladies: 5,887 yds. Rating: 72.8 Slope: 122

Tee Time: Call on Monday for weekend only.
Price: $11 - $13

Credit Cards:	■	Restaurant:	
Driving Range:	■	Lounge:	
Practice Green:	■	Meeting Rooms:	
Locker Room:	■	Tennis:	
Rental Clubs:	■	Swimming:	
Walkers:	■	Jogging Trails:	
Snack Bar:	■	Boating:	

COURSE DESCRIPTION

Charisma: that's what makes this desert course such a charm to play.

Be prepared to hit your drives accurately to get into good position. On your way you'll be facing tight fairways, high rough, and hundreds of trees. Another important factor to consider is the undulating terrain that the course was built upon. It's almost an impossibility to find your ball sitting on an even lie. You'll often have to play your approach shots from below and above your feet to small undulating greens.

When conditions are fair, the low cut Bermuda grass greens make it a pleasurable putting course.

DIRECTIONS

Going south on I-25 you'll need to exit at Mile Marker 159. Turn right on Bullock and another right three stop-signs down. This will take you directly to the course.

TAOS COUNTRY CLUB

P.O Box 254 (Hwy 570 West), Ranchos De Taos, NM 87557 / (505) 758-7300

BASIC INFORMATION

Course Type: Semi-private
Year Built: 1992 / 1993
Architect: Jep Willie
Local Pro: Glen McCargar

Course: N/A
Holes: 18 / Par 72

Back : 7,331 yds. Rating: 70.0 Slope: 128
Middle: 6,650 yds. Rating: 68.5 Slope: 125
Ladies: 5,486 yds. Rating: 70.0 Slope: 128

Tee Time: 7 days in advance.
Price: $25

Credit Cards:	■	Restaurant:	■
Driving Range:	■	Lounge:	■
Practice Green:	■	Meeting Rooms:	■
Locker Room:	■	Tennis:	■
Rental Clubs:	■	Swimming:	■
Walkers:	■	Jogging Trails:	■
Snack Bar:	■	Boating:	■

COURSE DESCRIPTION

Many wonderful things are happening to this charismatic golf course. Future plans include a new clubhouse complete with lockers, a fabulous restaurant, a lounge, and an additional championship golf course due out in May 1994.

This links style course offers many captivating mountain views you won't easily forget. If you're a double digit handicapper, I recommend playing the course from the middle tees, for the length of the course dictates many long drives to difficult landing areas, making it tough to place your ball in good position.

DIRECTIONS

Take Hwy. 68 north and turn left on Hwy. 570 (It's 3-miles south of Taos). Turn left on Hwy.570 and look for the course 1 1/4 miles down the road on your right.

NEW MEXICO

ALTERNATIVE COURSES

Bernalillo
Private

Albuquerque Country Club
601 Laguna Blvd. S.W.
Albuquerque, NM 87104
(505)

Four Hills Country Club
911 Four Hills Country Rd.
Albuquerque, NM 87123
(505) 299-9555

Tanoan Country Club
10801 Academy Rd. N.E.
Albuquerque, NM 87111
(505) 822-0433

Bernalillo
9-Hole

Puerto Del Sol Golf Course
1800 Girard S.E.
Albuquerque, NM 87106
(505) 265-5636

Bernalillo
Military

Tijeras Arroyo Golf Course
Kirtland Air Force Base
P.O. Box 18033
Albuquerque, NM 87117
(505) 846-1169

Chaves
Private

Roswell Country Club
Route 4 Box 275
Roswell, NM 88201
(505) 622-2050

Cibola
9-Hole

Zuni Mountain Golf Course
P.O. Box 2128
Grants Milan, NM 87021
(505) 287-9239

Curry
Military

Whispering Winds Golf Course
2206 Forest Dr.
Cannon Air Force Base, NM 88103
(505) 784-2800

Eddy
Private

Riverside Country Club
1700 W. Orchard Lane
Carlsbad, NM 88220
(505) 885-4253

Eddy
9-Hole

Artesia Country Club
P.O. Box 1305
Artesia, NM 88211
(505) 746-6732

Lea
Private

Hobbs Country Club
Carlsbad Hwy. West Box 760
Hobbs, NM 88240
(505) 393-5212

Lovington Country Club
E. Star Route Box 6
Lovington, NM 88260
(505) 396-6619

Lea
9-Hole

Eunice Municipal Golf Course
Carlsbad Hwy. P.O. Box 1235
Eunice, NM 88231
(505) 394-2881

Jal Country Club
N. 3 St.
Jal, NM 88252
(505) 395-2330

Lincoln
Private

Alto Lakes Golf & Country Club
1 Country Club Dr.
Alto, NM 88312
(505) 336-4231

Lincoln
9-Hole

Carrizozo Municipal Golf Course
Hwy. 380
Carrizozo, NM 88330
(505) 648-2451

Innsbrook Village Country Club
P.O. Box 1312
Ruidoso, NM 88345
(505) 258-3589

Otero
Military

Apache Mesa Golf Course
Holloman Air Force Base
Alamogordo, NM 88330
(505) 479-3574

Quay
9-Hole

Tucumcari Municipal Golf Course
P.O. Box 1188
Tucumcari, NM 88401
(505) 461-1849

Roosevelt
9-Hole

Portales Country Club
Box147
Portagles, NM 88130
(505) 356-8943

San Juan
Private

San Juan Country Club
5700 Country Club Rd.
Farmington, Nm 87402
(505) 327-4451

San Juan
9-Hole

Hidden Valley Country Club
P.O. Box 1450
Aztec, NM 87410
(505) 334-3248

Riverview Golf Course
P.O. Box 525
Kirtland, NM 87417
(505) 598-0140

San Miguel
Private

New Mexico Highland University Golf Course
Mills Avenue
Las Vegas, NM 87701
(505) 425-7711

Sandoval
Private

Rio Rancho Golf & Country Club
500 Country Club Dr. S.E.
Rio Rancho, NM 87124
(505) 892-8440

Santa Fe
9-Hole

Quail Run Country Club
3101 Old Pecos Trail
Santa Fe, NM 87501
(505) 986-2255

WHERE TO STAY IN NEW MEXICO

ALAMOGORDO
POPULATION: N/A

HOLIDAY INN ALAMOGORDO
1401 S. White Sands Blvd.
Alamogordo, NM 88310
(505) 437-7100

WHITE SANDS INN
1020 S. White Sands Blvd.
Alamogordo, NM 88310
(800) 255-5061

ALBUQUERQUE
POPULATION: N/A

ALBUQUEERQUE MARRIOTT HOTEL
2101 NE Louisiana Blvd.
Albuquerque, NM 87110
(505) 881-6800

AMBERLEY SUITE HOTEL
7620 NE Pan American Fwy.
Albuquerque, NM 87109
(505) 823-1300

BEST WESTERN AIRPORT INN
7620 NE Pan American Fwy.
Albuquerque, NM 87109
(800) 528-1234

BEST WESTERN FRED HARVEY HOTEL
7620 NE Pan American Fwy.
Albuquerque, NM 87109
(800) 227-1117

BEST WESTERN WINROCK INN
I-40 and Louisiana Blvd.
#18 Winrock Center
Albuquerque, NM 87109
(800) 866-5252

COURTYARD BY MARIOTT
1920 Yale Blvd.
Albuquerque, NM 87106
(800) 321-2211

DAYS INN
10321 NE Hotel Ave.,
Albuquerque, NM 87123
(505) 275-DAYS

DE ANZA MOTOR LODGE
4301 NE Central Ave
Albuquerque, NM 87108
(505) 255-1654

EL VADO MOTEL
2500 SW Central Ave.
Albuquerque, NM 87108
(505) 243-4594

HOLIDAY INN MIDTOWN
2020 NE Menaul Blvd.
Albuquerque, NM 87107
(800) HOLIDAY

HOLIDAY INN PYRAMID
5151 NE San Francisco Rd.
Albuquerque, NM 87109-4641
(800) HOLIDAY

HORNE'S HOWARD JOHNSON EAST
15 NE Hotel Circle
Albuquerque, NM 87109
(800) 877-4852

LA POSADA DE ALBUQUERQUE
125 NW 2 St.
Albuquerque, NM 87102
(800) 777-5732

LE BARON INN & SUITES
2120 NE Menaul
Albuquerque, NM 87107
(800) 444-REST

ALBUQUERQUE
Continued

QUALITY HOTEL FOUR SEASONS
2500 NE Carlisle
Albuquerque, NM 87110
(800) 545-8400

RADISSON INN ALBUQUERQUE
1901 SE University
Albuquerque, NM 87106
(800) 333-3333

RAMADA HOTEL CLASSIC
6815 NE Menaul Blvd.
Albuquerque, NM 87110
(800) 272-6232

RAMADA INN MARKET CENTER
25 NE Hotel Circle
Albuquerque, NM 87123
(800) 272-6232

RITEWAY INN
5201 NE Central Ave.
Albuquerque, NM 87108
(800) 888-8413

RODEWAY INN MIDTOWN
2108 NE Menaul
Albuquerque, NM 87107
(800) 228-2000

SHERATON OLD TOWN
800 NW Rio Grande Blvd.
Albuquerque, NM 87104
(800) 237-2133

ALBUQUERQUE - RIO RANCHO
POPULATION: N/A

BEST WESTERN INN AT RIO RANCHO
1465 Rio Rancho Dr.
Albuquerque-Rio Rancho, NM 87124
(505) 892-1700

BEST WESTERN INN AT RIO RANCHO
1465 Rio Rancho Dr.
Albuquerque-Rio Rancho, NM 87124
(505) 892-1700

ANGEL FIRE
POPULATION: N/A

INN AT ANGEL FIRE
Hwy. 434
Angel Fire, NM 87710
(800) 666-1949

LEGENDS HOTEL & CONFERENCE CENTER
P.O. Drawer
Angel Fire, NM 87710
(800) 633-7463

ARTISIA
POPULATION: N/A

BEST WESTERN PECOS INN
2209 W. Main
Artisia, NM 88210
(800) 676-7481

AZTEC
POPULATION: N/A

ENCHANTMENT LODGE
1800 W. Aztec Blvd.
Aztec, NM 87410
(505) 334-6143

BELEN
POPULATION: N/A

SUPER 8 MOTEL
428 S. Main St.
Belen, NM 87002
(800) 800-8000

CARLSBAD
POPULATION: N/A

BEST WESTERN CAVERN INN
17 Carlsbad Caverns Hwy.
P.O Box 128
Carlsbad, NM 88268
(800) 800-CAVERNS

BEST WESTERN MOTEL STEVENS
1829 S. Canal St.
Carlsbad, NM 88220
(800) 800-528-1234

CARLSBAD INN / HOLIDAY INN
601 S. Canal
Carlsbad, NM 88220
(505) 887-3541

CARSLBAD TRAVELODGE SOUTH
3817 National Parks Hwy.
Carlsbad, NM 88220
(800) 225-3050

PARK INN INTERNATIONAL
3706 National Parks Hwy.
Carlsbad, NM 88220
(800) 321-2861

CHAMA
POPULATION: N/A

BRANDING IRON MOTEL
Hwy. 17, W. Main, P.O. Box 557
Chama, NM 87520
(800) 446-2650

LITTLE CREEL LODGE
Hwy. 84, P.O. Box 645
Chama, NM 87520
(505) 756-2382

SPRUCE LODGE
Hwy.64 / P.O. Box 365
Chama, NM 87520
(505) 756-2593

CHIMAYO
POPULATION: N/A

HACIENDA RANCHO DE CHIMAYO
SR. 520
Chimayo, NM 87522
(800) 477-1441

CIMARRON
POPULATION: N/A

ST. JAMES HOTEL
Rt. 1, P.O Box 2
Cimarron, NM 87714
(505) 376-2664

CLAYTON
POPULATION: N/A

SUNSET MOTEL OF CLAYTON
702 S. First St.
Clayton, NM 88415
(800) 392-6691

CLOUDCROFT
POPULATION: N/A

THE LODGE AT CLOUDCROFT
P.O. Box 497
Cloudcroft, NM 88317
(800) 395-6343

CLOVIS
POPULATION: N/A

CLOVIS INN
2912 Mabry Dr.
Clovis, NM 88101
(800) 535-3440

HOLIDAY INN
2700 Mabry Dr., P.O. Box 973
Clovis, NM 88101
(505) 762-4491

CUBA
POPULATION: N/A

CUBAN LODGE
P.O. Box 238
Cuba, NM 87013
(505) 289-3269

DEL PRADO MOTEL (& FLORAL GIFT SHOP)
P.O. Box 507
Cuba, NM 87013
(505) 289-3475

DEMING
POPULATION: N/A

BEST WESTERN MIMBRES VALLEY INN
1500 W. Pine St.
Deming, NM 87013
(800) 528-1234

HOLIDAY INN OF DEMING
P.O. Box 1138
Deming, NM 88031
(505) 546-6308

DULCE
POPULATION: N/A

BEST WESTERN JICARILLA INN
P.O. Box 233
Dulce, NM 87528
(800) 742-1938

EAGLE NEST
POPULATION: N/A

LAGUNA VISTA LODGE
P.O. Box 65
Eagle Nest, NM 87718
(800) 821-2093

ESPANOLA
POPULATION: N/A

PARK INN CLUB & BREAKFAST
920 Riverside Dr.,P.O. Box 3617 FF
Espanola, NM 87533
(800) 766-7943

WESTERM HOLDIAY MOTEL
Rt. 3, P.O. Box 249
Espanola, NM 87532
(505) 753-2491

FARMINGTON
POPULATION: N/A

BASIN LODGE
701 Airport Dr.
Farmington, NM 87401
(505) 325-5061

BEST WESTERN, THE INN
700 Scott Ave.
Farmington, NM 87401
(505) 327-5221

HOLIDAY INN OF FARMINGTON
600 E. Broadway
Farmington, NM 87401
(800) HOLIDAY

GALLUP
POPULATION: N/A

BEST WESTERN, THE INN
3009 W66
Gallup, NM 87301
(505) 722-2221

GRANTS
POPULATION: N/A

BEST WESTERN, THE INN
1501 E. Santa Fe Ave.
Grants, NM 87020
(800) 528-1234

SANDS MOTEL
112 McArthur
Grants, NM 87020
(800) 424-7679

HOBBS
POPULATION: N/A

HOBBS MOTOR INN
Seminole Hwy.'s 62-180
Hobbs, NM 88240
(800) 624-5937

LAS CRUCES
POPULATION: N/A

A DAY'S END LODGE
755 N. Valley Dr.
Las Cruces, NM 88005
(505) 524-7753

BEST WESTERN MESILLA VALLEY INN
901 Avenida de Mesilla
Las Cruces, NM 88005
(800) 327-3314

BEST WESTERN MISSION INN
1765 S. Main
Las Cruces, NM 88001
(800) 528-1234

LAS CRUCES
Continued

DAY'S INN AT LAS CRUCES
2600 S. Valley Dr.
Las Cruces, NM 88005
(800) 553-4656

HOLIDAY INN DE LAS CRUCES
201 E. University
Las Cruces, NM 88001
(800) HOLIDAY

LA CRUCES-HILTON
705 S. Telshor Blvd.
Las Cruces, NM 88001
(800) HILTONS

PLAZA SUITES
301 E. University
Las Cruces, NM 88001
(800) 444-5250

ROYAL HOST MOTEL
2146 W. Picacho
Las Cruces, NM 88005
(505) 524-8536

LAS VEGAS, N.M.
POPULATION: N/A

COMFORT INN, THE
2500 N. Grand Ave.
Las Vegas, NM 87701
(800) 228-5150

INN ON THE SANTA FE TRAIL
1133 Grand Ave.
Las Vegas, NM 87701
(505) 425-6791

LORDSBURG
POPULATION: N/A

BEST WESTERN SKIES INN
1303 S. Main
Lordsberg, NM 88045
(800) 528-1234

LOS ALAMOS
POPULATION: N/A

HILLTOP HOUSE MOTEL
Trinity & Central
Los Alamos, NM 87544
(800) 462-0936

LOS ALAMOS INN
2201 Trinity Dr.
Los Alamos, NM 87544
(505) 662-7211

MESCALERO
POPULATION: N/A

INN OF THE MOUNTAIN GODS
Carrizo Canyon Rd.
Mescalero, NM 88340
(800) 545-6040

RATON
POPULATION: N/A

BEST WESTERN SANDS MANOR MOTEL
300 Clayton Rd.
Raton, NM 87740
(505) 445-2737

HOLIDAY CLASSIC MOTEL
301 Clayton Rd.
Raton, NM 87740
(800) 255-8879

MELODY LANE-MASTER INN
136 Canyon Dr.
Raton, NM 87740
(800) 421-5210

RED RIVER
POPULATION: N/A

ALPINE LODGE
Main & Mallette, P.O. Box 67
Red River, NM 87558
(800) 252-2333

GOLDEN EAGLE LODGE
E. Main St., P.O. Box 869
Red River, NM 87558
(800) 621-4046

LIFTS WEST CONDO-RESORT HOTEL
Main St., P.O. Box 318
Red River, NM 87558
(800) 221-1859

RIO COLORADO LODGE
P.O. Box 186
Red River, NM 87558
(800) 654-6516

RIVERSIDE, THE
P.O. Box 249,
Red River, NM 87558
(800) 432-9999

ROSWELL
POPULATION: N/A

BEST WESTERN EL RANCHO PALACIO
2205 N. Main
Red River, NM 88201
(800) 528-1234

BEST WESTERN SALLY PORT INN
2000 N. Main
Red River, NM 88201
(800) 528-1234

DAYS INN
Roswell, 1310 N. Main
Red River, NM 88201
(800) 325-2525

ROYAL MOTEL
2001 N. Main
Red River, NM 88201
(800) 423-3106

RUIDOSO
POPULATION: N/A

BEST WESTERN SWISS CHALET
1451 Mecham, Hwy. 48N
Ruidoso, NM 88345
(800) 47-SWISS

CREE MANOR INN
Paradise Canyon & Starlite Dr.
Ruidoso, NM 88345
(505) 257-4058

DAN DEE CABINS RESORT
310 Main Rd., P.O. Box 844
Ruidoso, NM 88345
(800) 345-4848

RUIDOSO
Continued

HIGH COUNTRY LODGE & RESORT
Alto, P.O. Box 137
Ruidoso, NM 88312
(800) 845-7265

RUIDOSO LODGE CABINS
P.O. Box 2316
Ruidoso, NM 88345
(800) 950-2510

SHADOW MOUNTAIN LODGE
107 Main Rd., P.O. Box 1427
Ruidoso, NM 88345
(800) 441-4331

VILLAGE LODGE & RESORT
1000 Mechem Dr.
Ruidoso, NM 88345
(800) 722-722-8779

SANTA FE
POPULATION: N/A

BEST WESTERN INN AT LORETTO
211 Old Santa Fe Trail
Santa Fe, NM 87501
(800) 727-5531

BEST WESTERN LAMPLIGHTER MOTEL
2405 Cerrillos Rd
Santa Fe, NM 87501
(800) 767-5267

BISHOP'S LODGE, THE
Bishop's Lodge Rd., P.O. Box 2367
Santa Fe, NM 87504
(505) 983-6377

EL REY INN
1862 Cerrillos Rd., P.O. Box 4759
Santa Fe, NM 87502
(505) 982-1931

ELDORADO HOTEL
309 W. San Francisco St.
Santa Fe, NM 87501
(505) 955-4455

GARRETT'S DESERT INN
311 Old Santa Fe Trail
Santa Fe, NM 87501
(800) 888-2145

GRANT CORNER INN
122 Grant Ave.
Santa Fe, NM 87501
(505) 983-6678

HILTON OF SANTA FE
100 Sandoval, P.O. Box 25104
Santa Fe, NM 87501
(800) 336-3676

HOTEL PLAZA REAL
125 Washington Ave.
Santa Fe, NM 87501
(800) 279-7325

HOTEL SANTA FE
1501 Paseo De Parlta
Santa Fe, NM 87501
(800) 825-9876

HOTEL SAINT FRANCIS
210 Don Gaspar
Santa Fe, NM 87501
(800) 666-5700

INN OF THE ANASAZI
113 Washington Ave.
Santa Fe, NM 87501
(800) 688-8100

INN OF THE GOVERNORS
234 Don Gaspar
Santa Fe, NM 87501
(800) 234-4534

INN ON THE ALAMEDA
303 E. Alameda
Santa Fe, NM 87501
(800) 289-2122

LA FONDA
100 E. San Francisco, P.O. Box 1209
Santa Fe, NM 87501
(800) 523-5002

LA POSADA DE SANTA FE
330 E. Palace Ave.
Santa Fe, NM 87501
(800) 727-5276

PUEBLO HEMOSA RESORT
501 Rio Grande
Santa Fe, NM 87501
(800) 274-7990

QUALITY INN
3011 Cerrillos Rd.
Santa Fe, NM 87501
(800) 221-2222

RANCHO ENCANTADO
Rt. 4, P.O. Box 57C
Santa Fe, NM 87501
(800) 722-9339

RESIDENCE INN BY MARRIOTT
1698 Galisteo St.
Santa Fe, NM 87501
(800) 331-3131

SANTA FE BUDGET INN
725 Cerrillos Rd.
Santa Fe, NM 87501
(800) 288-7600

SANTA FE MOTEL
510 Cerrillos Rd.
Santa Fe, NM 87501
(800) 999-1039

SILVER SADDLE MOTEL
2810 Cerrillos Rd
Santa Fe, NM 87501
(505) 471-7663

STAGE COACH MOTOR INN
3360 Cerrillos Rd.
Santa Fe, NM 87501
(505) 471-0707

SANTA ROSA
POPULATION: N/A

BEST WESTERN ADOBE INN
P.O. Box Drawer 410
Santa Rosa, NM 88435
(800) 528-1234

SOCORRO
POPULATION: N/A

SAN MIGUEL MOTEL
916 NE California Ave.
Socorro, NM 88435
(800) 548-7938

TAOS
POPULATION: N/A

BEST WESTERN KACHINA LODGE AND CONVENTION CENTER DE TAOS
P.O. Box NN
Taos, NM 87571
(800) 522-4462

EL MONTE LODGE
317 Kit Carson Rd.
Taos, NM 87571
(800) 828-TAOS

EL RINCON BED & BREAKFAST
114 Kit Carson Rd.
Taos, NM 87571
(505) 758-4874

HOLIDAY INN DON FERNANDO DE TAOS
1005 Paseo Pueblo Sur, P.O. Box DR
Taos, NM 87571
(800) 759-2736

HOTEL LA FONDA DE TAOS
P.O. Box 1447
Taos, NM 87571
(505) 758-2211

QUALITY INN
1043 Camino Del Pueblo Sur
P.O. Box 2319
Taos, NM 87571
(505) 758-2200

RANCHO RAMADA DE TAOS
615 Paseo Del Pueblo Sur
P.O. Box 6257
Taos, NM 87571
(800) 659-TAOS

SAGEBRUSH INN
P.O. Box 557
Taos, NM 87571
(800) 428-3626

SUPER 8 MOTEL
P.O. Box 6001
Taos, NM 87571
(800) 800-8000

TUCUMCARI
POPULATION: N/A

BEST WESTERN POW WOW INN
801 W. Tucumcari Blvd.
Tucumcari, NM 88401
(505) 461-0500

WHITE'S CITY
POPULATION: N/A

BEST WESTERN POW WOW INN
17 Carlsbad Cavern Hwy.
P.O. Box 128
White's City, NM 88268
(800) CAVERNS

WHITE ROCK
POPULATION: N/A

BANDELIER INN
132 St. Rd 4
White Rock, NM 87544
(800) 321-3923

EXCURSIONS

NORTHWEST NEW MEXICO

Aztec Ruins National Monument

This monument is devoted to the 12th-century pueblo ruins and features a fabulous *kiva* (an underground or partly underground chamber used for ceremonies) that is fully restored.

84 Rd. 2900, P.O. Box 640
Aztec, NM 87410
(505) 334-6174

El Morro National Monument

Spanish explorers and westbound pioneers decided to leave their mark on the world by signing their names on the monument's *Inscription Rock.*

St. Hwy 53
Ramah, NM 87321
(505) 783-4226

Jackson Lake State Waterfowl

Camping out will never be the same after you experience this beautiful park that runs along the **La Plata River**. Fishing, hunting, picnicking and relaxation are available throughout its many inviting locations.

P.O. Box 125
Bloomfield, NM 87413
(505) 632-2013

Acoma Pueblo Museum

Historical Indian artifacts, between the 1400's and today, are on display for your viewing pleasure. The exhibits are thoughtfully done and fun to look at.

P.O. Box 309
Pueblo of Acoma, N.M.,
(505) 552-6604

Aztec Museum

These 16th-century people had a rich and fascinating history. View some of their artifacts here and learn something about their way of life.

125 North Main
Aztec, N.M. 87410
(702) 758-6493

Carson McKee Museum

You can view historical artifacts that have been collected from all over the world. A wide selection of minerals and fossils are on display.

309 W. Main St.
Farmington, N.M.,
(702) 758-6493

Red Rock State Park

Don't miss the **Heritage Canyon** area; the sights are unbeatable. You'll find an informative visitors center along with great camping grounds.

Red Rock State Park
P.O. Box 328
Church Rock NM 87311
(505) 863-1337

Red Rock Museum

The beautiful collection of southwestern art in this museum is well worth the trip. You can view Indian *kachinas* (a carved doll portrayed in the costume of a spirit), silver, turquoise, pottery, rugs and more!

Address: same as **Red Rock State Park** above.

NORTH-CENTRAL NEW MEXICO

Cumbres & Toltec Scenic Railroad

You can take this eye-opening ride between the months of May and October It goes from Chama to Antonito, Colorado.

P.O. Box 789
Chama, NM 87520
(505) 756-2151

Randell Davey Audubon Center

Historical buildings, nature trails, and the incredible art of Randell Davey make up the finer points of this imaginative art center.

Upper Canyon Rd.
Santa Fe, NM 87501
(505) 983-4609

D. H. Lawrence Ranch & Shrine

This is the home of the late D.H. Lawrence, the notoriously controversial writer. The ranch has been turned into an educational and learning center for the public.

Call: (800) 732-8267

Lorreto Chapel

This wonderfully unique piece of architecture will bring you back to a part of history that has been long forgotten. It's a Gothic-styled cathedral, with an outstanding staircase design.

219 Old Santa Fe Trail
Santa Fe, NM
(702) 984-7971

Santa Fe Plaza

Great shops, engaging galleries, historical buildings, and so much more is available for you to explore and experience.

Call: (800) 777-CITY

Scenic Chair Lift Rides

You can take a chair lift to the **Agua Fria Mountain** to view **Wheeler peak, Moreno Valley**, and the surrounding **Cristo Mountains**.

Call: (800) 732-8267

Taos Institute Of Arts

Classes are available for Native American and Hispanic arts and crafts. Ask about their special workshops.

Call: (800) 732-8267

Center For Contemporary Arts in Taos

Many different art forms are in action, from stage acting to film movies. Other mixed media exhibits are featured too. Call for a list to confirm all showings.

Barcelona at Old Tacos Trail
Sante Fe, NM 87501
(702) 982-1338

NORTHEASTERN NEW MEXICO

Fort Union National Monument

Built during the 1800's, you'll find this fort along the **Santa Fe Trail** is an exciting look at an important part of our history.

Watrous, NM 87753
(505) 425-8025

Pecos National Historical Park

The park is home to 17th-century mission ruins. Bring your camera along for an interesting photo essay.

P.O. Drawer 418
Pecos, NM 87552
(505) 757-6414

Antonio Sanchez Cultural Center

The many traveling exhibits, artifacts, paintings, and photographs will open your eyes to the sheer beauty of the southwest.

166 Bridge St.
Las Vegas, NM 87701
(702) 425-8829

Conchas Lake State Park

If you've developed a love for fishing, you won't want to miss this wonderful location for Bass, Sunfish, Crappie, Catfish, and Walleye. A visitor center is readily at hand for further guidance.

Call: **(702) 868-2270**

CENTRAL NEW MEXICO

Indian Pueblo Cultural Center

Fascinating arts and crafts by pueblos, wonderful folk dances, an inviting museum and gift shop, and a great Indian restaurant are part of the attraction of coming to this cultural center.

2401 12th St. NW
Albuquerque, NM 87102
(505) 843-7270

Rio Grande Nature Center State Park

This park is home to a sanctuary filled with beautiful migratory birds. Other attractions include lush fauna and flora exhibits.

2901 N.W. Candelaria
Albuquerque, NM
(702) 344-7240

Rio Grande Zoological Park

You'll find over 1,000 species of animal life to view in their natural living environments. The **Amazon Rain Forest**, because of its many fascinating animals, is one of the most popular areas of the zoo.

903 S.W. 10th St.
Albuquerque, NM
(702) 843-7413

New Mexico Museum Of Natural History

This thoughtful museum is the most informative place to learn about the multiple facets of New Mexico. Some of the attractions include a walk through a simulated volcano and a cave from the IceAge. Live sea animals (including sharks) are an inviting and interesting part of the attractions.

1801 N.W. Mountain Rd.
Albuquerque, NM
(702) 841-8837

SOUTHEASTERN NEW MEXICO

Alameda Park Zoo

Alameda Park Zoo has many animals ranging from the exotic to the familiar

1321 N. White Sands Blvd.
Alamogordo, NM
(702) 437-8430

Lincoln State Monument And National Landmark

This is where Billy the Kid had his last escape. You'll find a restored frontier town and a museum to explore, too.

Hwy. 380
Lincoln, NM 88338
(702) 653-4372

Norman Petty Studios

Some of the most important people in the history of American music have recorded here.

206 Main St.
Clovis, NM
(702) 763-3435

Clyde W. Tombaugh Space Theater

You can view Omnimax quality movies, sit back and enjoy a laser light show or watch some of the educational programs designed for you and your family

P.O. 533
Alamogordo, NM 88310
(800) 437-2840

SOUTHWESTERN ARIZONA

Billy The Kid Sites

View his family cabin, the grave of his mother, and the famous **Star Hotel**, where legend has it that Billy used to wait tables.

Silver City, NM
(800) 548-9378

Gila Cliff Dwelling National Monument

This monument is an exceptional area to explore and is especially popular with landscape photographers. You'll find an endless array of beautiful sights.

Rt. 11, Box 100
Silver City, NM 88061
(505) 536-9461

Las Cruces Museum Of Natural History

A terrific display of southwestern natural history with an emphasis on the **Chihuahuan Desert.**

P.O. Drawer CLC
Mesilla Valley Mall, NM 88004
(702) 522-3120

Mineralogical Museum

Over 9,500 different forms of mineral specimens are on display along with fossils. It's a great place to bring your kids and watch their faces light up when they view the many colorful minerals that are on display.

Campus Station
Socorro, NM 87801
(505) 835-5246

NEW MEXICO INDEX

LEGEND

Public = **P**
Semi-private = **SP**
Private = **Italics**
Municipal = **M**
Military = **Mil.**
9-hole = **9H**
Executive = **E**

FROM THE AUTHOR -
I WANT YOUR INPUT!

It's possible that things may have changed at some of the golf courses I've selected by the time you visit. If changes have occurred, please let me know. And if you disagree with one of my recommendations, I'd like to hear that too. The address is listed below.

FROM THE PUBLISHER

Our goal is to provide you with a guide book that is second to none. As Jimmy reminds you above, however, things do change: phone numbers, prices, addresses, etc. Should you come across any new information, we'd appreciate hearing from you. No item is too small for us, so if you have any recommendations or suggested changes, please write us.

The address is:

Jimmy Shacky
c/o Open Road Publishing
P.O. Box 11249
Cleveland Park Station
Washington, DC 20008

COURSE NOTES

COURSE NOTES

COURSE NOTES

YOUR PASSPORT TO GREAT TRAVEL!
FROM OPEN ROAD PUBLISHING

THE CLASSIC CENTRAL AMERICA GUIDES

COSTA RICA GUIDE by Paul Glassman, 5th Ed. Glassman's classic travel guide to Costa Rica remains the standard against which all others must be judged. Discover great accommodations, reliable restaurants, pristine beaches, and incredible diving, fishing, and other water sports. Revised and updated. **$14.95**

BELIZE GUIDE by Paul Glassman, 6th Ed. This guide has quickly become the book of choice for Belize travelers. Perhaps the finest spot for Caribbean scuba diving and sport fishing, Belize's picture-perfect palm trees, Mayan ruins, tropical forests, uncrowded beaches, and fantastic water sports have made it one of the most popular Caribbean travel destinations. Revised and updated. **$13.95**

HONDURAS AND BAY ISLANDS GUIDE by J.P. Panet with Leah Hart and Paul Glassman, 2nd Ed. Open Road's superior series of Central America travel guides continues with the revised look at this beautiful land. **$13.95**

GUATEMALA GUIDE by Paul Glassman, 8th Ed. Glassman's treatment of colorful Guatemala remains the single best source in print. **$16.95**

OTHER TITLES OF INTEREST

PARIS GUIDE by Robert F. Howe and Diane Huntley. Brings you the heart of the romantic City of Light, plus new attractions, hotels, cafes, and great activities. **$13.95**

SOUTHERN MEXICO AND YUCATAN GUIDE by Eric Hamovitch. Complete coverage of beautiful southern Mexico and the Yucatan peninsula. Discover terrific beaches, majestic Mayan ruins, great water sports, and the latest on hotels, restaurants, activities, nightlife, sports and more! Available Fall 1994. **$14.95**

WALT DISNEY WORLD AND ORLANDO THEME PARKS by Jay Fenster. *The* complete guide to Disney World and all of Orlando's great theme parks (including Sea World, MGM Studios, Busch Gardens, Church Street Station, Spaceport USA, and more), shows you every attraction, ride, show, shop, and nightclub they contain. Includes 64 money-savings tips for hotel, airfare, restaurant, attractions, and ride discounts. **$12.95**

LAS VEGAS GUIDE by Ed Kranmar and Avery Cardoza. Great selection of hotels, restaurants, excursions, shopping, plus more pages of gambling advice than any other Vegas guide. **$5.95**

PLEASE USE ORDER FORM ON NEXT PAGE

ORDER FORM

Name and Address: _____

_____

_____

_____ Zip Code: _____

Quantity	Title	Price

Total Before Shipping _____

Shipping/Handling _____

TOTAL _____

Please include price of book plus shipping and handling For shipping and handling, please add $3.00 for the first book, and $1.00 for each book thereafter. Ask about our discounts for special order bulk purchases.

ORDER FROM: **OPEN ROAD PUBLISHING**
P.O. Box 11249, Cleveland Park Station, Washington, D.C. 20008